Investing With
Variable Annuities

Fifty Reasons Why Variable Annuities May Be Better Long-Term Investments Than Mutual Funds

John P. Huggard, J.D., CFP, ChFC, CLU
Huggard, Obiol and Blake, PLLC
Raleigh, North Carolina 27605

D1247406

Fifteenth Edition ver. 1

Printed in the United States

Huggard, John P.
          Investing with Variable Annuities / by John P. Huggard - 15th ed.
           270 pages
          Includes index.
          ISBN 978-0-9819467-4-0

Reader Inquiry Branch   Book orders
Parker-Thompson Publishing   (919) 832-2687
124 St. Mary's Street
Raleigh, NC 27605
(919) 832-9650

RESEARCH PROJECT DISCLAIMER

This book is the result of a research project conducted by the author over the last ten years. Statements and information in this book were compiled from sources that the author considers to be reliable or are expressions of the author's opinion. As an ongoing research project, this book is not intended to be complete, and therefore the author cannot guarantee its complete accuracy. This book is an ongoing research project designed to compare the relative benefits of owning variable annuities and mutual funds. The examples and data included are designed to provide useful information regarding the subject matter covered. This book is sold with the understanding that the author and the publisher are not engaged in rendering legal, financial or other professional services. Because laws vary from state to state, readers should not rely upon this or any other publication for financial or tax guidance but should do their own homework and make their own decisions. This book is not to be considered a solicitation of orders for financial products. Annuities are long-term investment vehicles designed for retirement purposes. Variable annuities are subject to market fluctuation, investment risk and possible loss of principal. Variable annuities are not insured or guaranteed by the FDIC. IRAs and qualified plans already have the tax-deferral found in annuities. For an additional cost, variable annuities can provide other enhanced benefits, including death benefit protection and the ability to receive a lifetime income. All guarantees made by variable annuity issuers are based solely on the financial strength of the issuing company. Annuities may impose tax penalties and contingent deferred sales charges for early withdrawal. The purchase of any investment, whether a mutual fund or variable annuity, should only be made after consultation with financial and tax professionals. The advice contained in this book (including any supplements) was not intended or written to be used, and it cannot be used by any taxpayer, for the purpose of avoiding any IRS penalties that may be imposed on the taxpayer. The advice contained in this book (including any supplements) was written for continuing education training only. This book is intended for use by professionals practicing in the areas of finance, law, insurance and accounting. This book is not and should not be made available for public use. A reader requiring legal or other expert advice should seek the services of a competent attorney, CPA, financial planner or other professional. Comments, criticisms and suggestions for improving this book are welcome. The author can be reached at (919) 832-2687 or johnphuggard@aol.com.

ABOUT THE AUTHOR

John Huggard is the senior member in the Raleigh law firm of Huggard, Obiol and Blake, PLLC. He limits his practice to consultation in the areas of estate planning and financial litigation. John is a retired college professor. For 32 years he taught introductory and advanced courses in law and personal finance at North Carolina State University. John was named an Alumni Distinguished Professor in 1994 and was a member of the university's Academy of Outstanding Teachers. John is a Board Certified Specialist in Estate Planning and Probate law and a Certified Financial Planner (CFP). John has also earned the Chartered Financial Consultant (ChFC) and Chartered Life Underwriter (CLU) designations. He is the author of *The Administration of Decedents' Estates in North Carolina* (Michie Pub. Co.), *The North Carolina Estate Settlement Practice Guide* (West Pub. Co.), *Living Trust, Living Hell: Why You Should Avoid Living Trusts* (Kendall-Hunt), *Investing with Variable Annuities – Fifty Reasons Why Variable Annuities May Be Better Long-Term Investments than Mutual Funds* (Parker-Thompson Pub.), and *The Truth About Variable Annuities – Debunking Variable Annuity Myths* (Parker-Thompson Pub.). Additionally, John has had many of his articles published in *Financial Planning, On Wall Street* and other financial magazines. John was named a North Carolina Super Lawyer by the *Charlotte City* magazine in 2007 and was named a Top U.S. Financial Advisor by Consumers' Research Council of America. John has been extensively interviewed or quoted in the *Wall Street Journal, Smart Money, USA Today, Variable Product Specialist* and other financial publications. John regularly lectures to professional groups on topics dealing with probate issues, investment taxation and financial planning. John received his undergraduate degree (Phi Beta Kappa) and law degree from the University of North Carolina at Chapel Hill and his master's degree from Duke University. John joined the U.S. Marine Corps in 1964 and served as a platoon sergeant in Viet Nam. He received a direct commission and served in the Navy Reserve JAG Corps for 30 years before retiring as a captain in 2005. John's hobbies include flying, competitive target shooting, motorcycling and deep ocean diving.

DEDICATION

*This book is dedicated to
the memory of
Betty Sampson Mossien,
my friend and aunt
who was taken from all
who loved her much too soon.*

ACKNOWLEDGMENTS

This book is the result of ten years of research. It would not have been possible to summarize this research in a readable format without the assistance and support of my colleagues at the university and the numerous CPAs, attorneys and financial professionals who provided me with data and constructive criticism over the years.

Special thanks go to my friend and assistant Donna R. Buck Spiers who reworked and corrected the original manuscript and each subsequent edition. To the extent that this edition has any clarity or cohesiveness is owed entirely to Donna's suggestions and corrections.

Readers are encouraged to contact the author with suggestions on how to clarify or improve on the contents of this book.

John Huggard

Huggard, Obiol and Blake, PLLC

Raleigh, North Carolina

(919) 832-2687

TABLE OF CONTENTS

PART I - INTRODUCTORY MATERIAL

PART II - THE TAX CONSEQUENCES OF MUTUAL FUND OWNERSHIP

PART III - THE COST OF OWNING MUTUAL FUNDS

PART IV - BENEFITS OF VARIABLE ANNUITY OWNERSHIP

PART V - DO VARIABLE ANNUITIES BELONG IN QUALIFIED PLANS?

PART I - INTRODUCTORY MATERIAL

[Summary: The material in Part I provides a discussion of terminology and how variable annuities work as well as the data and methodology used in this book to compare mutual funds and variable annuities. A discussion of articles appearing in the press relating to mutual funds and variable annuities is also included. In addition, a list of fifty reasons why variable annuities are better long-term investments than mutual funds is set out. The remainder of this book discusses these reasons in detail.]

- CHAPTER 1 -
WHY THIS BOOK?

§101. INTRODUCTION

For over 35 years I have practiced financial and estate planning law. During this period I have taught, researched and written about financial and estate planning topics. Nearly every article I have read over the years, both in the popular and financial press, has been, for the most part, informative and accurate. The only area where the press has consistently failed to be either informative or accurate in their reporting is in dealing with the issue of variable annuities. For several years I have read dozens of articles about variable annuities appearing in financial journals, newspapers and magazines that were clearly misleading and inaccurate. Hardly a month goes by that I don't find at least one article written in some publication containing several erroneous assumptions or misstatements about variable annuities.[1]

After collecting several of these articles and analyzing them, I noticed a distinct pattern had developed over the years. Nearly all of these articles compared variable annuities to mutual funds and concluded that investors should put their money in mutual funds and shun variable annuities. Another common denominator shared by these articles was the fact that the authors constantly repeated the same supposed shortcomings of variable annuities without offering any data to support their positions. For example, four points erroneously made by the authors of many anti-variable annuity articles include the following:

- Long-term mutual fund investors are taxed annually at capital rates of no more than 15%.
- Retired variable annuity owners in, for example, a 25% marginal tax bracket pay 25% in ordinary income taxes on withdrawals taken from their variable annuities.
- Variable annuities do not get a stepped-up basis and mutual funds do.[2]
- Variable annuities are more expensive to own than mutual funds.

Although the above statements, together with others, commonly appear in articles comparing mutual funds and variable annuities, they are not always accurate. The analysis discussed in this book demonstrates that the statements made above are more accurate when restated as follows:

---

[1] Most anti-variable annuity articles appear in the financial press. However, financial radio and television programs make unsupportable negative statements about variable annuities with about the same frequency as does the financial press.

[2] See §2502 for a definition of stepped-up basis.

- Many long-term mutual fund owners will not always be taxed on their annual mutual fund distributions at long-term capital gains rates of 15%. The actual income tax they will pay can be much higher.

- The income tax paid by retired variable annuity owners on withdrawals from their annuities will rarely exceed 15% even if they are in a marginal tax bracket as high as 25%.

- Variable annuities receive tax and other benefits that may be as advantageous as a step-up in basis.[3]

- The cost of owning a mutual fund more often than not will be *more* than the cost of owning a similar variable annuity.

§102. WHY ANTI-VARIABLE ANNUITY ARTICLES EXIST

I am often asked why inaccurate and misleading articles about variable annuities appear so frequently in the press. My research concludes that there are three major reasons for this. They are:

- The publishers of most periodicals know very little about variable annuities and seem to accept any negative article written about them without making an effort to have persons knowledgeable about annuities check submitted articles for accuracy.

- Most of those who write newspaper articles about variable annuities have almost no financial background or knowledge concerning variable annuities. Because they are intellectually lazy, they merely reformat prior negative articles written by others and repeat, without supporting data, what others have published in the past.

- Knowledgeable professionals who read inaccurate and misleading articles about variable annuities often don't challenge these articles by writing to the publishers who carelessly allow these articles to get in print. This failure to challenge inaccurate or misleading articles is often the result of not having data to support such a challenge. Hopefully, this book will supply the impetus and data that will allow financial professionals to challenge future articles about variable annuities that contain misleading or inaccurate information.

---

[3] See Chapter 25 on stepped-up basis.

2

- The *complete* failure of the variable annuity industry to defend its product against false, misleading and inaccurate news reporting.

§103. THE PURPOSE OF THIS BOOK

The primary purpose of this book is to examine non-qualified, actively managed, equity-based variable annuities and mutual funds sold by financial professionals to determine which investment is really the best one for long-term investors. The secondary purpose of this book is to dispel the many misconceptions that exist concerning variable annuities and demonstrate that our current tax and investment laws actually favor long-term investing in variable annuities rather than mutual funds. By investing in variable annuities, long-term investors will be able to grow their retirement accounts, reduce their tax burden and provide themselves with greater investment flexibility.

§104. BOOK DIVISION

This book is divided into five parts. They are:

- Part I - This section is an introduction to variable annuities and how they work.
- Part II - This section discusses the heavy income tax burden faced by mutual fund owners.
- Part III - This section examines the non-tax costs associated with mutual fund ownership.
- Part IV - This section discusses the many benefits of investing in variable annuities.
- Part V - This section examines why variable annuities may prove to be excellent investments for retirement accounts such as IRAs, 401(k)s, etc.

§105. CONCLUSION

For years the investing public has been bombarded with incorrect and incomplete information regarding both variable annuities and mutual funds. This book examines and corrects the many misconceptions that exist concerning these two investment vehicles. Hopefully, investors who take the time to learn about variable annuities and mutual funds will be better able to make appropriate long-term investment decisions.

- CHAPTER 2 -
PRO VARIABLE ANNUITY PRESS

§201. INTRODUCTION

Many financial professionals and knowledgeable investors complain about negative articles published in the popular and financial press that portray variable annuities as poor investments. It is probably fair to say that there will always be uninformed writers who will write negative things about any product. The good news is that there are a great number of variable annuity articles published every year that detail the benefits of investing in variable annuities.

§202. PRO VARIABLE ANNUITY ARTICLES

Articles addressing the advantages of variable annuities are published regularly and will most likely increase in the future as people begin to learn more about variable annuities. The following list is just a small sampling of the many pro variable annuity articles that have been published in the last few years.

- *Seniors Benefit from Living Benefits in a Variable Annuity*; Brian Massey; *Life Insurance Selling;* Sept. 2007; p. 98-102.

- *Confessions of a VA Critic*; Moshie Milevsky; *Research Magazine*; January 2007.

- *Annuities Are Getting Hotter - Once Shunned as Ugly Ducklings, Variable Annuities Have Grown into Sophisticated Swans*; Richard J. Koreto; *Financial Planning*; Mar. 1, 2001.

- *Annuities with Guarantees Soothing Queasy Clients*; Linda Koco; *National Underwriter*; Feb. 5, 2001; p. 6.

- *Why This Attorney Likes Variable Annuities*, Katherine Vessenes; *National Underwriter Life and Health*, May 14, 2007; p. 42.

- *Easy Riders*, David Port, *Senior Marketing Advisor*, October 2001; p. 34.

- *Diversify Your Clients' Portfolio with Annuities and Watch Their Assets Grow*, David Port, *Senior Marketing Advisor*, December 2001; p. 29.

- *Annuities with New Guarantees on Returns*; Kimberly Lankford; *Kiplinger's Retirement Report*; August 2007; p. 7.

- *The Beauty of VAs Shines Through – Especially Today*; Jacob Herschler; *National Underwriter, Life & Health/Financial Services Ed.*; October 2002; Vol. 106 Issue 40, p.11.

- *Annuities For the Wealthy? Yes, Indeed*; Michael J. Gilotti; *National Underwriter, Life & Health/Financial Services Ed.*; October 2002; Vol. 106

Issue 43, p. 24-26.

- *"New Opportunities in Tax-Deferred Annuities"* - An interview with Herbert K. Daroff, J.D., CFP, who is a business and estate planning advisor.

- *Variable Annuities Get a Second Look*; *Senior Market Advisor*; July 2004; p. 146.

- *Consider Variable Annuities*; Ryan Clark; *The Charlotte Observer* (NC); April 19, 2004; p.50.

- *Off Golden Pond*; Ben J. Stein; *The American Spectator*; October 2004; p.48.

- *Why Variable Annuity Sales Are Soaring*; John Huggard; *Senior Market Advisor*; December 2006.

- *Variable Annuity Guarantee Features Make Them Especially Attractive in Planning for Retirement*; Alan Peters; *Investment News*; November 28, 2005.

- *The Devil, the Deep Blue Sea, and the Variable Annuity*; Nick Murray; *Financial Advisor*; October 2005.

- *Annuity Guarantees Can Fit in Your Retirement Plan*; Humberto Cruz; *The Los Angeles Times*; September 6, 2006.

[Note: Chapter 47 discusses several studies showing the investment advantages variable annuities have over mutual funds.]

§203. PRO VARIABLE ANNUITY BOOKS

There are two books currently available to the public that address the benefits of variable annuity ownership. They are:

- *Creating Retirement Income*, Virginia Morris, Lightbulb Press 2002.

- *Income for Life*, Michael F. Lane, McGraw-Hill, New York 1999.

A great source of books and booklets dealing with all aspects of variable annuities is available from Richard Duff, J.D., CLU. Mr. Duff's website is www.RWDuff.com. Insured Retirement Institute (IRI), a trade organization for variable annuities, has many helpful books and booklets regarding variable annuities. (202-469-3000).

§204. REPORTS FOR VARIABLE ANNUITY PRODUCERS

Many variable annuity producers want more detailed information regarding variable annuities in order for them to better assist their clients in understanding the benefits of variable annuities. The author has written fifteen (15) reports that deal with many variable annuity issues in a detailed manner. Reports #1 - #5 are covered in this book. Reports #6- #15 are not. A brief description of these reports appears below:

- *Report #1:*

  "Variable Annuity Tax Deferral and Time Value of Money." This report discusses the benefit of income tax deferral provided by variable annuities. The report shows that, because of time value of money, when tax deferral is factored into the decision to invest in variable annuities or mutual funds, the variable annuity usually proves to be the better investment even though mutual funds may be subject to income tax rates that are lower than that of variable annuities.

- *Report #2:*

  "Why Federal Income Tax Laws Favor Variable Annuities Over Mutual Funds." This report discusses 16 reasons why variable annuity owners benefit from our tax laws more than mutual fund owners. The full deductibility of variable annuity losses, annuitization, transaction costs, the drawbacks of JGTRRA, avoiding income and estate taxes on variable annuities are a few of the topics covered.

- *Report #3:*

  "Do Variable Annuities Belong in Qualified Plans – A Lawyer's View." This report discusses whether variable annuities should be included in qualified plans. The arguments made against putting variable annuities in qualified plans are examined. The report demonstrates why these arguments have little merit. Examples of when variable annuities can be placed in IRAs, 403(b)s and other qualified plans are provided. Examples of when variable annuities should *not* be placed in qualified plans are also discussed. NASD's Notice to Members 99-35, the regulations governing this area, are included in the report and are fully discussed. A two page disclosure document is included to ensure regulatory compliance when placing a variable annuity in a qualified plan.

- *Report #4:*

  "The Tax Deductibility of Variable Annuity Losses." This report discusses the rules for fully deducting losses arising when variable annuities are sold. The procedure for properly deducting these losses is set out in the report. The tax law supporting this discussion and issues to be discussed with clients before such losses are taken are also included in the report.

- *Report #5:*

  "The Stepped-Up Basis – Mutual Funds vs. Variable Annuities." This report discusses the step-up in basis rules for mutual funds and variable annuities. The second most common reason for losing variable annuity sales is the belief that the step-up in basis provided by mutual funds is a major benefit. This report demonstrates that the step-up in basis provided by mutual funds is not as much of a benefit as many people believe. The step-up in basis provided by variable annuities under IRC §72(e)(4)(c)(i) is discussed and examples of how this step-up basis may be better than the step-up provided by mutual funds are included in the report. Alternatives to a step-up in basis such as the earnings enhancement benefit, spousal continuation, etc. are discussed.

- *Report #6:*

    "Variable Annuity Ownership – Who's Too Old?" This report addresses the issue of who might be too old to purchase a variable annuity. Many people believe that variable annuities should not be sold to senior investors (60+). The truth is that today's variable annuities are often the premium investment for investors in the age bracket of 55 to 75 and, in some cases, beyond.

- *Report #7:*

    "Mutual Funds vs. Variable Annuities – The True Annual Cost of Ownership." This report documents and summarizes all of the research done on the true cost of owning a mutual fund and variable annuity. The conclusion of this report and these studies show that the average actively managed mutual fund *more* expensive to own on an annual basis than an equivalent variable annuity. The major benefit of the report is the numerous citations to SEC, industry and academic studies that show the true cost of owning mutual funds and variable annuities.

- *Report #8:*

    "How To Do Net-to-Net Comparisons of Variable Annuities and Mutual Funds." This report shows advisors how to use a financial calculator to determine the *net* value of an investment in variable annuities or mutual funds. The value of a net-to-net analysis is that it shows clients what *they* will receive *after* factoring in all costs, taxes, fees, commissions, etc. Once a net-to-net analysis is completed, these later issues become moot.

- *Report #9:*

    "Eliminating Estate and Income Taxes From Retirement Accounts – An Opportunity for Financial Professionals." This report demonstrates how financial professionals can help clients, who own variable annuities and other retirement accounts, avoid estate and income taxes on these accounts. By using the technique outlined in this paper, financial professionals can sell large volumes of insurance and annuity products while helping their clients accomplish large tax savings.

• *Report #10:*

"The Impact of Commissions on Variable Annuity and Mutual Fund Performance." This report examines the impact commissions have on mutual funds and variable annuities and demonstrates that in most cases the performance of mutual funds is negatively impacted more by the commissions they impose than are variable annuities.

• *Report #11:*

"Variable Annuities and Mutual Funds – The Liquidity, Control and Flexibility Controversy." Many investors believe that variable annuities are less liquid than mutual funds and stocks. Additionally, they believe that variable annuities provide less control and flexibility than mutual funds and stocks. This report examines these three areas and demonstrates that variable annuities are as liquid as mutual funds and stocks and usually offer an investor more control and flexibility than other equity investments.

• *Report #12:*

"Suitability of Sub-Account Selection with Guaranteed Variable Annuities." This report discusses the suitability issues involved in selecting sub-accounts in variable annuities that provide guarantees against loss of principal. With principal protection guarantees, generally investors will want to be more aggressive. Investments that are too conservative may result in liability issues.

• *Report #13:*

"Mutual Funds – Calculating The True Annual Cost of Ownership." This report demonstrates that the typical mutual fund is three to four times more expensive to own each year than the 1.5% annual expense ratio that many mutual fund owners are led to believe is the only cost they incur when buying mutual funds.

• *Report #14:*

"Why I Own Variable Annuities." I taught law and finance courses at a major university for more than 32 years. In addition, I am a practicing tax attorney and hold the CFP, ChFC and CLU designations. A large portion of my retirement holdings are invested in variable annuities. Many people, over the years, have asked me to write this report setting out why I own variable annuities.

• *Report #15:*

"**Why Variable Annuity Sales Are Soaring.**" This report shows that the sale of variable annuities has consistently increased over the past 20 years. The most dramatic gains have occurred in the last few years. This report identifies who the buyers of variable annuities are (i.e., wealthy, educated investors) and sets out several reasons why variable annuity sales have been soaring.

> These reports are available from Parker-Thompson Publishing at (919) 832-2687. This book can also be purchased by calling Parker-Thompson Publishing.

§205. PRO VARIABLE ANNUITY WEB SITES

In addition to many pro variable annuity articles, there are several web sites that provide investors with positive information regarding variable annuities. One such web site is annuityiq. com.

§206. NEW BOOK: THE TRUTH ABOUT VARIABLE ANNUITIES

The author has written a second book about variable annuities. This book examines and debunks the 16 myths regarding variable annuities. Information about this book can be obtained by calling Parker-Thompson Pub. at (919) 832-2687.

§207. CONCLUSION

All investment vehicles are going to have supporters and detractors. One should expect to see both positive and negative articles being published about variable annuities. By having both the benefits and drawbacks of an investment made public, investors will be in a better position to make an informed investment decision. Intelligent investors should read as much as possible about a potential investment before making any investment decision. The biggest mistake investors make when considering variable annuities is to base their decision on a single negative article about these investments without trying to verify the accuracy of data used in the article.

- CHAPTER 3 -
ANTI-MUTUAL FUND PRESS

§301. INTRODUCTION

Financial professionals and investors sometimes claim that the popular and financial press is biased against variable annuities and seem to spend a great deal of time printing articles that favor mutual fund ownership. This is not necessarily the case. Each year, many articles are written that attempt to warn the investing public that much of what they hear about mutual fund investing may not be accurate.

§302. ANTI-MUTUAL FUND ARTICLES

Every year, many popular magazines and financial journals publish articles that address the negative aspects of mutual fund ownership. The following list is a small sample of such articles that have appeared in the last few years:

- *Tradings Hidden Costs*; Laura Santini; *Investment Dealers' Digest,* 08/14/2000; Vol. 66 Issue 33, p. 16.

- *SEC Probes Funds' Commissions*; Aaron Lucchetti; John Hechinger; *The Wall Street Journal*; 09/16/99, Vol. 234 Issue 54, p. C1.

- *Funds Cost More Than You Think*; *Smart Money Investment*; p. 28; May 2004.

- *Why Mutual Fund Investing Costs Matter*; Andrew Gluck; *Investment Advisor*; p. 37; March 2005.

- *Funds: The $20 Billion Tax Time Bonus*; Penelope Wang; *cnnmoney.com*; November 1, 2006.

- *Why Mutual Fund Expenses Matter*; *kiplinger.com*; February 2, 2003.

- *The Taxing Side of Mutual Funds*; *smartmoney.com*; November 28, 2006.

- *Hidden Expenses*; James M. Clash et al; *Forbes*; January 31, 2005.

- *Watch Out for Fund Expenses*; Michael Iachini; *Schwab Investing Insight*; October 6, 2006.

- *Trade-Happy Mutual Funds Can Cost You – Managers with High Turnover Post Weaker Returns on Average; Commission Expenses Tell a Tale*; Aaron Lucchetti; *The Wall Street Journal*; April 23, 2003.

- *SEC Warns About Mutual Fund Costs*; Robert McGough; Karen Damato; the *Wall Street Journal* - Eastern Edition; 11/05/98; Vol. 232 Issue 90; p. C1.

- *As Mutual Funds Lose Value, Many See Hikes in Fees*; Guy Halverson; *The Christian Science Monitor*; November 2002.

- *Mutual Fund Double Whammy: Taxes On Losses; Forbes.com*; December 2002.

- *When Funds Go Bad, They're Horrid*; Thomas A. Fogarty; *USA Today.com*; December 2002.

- *Mutual Funds: Time to Clean House; Business Week, Industrial/Technology Edition*; New York, January 2000; Issue 3665, p.188.

- *The Death of Mutual Funds, Sweeping Technological Changes Are Threatening To Bring The Mutual Fund Industry To Its Knees*; J.P. Vicente; *Redherring.com*; September 2000; Issue 82.

- *A Failing Grade For Mutual Funds*; James K. Glassman; *Washingtonpost. com*; December 2002.

- *Is That Mutual Fund A Tax Sinkhole?*; Robert Barker; *Businessweek.com*; December 2002.

- *Tax Bite Looms Larger for Returns*; Theo Francis; *The Wall Street Journal*; August 5, 2002, p. R1.

§303. ANTI-MUTUAL FUND WEB SITES

In addition to anti-mutual fund articles there are web sites that discuss the negative features of mutual funds. Three such sites are fundalarm.com, funddemocracy.com[1], and fool.com. The SEC's website sec.gov contains speeches by the SEC's former chairman Arthur Levitt and others that shed some interesting light on mutual fund investing.

§304. ANTI-MUTUAL FUND BOOKS

Contrary to popular belief, not everyone in the investment business believes mutual funds are a first rate investment. Many books have been written about the negative aspects of mutual funds. A sampling of these books include:

- *The Great Mutual Fund Trap*; G. Baer and G. Gensler; Banu Publishing, 2003.

- *Your Money, Your Choice...Mutual Funds - Take Control Now and Build Wealth*; Charles Jones, CFA; Prentice Hall, 2003.

- *The Trouble With Mutual Funds*; Richard Rutner. Elton-Wolf Publishing, 2002.

- *Common Sense on Mutual Funds: New Imperatives for the Intelligent Investor*; John Bogle; Wiley & Sons, 1999.

- *The New Common Sense Guide to Mutual Funds*; Mary Roland; Bloomberg Publishing, 2000.

---

[1] This website is the creation of a former SEC attorney.

§305. THE AUTHOR'S INVESTMENTS

This chapter was not intended to show mutual funds are not good investments. It was intended merely to demonstrate that there are those who will write negative articles about any investment, not just variable annuities. The author has a significant amount of his investment holdings in mutual funds. Most of these are in qualified accounts. A large portion of the author's investment holdings are in qualified accounts holding variable annuities. Individual stocks also comprise a large part of the author's holdings.

§306. CONCLUSION

As can be seen from the above articles, not everything written about mutual funds is positive. There are many writers that are committed to informing the public about the exaggerated benefits of mutual fund investing and the problems investors can confront when buying mutual funds.

- CHAPTER 4 -

FIFTY REASONS WHY VARIABLE ANNUITIES
MAY BE BETTER LONG-TERM INVESTMENTS THAN MUTUAL FUNDS

§401. INTRODUCTION

The primary purpose of this book is to help financial professionals determine for themselves that variable annuities may make better long-term investments than mutual funds. To this end, this book discusses fifty reasons why this is the case. These reasons are set out below in summary fashion. The chapters that follow will discuss each of these fifty reasons in detail.

§402. THE FIFTY REASONS

The following list sets out fifty reasons why variable annuities may be better than mutual funds as long-term investments. At the end of each item the chapter that discusses the stated reason is set out in parenthesis.

1. Non-qualified annuities grow tax-deferred, mutual funds don't. (Chapters 9 and 10).

2. Mutual funds rarely provide the annual 15% long-term capital gains rate that they claim owners can receive. On the other hand, variable annuity payments received in retirement are taxed at 15% even when the recipient's tax bracket is as high as 25%. (Chapter 8).

3. Mutual funds create an income tax trap for individuals purchasing funds late in the year. Variable annuities do not present a similar problem where late year purchases are made. (Chapter 12).

4. Mutual funds can make annual *taxable* distributions to fund owners even where their fund has gone down in value. Variable annuities do not generate income taxes when they have lost value. (Chapter 13).

5. Mutual fund ownership along with the annual distributions made by such mutual funds can subject the fund owner to taxation under the alternative minimum tax (AMT) structure. The AMT always results in increased income taxes. Variable annuity ownership cannot trigger the AMT in the same manner as mutual funds. (Chapter 16).

6. Variable annuities are easy to position so that at the owner's death the variable annuity will not be subject to either estate or income taxes. The same tax reduction techniques do not work nearly as well with mutual funds. (Chapter 18).

7. Mutual fund ownership can result in the loss of tax exemptions. This does not occur where variable annuities are owned. (Chapter 19).

8. Ownership of mutual funds can result in the loss of income tax deductions. Variable annuity ownership does not create the same tax loss. (Chapter 20).

9. Mutual fund ownership can cause the owner to lose tax credits. This does not occur where variable annuities are owned. (Chapter 21).

10. Variable annuities allow for restricted beneficiary designations and allow non-qualified "stretches" (Chapter 25).

11. Under the current tax climate, it is more likely that capital gains rates and capital gains holding periods will increase rather than decrease. If either capital gains rates or their holding period increase, it will raise income taxes for owners of mutual funds. Variable annuities, being tax-deferred, would be unaffected. (Chapter 24).

12. Beneficiaries of variable annuities will usually receive a larger amount by inheriting a variable annuity than a mutual fund even though the mutual fund beneficiaries receive a step-up in basis. Additionally, variable annuities have no stepped-down basis as do mutual funds. (Chapter 25).

13. The ownership of mutual funds can restrict or eliminate one's ability to fund other retirement accounts such as IRAs. Mutual fund ownership can also prevent one from converting a traditional IRA to a Roth IRA. Variable annuities present no such restrictions or limitations. (Chapter 26).

14. The ownership of mutual funds can, in many cases, cause Social Security to be subject to income taxes. Variable annuity ownership does not present the same problem. (Chapter 27).

15. When a variable annuity is sold at a loss, the tax treatment of that loss is more beneficial than an equal loss with a mutual fund. (Chapter 28).

16. The ownership of mutual funds may require the mutual fund owner to pay estimated taxes. Variable annuity ownership does not create the same tax problem. (Chapter 29).

17. Mutual funds are subject to state and local income taxes in those states that have such taxes. Variable annuities, because they are tax-deferred, are not subject to state and local income taxes while in the accumulation phase. (Chapter 30).

18. Variable annuities almost always prove to be less expensive to own than equivalent mutual funds. (Chapters 31-36). In addition, mutual fund costs tend to go up over time. Variable annuity costs are always fixed at the time the variable annuity is purchased and guaranteed not to go up. (Chapter 50).

19. The record-keeping requirements for owning mutual funds are significantly more complex than the record-keeping requirements for owning variable annuities. (Chapter 36).

20. Many states provide either complete or partial statutory protection to variable annuities from the claims of creditors. No state provides protection from creditors for mutual funds or stocks. (Chapter 37).

21. Mutual funds are commonly part of a decedent's estate which makes such funds available to all creditors of the estate. Variable annuities, on the other hand, are almost always non-probate property that do not pass through a decedent's estate and therefore are not subject to the reach of creditors of the decedent. (Chapter 37).

22. Mutual funds, because they are almost always part of a decedent's estate, are subject to the delays and expenses of probate. Variable annuities, because they pass outside of probate directly to beneficiaries, are not subject to similar delays and costs. (Chapter 38).

23. Attempting to position mutual funds so they will not pass through probate almost always results in additional taxes, costs or delays. (Chapter 38).

24. Mutual funds may disqualify the owner from obtaining tuition assistance for a child to attend college. Variable annuities do not present the same problem. (Chapter 39).

25. Owners of variable annuities can adjust their annuities so that they are not considered fully as an asset for Medicaid qualification. Typical mutual funds cannot be adjusted in a similar manner. (Chapter 40).

26. Variable annuities provide basic as well as enhanced death benefits to the beneficiaries of the variable annuity owners. Typical mutual funds do not provide any death benefit whatsoever. (Chapter 43).

27. Variable annuities provide dollar-cost averaging to variable annuity owners at no expense. Mutual funds, except for principal protected funds, do not provide this benefit on a cost-free basis to fund owners. (Chapter 44).

28. Mutual funds do not provide automatic asset rebalancing whereas variable annuities do. (Chapter 44).

29. Many variable annuities offer premium bonuses. Mutual funds do not offer similar bonuses. (Chapter 45).

30. Many variable annuities today provide guaranteed protection against loss of principal. Mutual funds, except for a few stable value funds, do not offer this same protection. (Chapter 45).

31. Many variable annuities today provide a guaranteed rate of return on fixed accounts within variable annuities. Mutual funds do not provide the same benefit. (Chapter 45).

32. Variable annuities can be used to keep a life insurance owner from having to sell a life insurance policy at a loss. Mutual funds cannot be used for this purpose. (Chapter 46).

33. Withdrawals can be made from variable annuities and used to purchase things such as retirement homes, yachts, etc. without having to pay income taxes on the withdrawals. (Chapter 48).

34. The risk of company insolvency rests with the owner of a mutual fund. Variable annuity owners are not exposed to similar insolvency risks. (Chapter 42).

35. Variable annuities allow the annuity owner to trade among different sub-account families on a commission-free basis. This is not a benefit extended to the owners of mutual funds. (Chapter 35).

36. A variable annuity owner may exchange his variable annuity for a completely different variable annuity without triggering income taxes on gains. A mutual fund owner cannot move his funds from one mutual fund company to another without triggering an income tax on gains. (Chapter 35).

37. Variable annuities provide long-term fixed income options. Mutual funds do not. (Chapter 50).

38. Beneficiaries of non-qualified variable annuities receive an income tax deduction under IRC § 691 when inheriting a variable annuity. Beneficiaries of non-qualified mutual funds do not receive a similar income tax deduction. (Chapter 25).

39. If the United States tax system is modified to include a flat tax, mutual fund owners will be at a disadvantage while variable annuity owners will reap a tax windfall. (Chapter 33). The same will occur with a national sales tax. (Chapter 22).

40. Variable annuities can provide their owners with a guaranteed stream of income for their entire lifetime. Mutual funds cannot provide the same benefit. (Chapter 6).

41. The exclusion ratio allows a variable annuity owner to use annuitization to shelter large portions of variable annuity payments from current income taxes. Mutual funds do not provide a similar exclusion ratio. (Chapter 6).

42. Mutual funds are subject to intangibles taxes in those states where intangibles taxes are levied. Variable annuities are universally exempt from intangibles taxes. (Chapter 30).

43. The owner of a variable annuity who elects to dollar-cost average into sub-accounts usually receives an interest rate well above the market rate on money waiting to be invested. Mutual fund owners who seek the benefit of dollar-cost averaging do not receive similar above market rates of interest on money awaiting investment. (Chapter 44).

44. Variable annuities allow owners to control precisely how much money will be withdrawn from their variable annuity and thus allow the variable annuity owner to control taxes. Mutual fund owners have no similar control. Mutual fund owners are subject to involuntary mutual fund distributions of capital gains and dividends each year whether they want such distributions or not. (Chapters 8 and 10).

45. If other mutual fund owners redeem their shares and leave a fund, this will have the impact of raising the potential tax burden of those mutual fund owners who remain in the fund. This tax trap is referred to as the embedded gain problem. Variable annuities contain no similar tax disadvantage. (Chapter 13).

46. Many variable annuities waive any surrender penalties when individuals suffer a serious illness, are required to go into a nursing home, lose their job, etc. Mutual funds do not provide a similar benefit where contingent deferred sales charges are imposed on mutual fund owners. (Chapter 17 and 45).

47. Variable annuities, when initially purchased, allow owners a period of time to revoke their purchase without cost. Mutual funds do not allow this benefit. (Chapter 41).

48. Some mutual funds dictate when a mutual fund owner may sell his mutual funds or impose a redemption fee when funds are sold. Variable annuities can be sold at any time without restriction. Variable annuities never charge additional redemption fees if one wants to sell their variable annuity. (Chapter 33).

49. There are costly tax traps associated with the buying and selling of mutual funds. Similar tax traps do not exist for variable annuities. (Chapter 14).

50. Mutual funds not only require annual taxation when the mutual fund is going up in value, but also impose income taxes when the mutual fund is going down in value. Variable annuities, being tax-deferred, impose no annual income taxes regardless of whether the variable annuity is increasing or decreasing in value. (Chapter 15).

§403. CONCLUSION

The above list demonstrates that there are many reasons why investors should consider owning variable annuities rather than mutual funds if they are long-term investors. This list is not exclusive and others may have additional benefits to add to this list. It is interesting to note that whenever proponents of mutual funds are asked to provide a list of benefits available to long-term mutual fund investors *vis-a-vis* long-term variable annuity investors, they are usually unable to list more than one or two reasons.

- CHAPTER 5 -

UNDERSTANDING VARIABLE ANNUITY TERMINOLOGY

§501. INTRODUCTION

One of the major hurdles to understanding the many benefits provided by variable annuities is the terminology used when describing these annuities. Financial professionals and investors must take time to make sure they fully understand the somewhat complex terminology encountered when dealing with variable annuities. Sadly, more variable annuity sales fail to materialize due to a misunderstanding of terminology than just about any other reason.

§ 502. CONFUSING TERMS

The three most confusing terms investors must contend with when trying to understand variable annuities are:

- Variable annuity (or deferred variable annuity);
- Annuitization; and
- Immediate annuity.

Investors cannot properly consider investing in variable annuities unless they understand the terminology associated with these annuities. For example, few investors really understand the difference between a variable annuity and annuitization. Many laypeople associate the word annuity with giving an insurance company a lump sum of money in exchange for a series of lifetime payments. They believe annuitization has something to do with variable annuities. Although the above terms are related, it is critical for investors to realize that these concepts are not interdependent. For example, one can own a variable annuity without ever being involved with annuitization. An immediate annuity is an annuity that pays money out to the annuity owner and has nothing to do with a variable annuity whose primary purpose is to accumulate wealth. The three terms set out above are discussed in the sections that follow.

§503. THE VARIABLE ANNUITY

In its simplest form a variable annuity is nothing more than a financial vehicle that allows an investor to purchase diversified investments[1] without having to pay income taxes on the gains made on these investments as long as they are held. Frequently, variable annuities are referred to as deferred annuities or deferred variable annuities because any income taxes owed on any gain made in the sub-accounts purchased through the variable annuity are deferred until withdrawn

---

[1] The investments made in variable annuities are technically called sub-accounts. These sub-accounts are substantially similar to mutual funds.

in the future. The word variable refers to the fact that a variable annuity can move up or down in value depending on the performance of the stock market and sub-accounts selected by the variable annuity owner. Like any other investment, a variable annuity owner is always free to close out his variable annuity and take the account value at any time.[2]

Example
Betty invested $12,000 a year in a variable annuity for 12 years. Her net return was fairly constant at 7%. At the end of 12 years, she had accumulated $229,688[3] and decided to cash out of her variable annuity to buy a small farm. The growth in her account was $85,687.[4] Betty paid $18,851 in income taxes at 22% on the growth and used the balance of nearly $211,000 to buy her farm.

Tax deferral merely delays income taxes until some future date when withdrawals are taken from the variable annuity. At that time, income taxes will be due. The major benefit of the tax deferral obtained with variable annuities is that a variable annuity owner's investments grow in value to a much larger amount than if they were held in a taxable investment because no income taxes are *currently* paid on gains. Once investors realize that variable annuities are essentially a way to purchase diversified investments without having to pay current income taxes, they are usually more receptive to learning about the many other benefits offered by variable annuities. For the remainder of this book, the term variable annuity will be used as a synonym for deferred annuity or deferred variable annuity. (See Chapter 9 for more on tax deferral).

§504. THE IMMEDIATE ANNUITY

An immediate annuity is simply the opposite of a variable annuity. As mentioned above, a variable annuity is a tax-deferred investment vehicle designed to accumulate wealth. An immediate annuity is not tax-deferred nor is it a wealth accumulation vehicle. An immediate annuity arises whenever a lump sum of money is transferred to an insurance company in exchange for the insurance company's agreement to pay a stream of income to the purchaser for a set number of years or for his lifetime. Most immediate annuities are designed to pay out the full amount used to purchase the annuity to the purchaser's survivors if the purchaser should die prematurely. When a variable annuity or other accumulated wealth is exchanged for an immediate annuity the process is called annuitization. A variable annuity owner may annuitize his variable annuity in the future if he elects, but is under no obligation to do so.

---

[2] Surrender penalties and IRS penalties may apply to early withdrawals from a variable annuity. A variable annuity owner who is a long-term investor, need not be concerned about these penalties.

[3] $12,000 per year x 7% x 12 years = $229,688.

[4] $229,688 - $144,000 = $85,687.

§505. ANNUITIZATION

Annuitization has little to do with investing in variable annuities. Anyone who has accumulated any type of retirement nest egg may transfer that nest egg to an insurance company for a guaranteed stream of income. This process of exchanging a lump sum of money for a guaranteed series of lifetime payments is referred to as annuitization. It does not matter whether the nest egg was accumulated by investing in variable annuities, stocks, bonds, real estate or any other form of investment.   It is critical for investors who buy variable annuities to realize that annuitization is *always an option* they have. Annuitization is *never* mandatory. Annuitization may be more advantageous to some individuals than others as the following example demonstrates:

Example

Jane's husband died ten years ago. The only asset he left Jane was a $100,000 life insurance policy. Jane invested the $100,000 in the stock market and doubled it over the ten years since her husband's death. Jane is now 72 and needs more than the $6,000 in income that she could get on her $200,000 from cash equivalents. Jane is no longer able to weather the ups and downs of the stock market. Additionally, Jane fears that she could outlive her $200,000 nest egg. Annuitization of Jane's $200,000 can solve all of her concerns. A $200,000 lump sum annuitized for the lifetime of a 72-year-old female could generate annual payments of $10,000 for the annuity owner's lifetime. This stream of payments is $4,000 more per year than what Jane could get with cash equivalents paying 3%. The insurance company would guarantee that, at a minimum, Jane's $200,000 would be paid to her or her beneficiaries if Jane died prematurely. Jane would also be guaranteed $10,000 a year for as long as she lived even if the total of these payments exceeded $200,000. Annuitization would also allow Jane to take advantage of the exclusion ratio which is discussed in §604 below. The exclusion ratio allows recipients of annuity payments to receive favorable current income tax treatment on their annuity payments. This means that Jane would pay income taxes on only a portion of her annuity income. Additionally, Jane's payments are fixed and guaranteed by the annuity issuer, thus freeing her from having to worry about what the stock market might do in the future.

As the above example demonstrates, annuitization by Jane of her $200,000 may well have been a good choice for her. However, for a 35-year-old, the election to annuitize $200,000 might not be as beneficial. Annuitization is discussed more fully in the next chapter.

§506. OTHER TYPES OF ANNUITIES

There are many different types of annuities. This book addresses only variable annuities. The immediate annuity was discussed above in §504. The following list sets out the other types of annuities that are available to the public:

- Fixed annuity – This annuity allows an investor to own a tax-deferred product that pays a set rate of return. They are often used as substitutes for money market accounts or bank CDs when an investor desires tax deferral.

- Income annuity – This annuity requires a payment today and will provide income for life at some age in the future.

- Indexed fixed annuity – This annuity is a fixed annuity that pegs the rate it pays to an index such as the S&P 500.

- Variable immediate annuity – This annuity is similar to an immediate annuity except that the payments can increase or decrease with the stock market's fluctuations because the owner's money is actually invested, at least partially, in the stock market.

§507. CONCLUSION

Investors need to understand that variable annuities are investment vehicles that allow the purchase of diversified investments that grow on an income tax-deferred basis. They are designed to accumulate wealth over time. Investing in variable annuities is independent of annuitization. Anyone with a retirement nest egg held in a variable annuity, stocks, bonds, CDs or any other investment is free to annuitize these sums or not. This book is primarily concerned with assisting financial professionals and their clients in understanding the many benefits of long-term variable annuity investing. Only where it would be important will the *optional* concept of annuitization be discussed.

- CHAPTER 6 -

ANNUITIZATION AND THE EXCLUSION RATIO

§601. INTRODUCTION

Annuitization is the process of exchanging a lump sum of money for a fixed stream of income that is guaranteed for a set period of time or one's lifetime. The exclusion ratio is applied to payments received when annuitization of a non-qualified variable annuity occurs. The effect of the exclusion ratio is to reduce current income taxes on the stream of income produced when annuitization occurs. There are other benefits available when one elects to annuitize a sum of money.

§602. ANNUITIZATION

Annuitization is always optional. It is never mandatory. Many investors believe if they buy a variable annuity they can only get their money back in the form of periodic payments over time or for their lifetime. This is not the case. Variable annuities are like most other investment vehicles. They can be liquidated by their owners for their net value at any time.[1] Annuitization is an attractive option for many, but not all variable annuity owners. Older people without spouses frequently find annuitization of assets to be financially beneficial.

§603. THE ANNUITIZATION PROCESS

Anyone with a lump sum of money can transfer it to an insurance or annuity company for an annuity contract that will return a stream of income to be paid monthly, quarterly or yearly, for a set number of years or for the lifetime of the purchaser. This process is called annuitization. When annuitization occurs, the annuity held by the owner is called an immediate annuity (which pays out income) to distinguish it from a deferred or variable annuity (which accumulates wealth).

The amount of an annuity payment is based on five factors:

- The amount transferred to the annuity company;
- The age of the annuitant;
- The length of time the payments are to be made;
- Whether the payments will be based on a single or joint life; and
- The frequency of payments (i.e. monthly, quarterly or annual payments).

---

[1] Surrender fees and IRS penalties may apply in some cases where a variable annuity is liquidated prematurely.

§604. THE EXCLUSION RATIO

If money used to buy an annuity has already been taxed, it will not be taxed at a later time when the money is taken out of the annuity. Such money is excluded from income taxation by use of the exclusion ratio. (Chapter 10 also discusses the exclusion ratio). The following simple example demonstrates how the exclusion ratio works:

> **Example**
> Jim bought a variable annuity for $200,000 when he was 55 years old. Today, he is 75 and his annuity is worth $600,000. He has decided to annuitize the $600,000 for a ten-year period. The annuity company has agreed to pay Jim $80,000 a year for ten years. Because 1/4 of the $800,000 expected payout was money that had previously been taxed, 1/4 of each $80,000 annuity payment ($20,000) will be excluded from taxation. Three-fourths of each annuity payment, or $60,000, will be deemed taxable income to Jim each year.[2]

If an annuity is not annuitized, all withdrawals for the annuity are considered fully taxable to the extent that they represent growth. Once all growth has been taxed any excess will be considered invested principal and will not be subject to income taxation. In the above example, Jim could have opted not to annuitize his annuity and simply taken withdrawals as needed. Once all of his growth was taxed (approximately $400,000)[3] his $200,000 principal investment could be withdrawn without Jim having to pay income taxes on this amount.

§605. CALCULATION OF THE EXCLUSION RATIO

The calculation of the exclusion ratio is difficult. Annuity companies are glad to make this calculation for investors and financial professionals. Based on the data supplied, an annuity company can determine what amount of each annual payment generated by an immediate annuity would be excluded from income taxation by the exclusion ratio and what portion would not be excluded. Such a calculation should be requested by anyone considering the annuitization of a variable annuity or other sums of money.

§606. BENEFITS OF ANNUITIZATION

Annuitization is an option that may be of value to certain people. The following six benefits are available when annuitization is elected. If these benefits would be of value to an investor then annuitization should be considered.

- A guaranteed stream of income is paid;
- The stream of income provided is guaranteed to be paid for a set

---

[2] It is assumed that this variable annuity is guaranteed for a 10 year period.

[3] This $400,000 will also grow during withdrawals and may increase in value to an amount in excess of $400,000.

number of years or the life of the purchaser (or the life of the purchaser and another person if desired);

- Payments are fixed and not subject to stock market fluctuations;[4]
- The stream of income can be adjusted for inflation;
- The annuity can be designed so it will pay the full initial investment (i.e. premium) to the purchaser or his beneficiaries; and
- A large part of the income stream provided by the annuity may be excluded from income taxes by application of the exclusion ratio.

In a study conducted by *Kiplinger's Personal Finance* magazine, the advantages of annuitization were discussed. In the article, a hypothetical investment of $10,000 was placed into both a typical variable annuity and a no-load mutual fund. Annual expenses for the annuity were set at 1% above the annual expense of owning the mutual fund and it was assumed that the annuity charged a $30 annual maintenance fee. A 32% average tax rate was assumed. The mutual fund's annual distribution was 30% ordinary income, 30% long-term capital gain and 40% unrealized capital gain. The hypothetical fund owner sold 25% of his portfolio each year and reinvested the proceeds. A 12% return on investment was assumed for both investments. The study concluded that at the end of 30 years the hypothetical annuity owner following annuitization would receive an after-tax retirement income of $13,703 for 20 years. If the fund owner cashed out of his fund, paid taxes and purchased a 20-year immediate annuity with the net proceeds, he would receive an after-tax retirement income of less than $9,200 or one-third less than the variable annuity owner!

§607. OPTING FOR ANNUITIZATION

There are many cases where annuitization can be quite attractive. The following examples examine cases where annuitization is elected and where it is not.

Example #1
Bob, a widower, is 73 and has a variable annuity worth $210,000. He bought it 12 years ago for $93,000. Bob has other retirement income of $35,000 and would like $20,000 more that he can count on for his retirement. Bob's financial planner suggested that Bob annuitize his $210,000 variable annuity and purchase an immediate annuity guaranteeing payments for life or ten years, whichever is longer. Assuming a life expectancy of 83 and using a 4% annuitization rate, Bob would receive the following benefits:

---

[4] Immediate annuities can be purchased that will base payments on stock market performance. Not to confuse things, but these annuities are called variable immediate annuities.

- Bob would receive $22,100 a year in guaranteed payments;

- Bob would receive his $22,100 for as long as he lived;

- The annuity company would pay out a *minimum* of $221,000 (or ten payments) either to Bob or his beneficiaries;

- Bob's payments would not be affected by stock market gyrations;

- Bob could opt to have his payments adjusted for inflation if needed; and

- A large part of each $22,100 annual payment received would be excluded from income taxes by applying his exclusion ratio.

Example #2

Ellen is 71 years old and single. She has a mutual fund portfolio she purchased twelve years ago that is now worth $189,000. She initially invested $93,000 in the funds. Ellen has $35,000 in other income and would like $20,000 more that she can count on for her retirement. Ellen's financial planner suggested that Ellen live off the distributions of her mutual funds. If Ellen makes this election she will have the following problems:

- Any annual income from her funds will not be guaranteed to produce the needed $20,000;

- She would not have a guarantee that she would not outlive her money;

- She would have no guarantee as to what she would receive each year or what would pass to her beneficiaries in case of her death;

- Her income would depend on what the stock market was doing;

- She would not be guaranteed fixed payments that could be adjusted for inflation; and

- She would not be able to control her mutual fund distributions and therefore her income tax liability.

As the above examples demonstrate, the option to annuitize can provide some attractive benefits that cannot be obtained from an equal amount of non-annuitized money. Mutual fund proponents argue that investors with large mutual fund holdings may purchase an immediate annuity or annuitize their mutual fund portfolio at any time just like a variable annuity owner can. This statement is misleading for two reasons:

- Because mutual fund portfolios are taxed annually, they will have much less in them at retirement to annuitize than a variable annuity; and

- There are usually transaction costs (commissions or income taxes) to pay when large mutual fund portfolios are liquidated. This also reduces the amount available for annuitization.

For the two reasons stated above it is highly unlikely that a mutual fund investor would be able to obtain the same benefit from annuitization as would a variable annuity owner. See Chapter 9 for more on tax deferral.

§608. REVOCABLE ANNUITIZATION

One of the major objections to annuitizing money is that such an election is usually irrevocable. The annuity industry has responded to this concern by allowing one to annuitize on revocable basis.[5] Recently, more variable annuity companies have begun to offer revocable annuitization. Annuity companies that currently offer revocable annuitization are receiving almost no requests for revocation from investors who have elected to annuitize assets. It seems that once investors begin to enjoy the benefits of annuitization they have little reason to reverse this process.

§609. CONCLUSION

Investors need to understand that they may invest in variable annuities without the requirement that they formally annuitize their annuity in the future. The option to annuitize, along with the exclusion ratio, may prove helpful in the future to some variable annuity owners. Where annuitization provides benefits to a variable annuity owner he should discuss the possibility of annuitization with his financial professional. Annuitization is an option that is available and should be considered by those investors who need the guarantees provided by annuitization. The annuitization of a variable annuity will always be more beneficial than the annuitization of a similar mutual fund portfolio.

---

[5] The annuity industry also refers to revocable annuitization as commutation. See §1004 below.

- CHAPTER 7 -

METHODOLOGY AND COMPARISON DATA

§701. INTRODUCTION

Comparing mutual funds and variable annuities can be a difficult task unless reasonable data and assumptions are used in making such comparisons. This chapter discusses the data and methodology used to compare mutual funds and variable annuities in this book.

§702. WHAT IS BEING COMPARED

This book compares equity-based, non-qualified variable annuities sold by financial professionals with actively managed, equity-based, non-qualified mutual funds sold by financial professionals.[1] See §702B for the comparison of qualified variable annuities and mutual funds. To compare no-load mutual funds with variable annuities sold by financial professionals or vice versa would not be a valid comparison. If one wants to compare no-load mutual funds with variable annuities, then the variable annuities selected for comparison should also be no-load variable annuities sold directly to the public.

§702B. COMPARING QUALIFIED VARIABLE ANNUITIES AND MUTUAL FUNDS

It is critical to understand that all of the material in this book can be applied to the comparison of *qualified* variable annuities and mutual funds. When qualified variable annuities and mutual funds are compared, all of the tax issues relating to variable annuities and mutual funds become moot because both products are treated identically for tax purposes. For example, investors owning non-qualified mutual funds may believe that those who inherit their mutual funds will be better off tax-wise because such beneficiaries will receive the tax benefit provided by the step-up in basis which is not available to those who inherit variable annuities. This common myth becomes completely moot if the mutual funds and variable annuities being compared are *qualified*. The reason for this is that the tax treatment beneficiaries receive when they inherit *qualified* mutual funds or variable annuities is *identical* because the step-up in basis rule does not apply to qualified mutual funds that are inherited. In short, if qualified mutual funds and variable annuities are being compared, their tax treatment is identical and therefore other characteristics, such as the cost of ownership, are the only comparisons that are relevant.

---

[1] The term non-qualified is used to refer to mutual funds and variable annuities not held in a retirement account such as an IRA, Roth IRA, 401(k), 403(b), etc.

§703. ANNUAL OWNERSHIP COSTS OF MUTUAL FUNDS AND VARIABLE ANNUITIES

Both mutual fund and variable annuity companies charge an annual expense that is used to pay their investment managers and other related expenses. On average, mutual funds have annual expenses of 1.5% (which includes 12b-1 fees) while variable annuities have average annual expenses of 2.2% (which includes 12b-1 fees). This 2.2% figure also includes a mortality and expense (M&E) charge which averages 1.3% for the typical variable annuity. Investors should feel free to adjust these percentages to better reflect their actual situation. For example, if an investor wants to compare a mutual fund with an annual expense of 1.4% with a variable annuity with an annual expense of 2.1%, then these actual figures should be used to make comparisons. Annual expenses for mutual funds (technically called annual expense ratios) are usually imposed quarterly on the mutual fund's account value. This book, for simplicity purposes, will levy such expenses only once at year's end. Variable annuity expenses and M&E charges are also assessed quarterly against account values. They too will be levied annually in the comparisons made in this book.

§704. ANNUAL GROSS RATE OF RETURN

The rate of return is the easiest piece of comparison data to establish. As long as both the variable annuities and mutual funds being compared use identical and reasonable rates of return a valid comparison can be made. Unless stated to the contrary, the examples that compare mutual funds and variable annuities in this book use a 10% gross rate of return. The 10% gross rate of return was selected because it is realistic and reasonable given that the overall market for more than three decades (as measured by the S&P 500) has produced annual returns slightly in excess of this 10% figure.

§705. COMMISSIONS AND LOADS

In addition to annual management expenses averaging 1.5% mutual funds usually charge commissions in one of four ways:

- Up-front commissions of from 2% to 6% (commonly called A-share loads).

- Deferred sales charges where no up-front commission is charged but instead, the annual expense of owning the fund is increased by approximately 1%. (Commonly called B-share loads).

- An additional fee added to the cost of the mutual fund of .75% to 1.50% until the fund is sold (commonly called C-share loads).

- An annual money management fee paid to a fee only financial planner to select and manage an investor's mutual fund portfolio.

There are other commission structures for mutual funds, but the four listed above are the most common. Rather than assume investors pay commissions only in one of the four ways mentioned above, the examples in this book will alter these methods. The method of paying commissions will be specified in the examples. In some cases, commissions or loads may even be ignored to cover those situations where one has obtained their mutual funds by gift or inheritance or in some other manner where a commission or load may not have been paid by the current owner. It is important for investors to use the actual commission or load they are paying, or will pay, for their mutual funds when comparing these funds to variable annuities. Mutual fund commissions are discussed more fully in Chapter 34. Commissions on variable annuities are paid differently than for mutual funds. As a basic rule, the variable annuity companies pay commissions directly to the professionals who sell their annuities. Variable annuity companies pay commissions to the seller of their variable annuities based on the assumption that the buyers of their variable annuities will be long-term investors. For this reason, variable annuities have holding periods. If a variable annuity purchaser buys a variable annuity with a holding period of six years and sells his variable annuity before this period expires, he will be charged a contingent deferred sales charge or CDSC that is designed to help the variable annuity issuer recoup some of the commission it advanced to the financial professional involved when the annuity was purchased. CDSCs usually run for an average of six years and decline 1% a year until they disappear. This book will assume a 7% CDSC that declines 1% a year for seven years unless otherwise noted.

§706. ANNUAL INCOME TAXATION OF MUTUAL FUNDS

Mutual funds are taxed each year based on realized (i.e. actual) gains resulting from the purchase and sale of investments by the mutual fund company. Distributions of realized gains are allocated to fund owners proportionately based on their ownership interest in the fund. For example, a fund holder with $100,000 worth of a mutual fund would get a distribution that is ten times larger than a fund owner who owned only $10,000 worth of the fund. Realized gains are reported to both the IRS and fund holders annually. Fund holders must report these realized gains on their income tax returns and pay taxes on them. Several of the country's leading researchers who have studied the impact of income taxes on mutual fund ownership have put the current average annual income tax loss at 20% of a fund's annual net gain. Tom Roseen, a senior research analyst with Lipper, Inc., recently authored a detailed study of the reduction in annual mutual fund gains resulting from federal income taxation.[2] This current research demonstrates that federal income taxes, on average, reduce mutual net fund gains by 20%. Joel Dickson, who heads Vanguard's Active Quantitative Equity Group. agrees that the current annual federal income tax loss on gains generated by the typical equity mutual fund is approximately 2.0%, as does Robert Arnott, who is the Chairman of Research Affiliates, L.L.C. and the former editor of *Financial Analysts Journal*. This book uses a 20% income tax loss figure in its examples where mutual funds and variable annuities are being compared. Section 804 also discusses the tax liability of mutual fund ownership. Regardless of the tax loss assumed in this book, investors should use their *actual* annual tax loss when comparing a potential mutual fund investment with a potential variable annuity investment. The following example demonstrates the use of a 10% annual net rate of return for a mutual fund reduced by 2% for income taxes.

Example
Paul purchased a mutual fund for $100,000. He held it for ten years. The annualized net rate of return was 10%, but this return was reduced to 8% due to the imposition of annual income taxes. Paul's mutual fund would be worth $215,892 after ten years.[3] This example ignores any non-tax costs associated with the purchase of the mutual fund (i.e. commissions, etc.).

As mentioned, an investor should always use his actual income tax loss when comparing mutual funds and variable annuities. For example, if an investor owns $100,000 worth of a mutual fund that distributes 10% of its value resulting in income taxes of $2,000, he should use a 2% annual tax loss figure in any calculations he makes regarding his mutual fund. On the other hand, if he pays $3,000 in income taxes, then he should use a 3% annual tax loss instead.

§707. TAXATION OF MUTUAL FUNDS WHEN SOLD

Not all of a mutual fund's annual growth is paid out in realized gains. Some gains are paper gains or unrealized gains that are not taxed currently. They will be taxed at a later time when these paper gains are realized or the fund is sold. The following simplified example demonstrates how realized and unrealized gains are taxed to mutual fund owners.

Example
Ron invested $100,000 in a mutual fund. A year later, the fund had increased in value by 10% to $110,000. Of this $10,000 gain, only 60%, or $6,000, was realized gain. The other 40%, or $4,000, was unrealized gain and is not subject

---

[2] The most detailed study on mutual fund income taxes is Lipper, Inc.'s "Taxes in the Mutual Fund Industry - 2010 - Assessing the Impact of Taxes on Shareholders' Returns." Tom Roseen was the senior researcher on this project. The annual tax loss referred to in this chapter deals only with *federal* income taxes. State and local income taxes are discussed in Chapter 30.

[3] $100,000 x 10 years x 8% = $215,892.

to current taxation. When Ron reports the $6,000 realized gain on his tax return, he will be able to add this $6,000 to his original $100,000 purchase price of his fund. This process is referred to as making an upward adjustment to cost basis. This prevents a mutual fund owner from paying taxes on a realized gain previously taxed when the mutual fund is later sold. For example, Ron's cost basis after reporting and paying taxes on the $6,000 realized gain he made will now be $106,000. If Ron sells his fund tomorrow for $110,000, he will have to pay taxes only on the remaining profit of $4,000. The $4,000 would represent the unrealized gain that would become a *realized* gain when the fund was sold by Ron. Non-tax costs are ignored in this example.

§708A. TAXATION OF VARIABLE ANNUITIES

The major advantage of owning variable annuities is that, unlike mutual funds, variable annuities grow income tax-deferred. Income taxes are paid on the gains earned by the variable annuity at ordinary income tax rates when these gains are withdrawn in the future.

Example
Alice purchased a variable annuity for $100,000 and held it for ten years. The annuity increased at an annual net rate of return of 7.3%. After ten years, Alice's variable annuity was worth $202,301.[4] Of this amount, $102,301 is profit and if subject to income taxation at 25%, it would reduce the gain to $76,726. This amount combined with the original purchase price of $100,000 would make the variable annuity worth $176,726 on an after-tax basis. In this book, variable annuity gains are reduced by the average tax bracket that would be most appropriate for the facts presented. For clarity, non-tax costs were ignored in this example.

§708B. TRADING COSTS

Both mutual funds and variable annuities have trading costs. These are the costs incurred by mutual fund and variable annuity companies to buy and sell investments. Studies have shown that trading costs for mutual funds can reach 1% or more.[5] The trading costs for variable annuities are slightly lower at an average of 0.7%.[6] This minor difference is a result of the slightly greater selling activity of mutual funds. Every quarter (especially in the last quarter of the year) mutual fund companies engage in "window dressing" which involves the massive selling of losing positions in order to reduce potential capital gains taxes for the fund's owners as well as dress up the books with more gaining transactions than losing transactions.

---

[4] $100,000 x 10 years at 7.3% = $202,301.

[5] *Better Investing*, July 2001, p. 9 citing a Plexis Group Study. Bottom Line / Retirement Newsletter, Dec. 2007, interview with Ric Edelman for the article titled "Don't Let Investment Fees Eat You Alive."

[6] The turnover for variable annuities is 84% according to *Morningstar Principia*. For mutual funds it is 118. Thus trading costs for variable annuities would be approximately 71.1% that of mutual funds. Trading costs for mutual funds average 1.0% per year. Trading costs for variable annuities would be approximately 71.1% of the average mutual fund trading cost of 1% or 0.7%.

The comparisons in this book will use 0.7% as the trading cost for mutual funds and 0.5% for variable annuities. Actual trading costs should be used when non-hypothetical comparisons are being made.

§708C. MISCELLANEOUS MUTUAL FUND AND VARIABLE ANNUITY COSTS

Both mutual funds and variable annuities have some minor costs associated with their ownership. Mutual funds often impose annual administrative costs and miscellaneous fees. Variable annuities impose similar administrative costs and fees. These miscellaneous fees for mutual funds and variable annuities are usually quite small. In many cases these costs are waived or reduced. These minor fees will be ignored in the comparisons made in this book. However, it must be remembered that any miscellaneous costs actually charged in real comparisons must be factored into such comparisons.

§709. USING THE COMPARISON DATA

Unless stated otherwise, the comparisons made in this book will set the gross annual return for both mutual funds and variable annuities at 10%. Commissions will be set at 5% for A-share mutual funds and will be reduced for break-points. Annual expense ratios for mutual funds, including 12b-1 fees will be set at 1.5% and trading costs at 0.70%. Annual management fees for variable annuities will be set at 1.0%, mortality and expense fees (M&E) will be set at 1.2% and trading costs at 0.5%. Annual taxes imposed on mutual funds will be set at 20% of the fund's *net* gain. Unrealized gains for mutual funds will be taxed as if 30% of the mutual fund gain at liquidation is unrealized gain that becomes realized at sale. These gains will be taxed at appropriate long-term capital gains rates. Variable annuities will be taxed at a rate of 25% subject to adjustment if the facts of an example so dictate.

> **Example**
> Ben, who is 50, was interested in buying a mutual fund for $25,000. He planned on holding the fund for ten years. (Sara, Ben's wife wanted him to buy a variable annuity). Ben and Sara pay income taxes at 25%. Ben's commission to buy the fund was 5%, the annual expense ratio was 1.5%, trading costs were 0.7% and income taxes would reduce the fund's net rate of return by 20%. Based on this information, the mutual fund Ben was considering would have a net rate of return of 6.064%. This is calculated as follows:
>
> > $25,000 less 5% commission = $23,750. $23,750 + 10% gross return = $26,125 less 2.2% (annual expenses and trading costs) = $25,550.50. $25,550.50 less $23,750 (amount invested) = $1,800.50 gain less 20% income tax = $1,440 ÷ $23,750 (amount invested) = 6.064% net rate of return.

Example

Sara (Ben's wife), who is 50, was interested in investing $25,000 in a variable annuity. (Her husband Ben [in the last example] thought a mutual fund would be a better investment.) Sara and her husband pay income taxes at 25%. Sara planned on holding the annuity for ten years. The annuity charged no commission but had a 7% CDSC that declined 1% a year. The combined annual expense (1.0%) ratio and M&E (1.2%) were 2.2% and trading costs were 0.5%. Based on this information, the variable annuity Sara was considering would have a net rate of return of 7.030%. This is calculated as follows:

> $25,000 + 10% gross return = $27,500 less 2.7% (annual expenses, M&E and trading costs) = $26,758 - $25,000 investment = $1,758 gain ÷ $25,000 = 7.030% net rate of return.

Once a net rate of return is determined it can be used to calculate investment results over time. The results must be reduced for any income taxes due upon the sale of the investments being compared.

Example

In the previous examples, it was determined that the net rate of return that Ben could get from his mutual fund was 6.064% and that Sara could get a net rate of return of 7.030%. By applying these rates of return to the amounts invested, ending values ten years form now can be determined as follows:

- Ben's Mutual Fund: 6.064% x 10 years x $23,750 = $42,790

- Sara's Variable Annuity: 7.030% x 10 years x $25,000 = $49,317

The ending values determined above must be reduced by any income taxes that would be owed if these two investments were liquidated.

- Ben's Mutual Fund: $42,790 (ending value) - $23,750 (investment) = $19,040 in gain. Assuming 30% of the gain is long-term capital gains or $5,712. At a 15% tax this capital gain would generate a tax of $857. Ben's net (after-tax) mutual fund value after ten years would be $41,933 ($42,790 - $857).

- Sara's Variable Annuity: $49,317 (ending value) - $25,000 (investment) = $24,317 - 25% income tax = $18,238 + $25,000 (investment) = $43,238 net (after-tax) variable annuity value after ten years.

§710. THE 20% FEDERAL INCOME TAX LIABILITY – DETAILED EXPLANATION

As mentioned above, the typical, actively managed, equity-based, non-qualified mutual fund loses 20% of its net gain every year to federal income taxes. Some readers may assume that if a 20% tax liability is imposed on a mutual fund's net gain, that 100% of the fund's gain is subject to federal taxation in a given year. This is an inaccurate interpretation. What researchers have found is that *regardless* of a fund's net gain (e.g. 8%, 9%, 10%, etc.), twenty percentage points of that net gain on *average* are lost to the IRS each year. In some cases the loss could be 30% on a fund returning a net 10% while a tax loss of 20% might be found with a mutual fund returning a net 9%, and so on. The point the researchers are trying to make is *regardless* of a fund's annual return, the fund will lose on average twenty percentage points of its net gain to the IRS. This 20% tax loss is an *annual* tax loss and in no way eliminates the requirement that a fund owner pay income taxes on unrealized gains that become realized when the mutual fund is sold.

There are two major reasons why annual mutual fund income taxes exceed 15%:

- Mutual funds do not automatically guarantee annual taxation at a 15% rate. The primary reason for this is that distributions from mutual funds are rarely comprised of nothing but long-term capital gains and qualifying dividends. In most cases, a mutual fund's annual distribution will be made up of both short-term capital gains (including non-qualified dividends) and long-term capital gains (including qualifying dividends). If a mutual fund owner pays federal income taxes on his ordinary income at 33% and receives a distribution that is 70% long-term capital gains (including qualifying dividends) and 30% short-term capital gains (including non-qualifying dividends) his annual federal income tax liability on his mutual fund distribution is 20.4%, not 15%.

- Even where mutual fund distributions, due to low turnover, are taxed annually at 15%, the effective income tax liability on a mutual fund can still exceed 15% because mutual fund owners often pay federal income taxes on their annual mutual fund distribution regardless of whether the mutual fund goes up in value, remains constant or declines in value. If income taxes are paid when mutual returns are flat or have decreased in value, this will increase the effective income tax rate paid on those mutual fund distributions that have gone up in value. It is for this reason that a nominal 15% income liability can actually be much larger.

Example

Frank owns three mutual funds. He invested $20,000, after commissions, in his three mutual funds on January 1. Over a one-year period, Frank's mutual funds performed as follows:

(1) Mutual Fund #1: $20,000 invested. By year's end the value of the fund was up to $24,000. For the year, a distribution of $2,000 was made and not reinvested. After this distribution, Frank's first mutual fund had its value reduced to $22,000 to account for the distribution made.

(2) Mutual Fund #2: $20,000 invested. By year's end the value of the fund was unchanged at $20,000. For the year, a distribution of $1,500 was made and not reinvested. After this distribution Frank's second mutual fund had its value reduced to $18,500 to account for the distribution made.

(3) Mutual Fund #3: $20,000 invested. By year's end the value of the fund was down $1,000 to $19,000. For the year, a distribution of $1,500 was made and not reinvested. After this distribution, Frank's third mutual fund had its value reduced to $17,500 to account for the distribution made.

Frank's mutual funds were only worth $58,000 ($22,000 + $18,500 + $17,500) one year after buying them. Of this amount, Frank received $5,000 in cash distributions ($2,000 + $1,500 + $1,500). Thus by year's end, Frank had a net gain of $3,000 ($5,000 in cash distributions less $2,000 downward adjustment in value). Frank had to report his $5,000 in cash distributions and pay taxes on this amount. Although his tax liability was 15% (long-term capital gains) or $750, this $750 tax was incurred on a net gain in value of $3,000. Thus, the effective tax rate was not 15%, but 25% ($750 ÷ $3,000).

§711. ANNUAL MUTUAL FUND INCOME TAXES – THE SOURCE FOR PAYMENT

In the examples used in this book, the average annual federal income tax liability of 20% is paid out of the mutual fund. This is rarely done in actual practice. The majority of mutual fund owners usually pay any annual income taxes from sources *other than* the mutual funds themselves. The reason this book assumes that taxes are paid out of the mutual funds that generate the income tax due is that it makes the math needed to do various comparisons much easier. If it were assumed that taxes were paid from other sources, a computer would be needed to make accurate comparisons rather than a calculator. In this book it will be assumed all costs and taxes are paid from a variable annuity when it is surrendered. This will make comparisons easier to understand.

When annual income taxes are paid out of the mutual funds that generate them, the owner has "freed-up" the out-of-pocket taxes he would have paid. The value of these freed-up payments must be factored into any comparison between where mutual fund taxes are paid out of the mutual fund or paid from separate sources. For example, if an investor purchases a mutual fund for $30,000 and holds it for seven years, his net after-tax and after-cost ending value will be

$46,741 if annual taxes (including liquidation taxes) are paid from other sources. If the annual taxes (including liquidation taxes) are paid from the mutual funds themselves, the net ending value will be $42,448. However, in this last situation, the fund owner does not have to pay income taxes out of his pocket each year and therefore the amount of these tax payments may be invested elsewhere. If these tax payments could be invested at an after-tax return of 8%, these payments will grow to an after-tax value of $4,548 in seven years. If this $4,548 is accounted for, the real ending value of the mutual funds which were reduced every year to pay annual income taxes increases to $46,996 which is almost exactly the ending value of the mutual fund investment where income taxes were paid from other sources. Another simple example might be helpful. A $10,000 mutual fund investment subject to the costs and taxes discussed in §709 above would be worth $10,076 (6.064% x 1 year x $9,500) a year later if income taxes are paid from the mutual fund. The same $10,000 would grow to $10,220 (7.580% x 1 year x $9,500) if income taxes were paid from another source. After reducing this figure by $144 for income taxes ($720 gain less 20% tax) paid from another source, the mutual fund would be worth exactly $10,076. Again, whether income taxes are paid from a mutual fund itself or from another source, the economic impact does not differ significantly. As can be seen, whether taxes are paid from a mutual fund or from other sources, when all economic aspects are factored in, the net ending value of the mutual fund will be nearly identical. (Chapter 10B expands on this topic).

§712. SKEWING OF COMPARISON DATA

The data selected for the comparison of mutual funds and variable annuities in this book has been skewed in favor of mutual funds in almost all regards. For example:

- An annual income tax loss of 20% of net gains was selected because it is slightly lower than the annual tax loss figure many mutual fund owners pay over time. Mutual fund owners frequently lose more to annual income taxes than the 20% figure used in this book. For one to have a 20% annual tax loss on his mutual fund's net gain merely requires the payment of $200 a year in taxes per $10,000 worth of funds returning a net 10%. Many mutual fund owners pay taxes well in excess of this amount.

- A gross 10% annual rate of return was selected because it represents a return that is slightly less than the stock market's long-term rate of return.

- It is assumed that when any variable annuity compared in this book is surrendered, it is surrendered all at one time and all income taxes are paid in a lump sum at the owner's highest marginal tax rate. This rarely occurs. When annual withdrawals are taken from a variable annuity instead of a lump sum, income taxes are greatly reduced.

- The fact that sub-accounts held in variable annuities may perform better than their counterpart mutual funds held outside of variable annuities (see §4703) is ignored in all calculations.

- Gains on the sale of mutual funds will be deemed to contain only 30% unrealized capital gains although this figure can be higher.

- The time value of money advantage of variable annuity tax deferral, although a major benefit is ignored in nearly all comparisons made in this book where it would be available. (See Chapter 10B).

- The commissions and loads on mutual funds used in the many hypothetical examples in this book do not exceed 1% a year. In reality, mutual fund commissions can easily exceed 1%. In *The Great Mutual Fund Trap* by Baer and Gensler (at p. 101) the authors found the average annual mutual fund commission to be nearly 1.4% a year.

- State and local income taxes are ignored in the examples in this book although Chapter 30 demonstrates that annual state and local income taxes can add as much as 0.5% to the annual cost of owning a mutual fund.

- The typical holding period for mutual funds is three years. This book often assumes holding periods of 15 to 25 years without imposing any additional commission costs or taxes on the fund owner for trading that would most likely occur.

- Rebalancing is commission-free with variable annuities and does not trigger an income tax. Rebalancing with mutual funds is often commission-free but will always generate an income tax where gains are realized. Although rebalancing with mutual funds and variable annuities is common, any tax cost involved with such rebalancing will be ignored for comparisons made in this book.

- All comparisons are made in upward moving markets. In reality the stock market has down years. These down years negatively affect the taxation of mutual funds but not variable annuities. (See Chapter 15 below.)

- Variable annuities include a cost for their death benefit. Mutual funds have no such benefit. The cost of the death benefit has *not* been taken out when variable annuities and mutual funds are compared.

Financial professionals reading this book should use the material discussed as a basic guide to comparing mutual funds with variable annuities. Once a basic understanding is accomplished, the *actual* data for a specific client can be used with *actual* mutual funds or variable annuities being considered by a client. Only by making accurate comparisons based on a client's *actual* data can a professional help determine whether a mutual fund or variable annuity is the best investment for their client.

§713. CONCLUSION

When comparing variable annuities and mutual funds on a hypothetical basis, reasonable and consistent data must be used. By using actual data, financial professionals can determine whether variable annuities or mutual funds are the better long-term investment for their clients. Only when a fair and impartial comparison of variable annuities and mutual funds is made, are investors able to make proper long-term investment decisions. It should be remembered that no existing method of determining the net ending value of a mutual fund or variable annuity is flawless. One need only review the web site for the SEC and FINRA and examine the mutual fund calculators they provide to the public to realize this. Good financial professionals should create a method for obtaining net ending values for mutual funds and variable annuities that they are comfortable with and can improve over time. Section 3409 sets out charts that can help with this process.

PART II - THE TAX CONSEQUENCES OF MUTUAL FUND OWNERSHIP

[Summary: Once income, gift and estate taxes are taken into consideration, investors will realize that long-term investing in variable annuities will produce better financial results than investing in mutual funds.]

- CHAPTER 8 -
THE CAPITAL GAINS MYTH

§801. INTRODUCTION

The common belief that mutual funds are taxed annually at a maximum 15% capital gains rate if held for more than a year is a myth. Similarly, the fact that one owns variable annuities and is in a 25% marginal tax bracket does not mean the variable annuity owner will pay his taxes at 25% or that he will pay 25% tax on his variable annuity withdrawals.

§802. THE MYTH OF THE 15% CAPITAL GAINS TAX

Many mutual fund investors have been led to believe that long-term ownership of these funds results in a maximum annual long-term capital gains tax rate of 15%, while withdrawals from variable annuities are subject to significantly higher ordinary income tax rates. Mutual fund proponents argue that the difference between the capital gains rate of 15% on mutual funds and the ordinary income tax rate of 25% or more on variable annuities makes mutual funds more attractive to own than variable annuities as long-term investments.[1] The assumption that holding appreciating mutual funds for more than a year will result in a maximum annual long-term capital gains tax of 15% is not accurate. Legally, mutual fund companies must, on an annual basis, distribute nearly all realized gains made by their funds to the funds' owners. These distributions are usually made late in the year and are reported to the IRS and fund owners on IRS Form 1099-DIV. Mutual fund owners use these forms to report fund gains on their individual income tax returns. Whether gains from holding a mutual fund receive 15% long-term capital gains tax treatment each year is exclusively a function of how long the mutual fund *company* holds the underlying investments it purchases and has almost nothing to do with how long a mutual fund *owner* holds his or her fund. For example, if one has owned a mutual fund for three years and the fund's managers do not hold a significant amount of the fund's investments for more than a year, a large portion of the fund's realized appreciation for that year will be taxed to the fund owner as ordinary income and not at the more favorable 15% long-term capital gains tax rate.

§803. THE TURNOVER RATIO

The frequency with which a mutual fund buys and sells investments is referred to as its turnover ratio. A turnover ratio of 100 means that on average, a mutual fund company

---

[1] The taxes mentioned in this and subsequent chapters refer only to federal capital gains and ordinary income taxes. State and local income taxes are discussed in Chapter 30.

sells and replaces its entire portfolio once a year. A turnover ratio of less than 100 means that a mutual fund company, on average, takes more than a year to completely turn over its entire portfolio. Thus, a mutual fund company with a turnover ratio of 50 would, on average, completely turn over its portfolio every two years. A mutual fund company with a turnover ratio of more than 100 means the company, on average, takes less than a year to turn over its entire portfolio. Therefore, a mutual fund company with a turnover ratio of 200 would completely sell its portfolio and replace it with new investments, on average, every six months. By dividing a mutual fund's turnover ratio into 1,200 one can determine, on average, how many *months* investments are held by the mutual fund company. For example, a mutual fund with the current average turnover ratio of 118 (Morningstar) holds its investments for approximately ten months. As a general rule, the higher a fund's turnover ratio the higher the potential ordinary income tax burden for the owner.

Because some part of a mutual fund's distribution is usually short-term capital gains, taxation at the 15% capital gains rate is not likely. The following example demonstrates this:

Example
Paul and Sue are young professionals who each have taxable incomes of $70,000. In early January of 2011 they determined that they would owe federal income taxes of $27,363 on their combined incomes for 2010. This would be a tax liability of 19.54%. Shortly thereafter, Paul and Sue each received a $15,000 distribution from their mutual fund. Half of each distribution was long-term capital gains and dividends while the other half was short-term capital gains. When these distributions were added to Paul and Sue's income for the year, their taxes rose by $6,450 to $33,363. With their taxable income at $170,000, their tax liability rose slightly to 19.62%. Both Paul and Sue were disappointed that they did not receive more benefit from the 15% tax treatment they believed they would get as mutual fund owners.

It must be remembered that it is a mutual fund company's investment activity and not the length of time an investor holds his mutual fund that dictates the rate at which the investor will pay income taxes on the annual increase in the value of his mutual funds. A more accurate comparison of the income tax impact of owning mutual funds and variable annuities can be made once this in understood. Another misunderstanding mutual fund owners have is assuming that a turnover ratio of less than 100 means that all investments held by a mutual fund company are held for at least a year before being sold thereby obtaining the more favorable 15% long-term capital gains tax treatment. This is not true. A turnover ratio of 100 signifies nothing more than, *on average*, a mutual fund company sells and replaces its whole portfolio once a year.

This means that some of the investments sold by the mutual fund company may have been held for less than a year while others may have been held for more than a year. Simply stated, a low turnover ratio may not provide mutual fund owners with complete protection from having to pay ordinary income taxes on some portion of their mutual fund gains.

§804. REVIEWING THE 1099-DIV FORM

Investors should review their Form 1099-DIV each year when it is received from their fund company. These forms show what portion of a distribution is taxed at long-term capital gains rates and what portion is taxed as ordinary income. Reviewing these forms can be quite sobering. Many investors, for the first time, are able to confirm that a large part of their mutual fund distributions are taxed at rates well above the 15% long-term capital gains rate. For example, a mutual fund distribution which is comprised of 50% short-term capital gain subject to a 35% tax and 50% long-term capital gain subject to a 15% tax will actually result in an average tax of 25%. Investors must realize that long-term ownership of mutual funds does not guarantee the 15% long-term capital gains rate often cited by fund proponents. Once investors realize that they may be subject to ordinary income taxation on a large portion of their mutual fund gains, the advantage of deferring this tax by buying variable annuities should be investigated.

§805. THE ANNUAL TAX LOSS ON MUTUAL FUNDS

As discussed above, the typical equity-based mutual fund loses approximately 20% of its net gain to the IRS each year.[2] The tax loss suffered by mutual fund owners each year has historically been reported in such a way that mutual fund owners rarely, if ever, have been able to determine the annual tax cost of owning their funds. For example, mutual fund companies, until recently, reported mutual fund returns on a before-tax basis. The Securities Exchange Commission became so concerned about the public not being aware of the tax cost of mutual fund ownership that they now have strict rules regarding how mutual fund companies must report their returns. The major thrust of these disclosure rules require mutual fund companies to report mutual fund returns on both a before- and after-tax basis so the investing public can better realize what the real tax cost is for owning mutual funds.

§806. THE IMPACT OF ANNUAL TAXATION ON MUTUAL FUND OWNERSHIP

Although several studies have shown that the average mutual fund can lose more than 20% of its annual net return each year to taxes, this book will use a tax loss figure of 20%. As

---

[2] See footnote 2 in Chapter 7 *supra*.

47

mentioned earlier, this book will also assume that mutual funds increase in value at an annual rate of 10% after annual expenses. By using these two figures, the examples in this book will provide mutual fund owners with the 20% tax liability that more closely reflects what many mutual fund owners actually pay in annual taxes each year.

Example
Bob invested $100,000 in a mutual fund. It increased in value to $110,000 in a year. Bob lost 2% of his 10% or 20% of his gain to taxes. Bob's after-tax return would be $108,000. (Non-tax costs are ignored in this example.)

The figures discussed above are used for hypothetical comparison purposes only. Professionals should always use the *actual* rates of return and tax cost of any mutual fund they are comparing with any other potential investment such as a variable annuity. For example, if an investor is able to obtain a 12% net rate of return on his mutual funds rather than 10% and loses only 17% of that return to taxes instead of 20%, he should use these figures rather than the hypothetical comparison figures the author has chosen.

§807. TAX-EFFICIENT FUNDS

Mutual fund proponents claim that the negative tax impact of owning mutual funds with high turnover ratios can be eliminated by purchasing funds with low turnover ratios so that the more favorable 15% long-term capital gains tax rates can be obtained by fund owners. This solution is unrealistic for several reasons. Among them are: a) most mutual fund purchasers have no idea what a turnover ratio is or what its tax implications are; b) buyers of mutual funds pick their funds based on potential return and not turnover ratios; c) mutual funds cannot completely control their turnover ratios. For example, a fund with a favorable turnover ratio can have its turnover ratio increased dramatically if redemptions by fund holders are larger than normal thus forcing the fund to sell shares it may not have held for more than a year; and d) funds with low turnover ratios still generate short-term capital gains or dividends each year, both of which are taxed to fund owners as ordinary income. Buying "tax-efficient" mutual funds won't help in most cases. In the August 1999 issue of *Mutual Funds* magazine, 19 of the most tax-efficient mutual funds were examined. Although these funds did greatly reduce the problems associated with the taxes discussed above, these tax savings came at a high cost. The average tax-efficient fund listed in the study returned an average of 13% over a one-year period while the stock market as a whole was up twice that amount for the same period. Additionally, 15 of these tax-efficient funds had front-end loads and nine had annual expense ratios from 1.1% - 2.0%.

In the January 1999 issue of *Kiplinger's Personal Finance Magazine* an article written by

Steven Goldberg addressed the topic of tax-efficient mutual funds. The author noted that:

- The after-tax difference between relatively tax-efficient funds and tax-inefficient funds was small; and

- Tax-efficiency is short-lived. Research indicates that 40% of tax-efficient funds in one year were not tax-efficient three years later.

Many "tax-efficient" funds are doing nothing more than selling losing investments to offset investment gains. Although such transactions do reduce income taxes for these funds, they also reduce the fund's overall performance.

Money's March 2000 issue points out that performance is the number one factor investors relied on when considering a mutual fund purchase and not tax-efficiency. *Money* stated, "virtually 100% of all new money goes into funds with Morningstar rankings of four or five stars." The problem with this is that, generally speaking, the better the performance rating of a fund, the higher the turnover ratio and thus the higher taxes.

§808. MUTUAL FUNDS EXPOSE INVESTORS TO HIDDEN INCOME TAXES AND COSTLY INCOME TAX TRAPS

Mutual funds have hidden tax costs that variable annuities do not pose. For example, mutual fund distributions may cause taxpayers to lose certain income tax credits, exemptions or deductions. The loss of income tax credits, exemptions and deductions will be discussed more fully in Chapters 19 to 21. When credits, exemptions or deductions are lost, income taxes are increased. These hidden income tax costs must be added to the cost of owning mutual funds. When such costs are taken into consideration, they make mutual fund ownership much less attractive. The following example demonstrates how mutual funds generate hidden tax costs:

Example:
Bill and Judy have three children who are under age 17. Their adjusted gross income is $110,000. At this level of income they are eligible for a $1,000 child tax credit for each of their three minor children or $3,000. Bill and Judy just received a distribution notice from a mutual fund they own requiring them to report an additional $30,000 of income. The tax on this distribution generated an additional income tax of $5,400 or 18% of the mutual fund's distribution. This additional income will reduce their child tax credit by half to $1,500.[3] The loss of the $1,500 credit will increase the effective tax on the mutual fund from 18% ($5,400 tax on $30,000) to 23% [$5,100 ($5,400 + $1,500) ÷ $30,000].

§809. TAX PREPARATION SOFTWARE

Investors desiring to determine exactly what their true tax liability is on their mutual fund holdings should consider purchasing tax preparation software. The software can be used

---

[3] $140,000 - $110,000 phaseout cap = $30,000 ÷ $1,000 = $30 x $50 = $1,500.

to compare a tax return *with* a mutual fund distribution to a return *without* the distribution. The software will adjust for lost credits, deductions, exemptions, etc. By comparing the two returns, the true tax burden of owning a mutual fund can be determined. For example, if a tax return containing a $10,000 mutual fund distribution results in a tax of $3,300 and the same return without the distribution results in a tax of $1,400, the difference (i.e. $1,900) can be attributable to the inclusion of the $10,000 mutual fund distribution. The fund owner then knows his true tax burden on his mutual fund is 19%, not 15%.[4]

§810. CAPITAL GAINS RATES – TEMPORARY NATURE

The current 15% long-term capital gains rate is scheduled to increase to 20% after December 31, 2012.

§811. CONCLUSION

This chapter hopefully demonstrated that mutual fund owners can pay much more than the 15% long-term capital gains rate they have been led to believe they would receive by investing in mutual funds for the long-term. Variable annuities, because they are tax-deferred, do not trigger current taxes. It is this tax deferral that makes variable annuities an attractive long-term investment vehicle. The next chapter explores the issue of tax deferral.

> For more information on income taxation of mutual funds and variable annuities, please see the Report #2 titled "Why Federal Income Tax Laws Favor Variable Annuities Over Mutual Funds." This report is available by calling Parker-Thompson Publishing at (919) 832-2687.

---

[4] Depending on income levels, this burden can easily exceed 25%.

- CHAPTER 9 -
THE MAGIC OF INCOME TAX DEFERRAL

§901. INTRODUCTION

The major benefit of owning variable annuities rather than mutual funds is that variable annuities grow income tax-deferred. It is important for investors to understand the advantage of tax-deferral.

§902. HOW INCOME TAX DEFERRAL WORKS

The income tax deferral provided by a variable annuity simply means the owner does not have to pay income taxes on the growth of his variable annuity until he withdraws money from the variable annuity in the future.[1] Mutual funds owners do not receive the benefit of tax deferral but instead must pay income taxes each year on annual distributions made by their mutual fund company. All financial professionals know that money that grows tax-deferred will grow to a larger amount than money placed in a similar investment that is not tax-deferred. For example, $50,000 invested at 10% for 25 years grows to $396,379 *after taxes* if held in a tax-deferred investment like a variable annuity.[2] The same $50,000 invested in a mutual fund earning an after-tax rate of return of 8% grows to $329,264 due to the burden of re-occurring annual income taxes.[3] On these facts, the mutual fund would contain $67,115 less than the tax-deferred variable annuity on an after-tax basis. Because of this, the variable annuity owner can pull out *larger* amounts from his variable annuity and control his income taxes. In doing so, many retired couples can keep their total tax burden to 15% although in a 25% marginal tax bracket. As Chapter 6 points out, by using annuitization and taking advantage of the exclusion ratio the variable annuity owner's annual tax burden can be reduced even more. As subsequent chapters will point out, the non-tax costs of the typical mutual fund will exceed those of a variable annuity. When factored in, these non-tax costs will result in the variable annuity yielding a larger net return than the example discussed above reflects.

§903. HOW TAX DEFERRAL INCREASES FUTURE INCOME

Tax-deferred investments, like variable annuities, together with their lower costs, almost always provide more after-tax income than taxable investments like mutual funds. This is true

---

[1] The income tax referred to in this and subsequent chapters is the federal income tax. State and local income taxes are also deferred when variable annuities are owned.

[2] $50,000 x 25 years x 10% = $541,735 less $145,356 in income taxes (29.56% average tax rate on $491,735) = $396,379.

[3] $50,000 x 25 years x 8% = $342,423. Unrealized capital gains due on sale are assumed to be 30% of growth ($87,727) subject to a tax of 15% = $13,159. $342,423 - $13,159 = $329,264.

even if the owner of the tax-deferred investment is in a high income tax bracket.

Example

Dave and Donna are 55 year-old twins. Fourteen years ago, Dave decided to put $15,000 a year into a mutual fund portfolio. At this same time, Donna elected to put $15,000 a year into similar investments in a variable annuity. Dave and Donna both received an average annual return of 10%. All costs for both the mutual fund and the variable annuity fall in the normal range for such investments (see §709 above). Today, Dave's mutual fund account has $319,054 in it.[4] Donna's variable annuity, due to tax deferral, contains $362,807.[5] If Dave and Donna take 10% from their respective nest eggs each year and pay 15% and 20% respectively in income taxes on those distributions or withdrawals, Dave will net $27,119[6] and Donna will net $29,025.[7] Donna's net retirement income will exceed Dave's by $1,906 each year. In addition, Donna's nest egg will be larger than Dave's by $43,753.[8] (Assuming 30% of Dave's mutual fund gain of $109,054 is unrealized capital gains subject to a 15% tax, his mutual fund portfolio would be worth $314,147 if he cashed out his fund all at once.[9] At an average tax of as much as 30% Donna's variable annuity would be worth $316,965 if it was liquidated all at once.[10]).

§904. CONCLUSION

What this chapter demonstrates is that the income tax deferral provided by variable annuities can be so beneficial that, standing alone, it can result in wealth creation that cannot be matched by mutual funds. Investors must consider tax deferral when comparing potential investments in mutual funds and variable annuities. When this is done, the investment that will provide the most after-tax income will quite frequently prove to be the variable annuity.

---

[4] $14,250 x 6.064% x 14 years = $319,054 (see §709).

[5] $15,000 x 7.03% x 14 years = $362,807.

[6]   10% x $319,054 = $31,905 less 15% = $27,119.

[7]   10% x $362,807 = $50,991 less 20% = $29,025.

[8] $362,807 - $319,054 = $43,753.

[9] $319,054 - $210,000 = $109,054 x .3 x .15 = $4,907. $319,054 - $4,907 = $314,147.

[10] $362,807 - $210,000 = $152,807 - 30% = $106,965 + $210,000 = $316,965.

- CHAPTER 10 -

TAXATION OF VARIABLE ANNUITIES

§1001. INTRODUCTION

The last chapter demonstrated the tremendous advantage of income tax deferral that is available to those who elect to invest in variable annuities. The importance of tax deferral will become even more evident as the taxation of variable annuities is discussed below.

From Chapter 8, it was shown that the commonly held belief that long-term investing in mutual funds will result in annual taxation at a 15% capital gains rate is not always the case. Just as inaccurate are statements made about the taxation of variable annuities. Many variable annuity detractors claim that variable annuity owners in, say a 25% marginal tax bracket, will pay 25% in ordinary income taxes on withdrawals made from their annuities. Statements such as these are misleading and often cause investors to make incorrect investment decisions.

§1002A. TAXATION OF VARIABLE ANNUITIES

Investors who invest in variable annuities over a long period do not pay current income taxes on the growth in their variable annuities. This benefit occurs because variable annuities are income tax-deferred wealth accumulation vehicles. Variable annuity owners realize that at some point in the future they will want to withdraw money from their annuities. When this occurs, income taxes become due as money is withdrawn from the variable annuities. The proponents of mutual funds want potential variable annuity owners to believe that if they are in a 25% marginal tax bracket they will pay 25% in ordinary income taxes on their variable annuity withdrawals. Such statements, although frequently made, are highly misleading.

The 25% income tax rate mentioned and so frequently quoted by mutual fund advocates is a *marginal* tax bracket. Much of the taxable income of all taxpayers in a 25% *marginal* tax bracket is taxed at rates much lower than 25%. What this means, for example, is that married taxpayers who are in a 25% marginal tax bracket and who have large incomes will rarely pay anything close to 25% in income taxes even if much of their income comes from annuity withdrawals subject to ordinary income taxes. The following example demonstrates this.

> **Example:**
> For the year 2010, John and Mary Smith, both 62, have a combined gross income of $100,000.[1] Their itemized deductions are $16,350 and combined personal

---

[1] The tax liability on variable annuities should be of great importance to retired couples. Only a very small portion of the retired persons in the U.S. have gross incomes that would put them in a 25% marginal tax bracket. Most retired persons pay taxes at a 15% average tax rate.

exemptions are $7,300. Their taxable income is $76,350. They are in the 25% marginal tax bracket. The Smith's tax burden on their taxable income would be calculated as follows:

$$\begin{aligned}
\$ \ -0- \ - \$16,750 \times 10\% &= \$1,675.00 \\
\$16,750 - \$68,000 \times 15\% &= \$7,687.50 \\
\$68,000 - \$76,350 \times 25\% &= \underline{\$2,087.50} \\
& \ \$11,450.00
\end{aligned}$$

As can be seen from the above example, a tax of $11,450 on a taxable income of $76,200 results in a *maximum* average ordinary income tax of 15%.[2] This example is significant because it demonstrates that married investors in a 25% marginal tax bracket who have gross incomes of as much as $100,000 and taxable incomes in excess of $76,000 will pay a *maximum* average ordinary income tax of 15% on their *taxable* income regardless of how much of this income is derived from variable annuity withdrawals including all of it! If the Smiths had larger itemized deductions, their gross income could easily exceed $100,000 and their maximum average income tax would still not exceed 15%. An example involving a single investor may be helpful:

Example
Sally, who is 64, has a gross annual income of $48,750 that comes solely from fully taxable withdrawals from a variable annuity she owns. Her itemized deductions and personal exemption come to $10,600. Her taxable income is $38,150 which puts Sally in a 25% tax bracket for 2010. Based on a taxable income of $38,150 Sally will pay $5,744 in income taxes. Based on these facts, Sally's income tax burden will be 15%. This is a far cry from her marginal tax bracket of 25%.

A good question investors should ask themselves is:

> If the stream of income I will have in retirement from a variable annuity will most likely be taxed at 15%, why should I pay taxes each year on a mutual fund portfolio from 15% to 20% or more which will reduce my retirement nest egg while providing me with the same 15% tax liability I'll get with a variable annuity when I'm in retirement?

§1002B. THE MARGINAL TAX RATE DECEPTION

People who know little about taxation of investments can often fall for a trap set by the detractors of variable annuities. These detractors almost always treat variable annuity income as

---

[2] $11,450 ÷ $76,350 = 15%. In actual practice, tax tables would be used. These tables would reflect a slightly different tax but the average tax would still be 15%.

if this income is received late in the year. By doing so they can claim it is subject to the owner's highest marginal tax bracket. This scam is defective for two reasons:

- Ordinary income earned by taxpayers is never segregated and taxed at different marginal tax rates. All ordinary income is totaled and taxed at *average* tax rates which blend the various tax brackets so all ordinary income benefits by being taxed at the same average "blended" tax rates.

- If the faulty logic of variable annuity detractors was correct, a variable annuity owner could withdraw $16,750 (2010) from his variable annuity in early January before he earned any other income. He could then claim that this variable annuity income, because it was received early in the year, would be subject to the lowest 10% tax bracket!

The following example discusses this issue:

Example

Bill and Sara, age 61, recently retired. They have $335,000 to invest and plan to withdraw 5% or $16,750 from this investment to supplement their retirement. It is assumed that the investments will return at least 5% a year. Including income from their investment, Bill and Sara will have a gross income of $100,000 for 2010. Of this amount, $16,750 would be investment income and $83,250 is pension income. After deductions and personal exemptions of $15,400, they are left with a taxable income of $84,600. Bill and Sara were considering investing their $335,000 in a variable annuity but were advised not to by a stockbroker who pointed out that the variable annuity withdrawal would be taxed at 25%. The stockbroker, who wanted to sell mutual funds to Bill and Sara, prepared the following chart for them:

INCOME SOURCE	AMOUNT	INCOME TAX
Pension Income	$16,750	10%
Pension Income	$51,100	15%
Variable Annuity W/D	$16,750	25%

Bill and Sara talked with another financial advisor who told them he could sell them a variable annuity that would only be taxed at 10%. The advisor stated this could be accomplished if Bill and Sara were to take their annual $16,750 variable annuity withdrawal during the first week in January. This would make it the first income earned for the year. To prove this, the advisor provided the following chart to Bill and Sara:

INCOME SOURCE	AMOUNT	INCOME TAX
Variable Annuity W/D	$16,750	10%
Pension Income	$51,100	15%
Pension Income	$16,750	25%

Neither the stockbroker nor the financial advisor are providing accurate tax advice. The truth of the matter is that the income tax liability for Bill and Sara will be *identical* under the two scenarios described. In both cases, they would report $84,600 in taxable income and pay an income tax of $13,519 (2010) or 16% of their taxable income.

Making financial decisions "at the margin" can be misleading. The following two examples demonstrate this.

Example #1

Betty wants to purchase a new sports car. She is very concerned with fuel costs. One sports car she is considering has a 15 gallon gas tank. Gas costs $3.00 a gallon. An identical sports car has the same size gas tank but requires a quart of special additive be added to the car every time the gas tank is filled. A quart of gas costs $.75 ($3.00 ÷ 4), however a quart of the special additive costs $1.50. Which of the following statements is true?

- It costs twice as much to fill the gas tank on the second sports car as it does the first.

- The cost to fill the gas tank on the first sports car is $45.00 ($3.00 x 15) and $45.75 ($3.00 x 14¾ + $1.50) to fill the gas tank of the second car.

Technically, both of the above statements are true. However, if Betty relies on the *first* statement, she would most likely not consider purchasing the second sports car. If Betty relies on the *second* statement she will realize that the *total* cost to fill the gas tank of either car is nearly the same. Betty would most likely make her decision to buy either sports car on some feature other than fuel consumption.

Example #2

Jack recently purchased a hotel for $15 million. He wants to completely refurbish it. Which of the following methods would be best for Jack to use in selecting one of two companies to do the refurbishing work:

- Ask each company what the cost of the last item of work they will perform will cost (i.e., carpeting the hotel); or

- Ask each company what the *total* cost of doing *all* of the refurbishing work will be?

In the second example, Jack would be foolish to pick a refurbishing company based only on the marginal cost of installing carpet. One company could have a carpet cost that is half that of the other company, yet the *total* refurbishing costs could be significantly higher for the company providing the lowest cost for carpeting. Jack would be better off deciding which company to use based on the *total* cost of refurbishing his hotel.

Making financial decisions based on marginal tax rates can also be misleading. For example, a couple in a 25% marginal tax bracket may believe that a variable annuity withdrawal might be taxed at a higher rate than might a mutual fund distribution which would be taxed at 15%. However, it is quite possible for someone to be in a 25% marginal tax bracket and yet have a tax liability of only 15% on all of their income regardless of source. The John and Mary example in §1002A above demonstrated this. By understanding the limitations of marginal tax brackets, investors can make more informed investment decisions.

§1002C. MUTUAL FUND SALES AND CAPITAL GAINS RATES

When mutual funds are liquidated they are normally taxed at 15%. However, under current tax law this 15% could increase in the future. The rate has been extended to December 31, 2012. However, with the ever-increasing federal deficit, many financial and tax experts predict the capital gains rate increase will become permanent and could increase before the end of 2012. Recently, an effort by Congress to make the 15% capital gains rate permanent failed.

§1003. TAX BENEFIT OF ANNUITIZATION

If a variable annuity owner elects to annuitize an annuity he owns, his annual tax burden on any stream of income produced will be reduced significantly. This income tax reduction arises due to the application of the exclusion ratio. The exclusion ratio ensures that money invested in a variable annuity that has already been taxed is not taxed again when it is withdrawn at a later time.[3] The following example demonstrates a taxpayer's annual income tax liability where the exclusion ratio is not used:

> **Example #1**
> Doug, who is 65 and retired, has a variable annuity worth $500,000. His investment in the annuity is $250,000. Doug's $250,000 investment in his annuity was previously subjected to income taxes. Doug has elected to take money out of his annuity as he needs it. Because Doug has not formally

---

[3] The exclusion ratio which was discussed in Chapter 6 applies to non-qualified annuities only. Qualified annuities (IRAs, 403(b)s, 401(k)s, etc.) are fully funded with money that has never been taxed. For this reason, 100% of the withdrawals from these sources are taxed as ordinary income. IRAs are treated in the same manner as are SEPs, 457s, etc., although they, technically, are not before tax dollar contributions.

annuitized his contract, any withdrawals he makes above his $250,000 cost basis will be considered gain and are subject to ordinary income taxes until all gains are taxed. After that, withdrawals would be deemed principal and would not be taxed. It is assumed that Doug will pay taxes at 20%. Assuming Doug wants to withdraw $35,000 from his variable annuity, he will pay $7,000 in taxes, or 20% of the withdrawal.[4]

The next example demonstrates the basic advantage of annuitization:

Example #2
Debbie, who is 65 and retired, has a variable annuity worth $500,000. Her total investment in the variable annuity is $250,000 which was made with money already subject to income taxation. Assume Debbie annuitizes her annuity so as to receive $35,000 a year for 20 years.[5] Each payment of $35,000 would be considered 64.3% growth and 35.7% investment based on Debbie's $250,000 investment and the annuity's expected payout of $700,000 ($35,000 x 20 years). As Debbie receives each payment of $35,000, she will be taxed only on $22,500 (64.28571% x $35,000). Assuming her average income tax on $22,500 is 20% and the other $12,500 is untaxed, Debbie's $35,000 stream of income will be subject to an average tax of 12.86% ($4,500 ÷ $35,000). In the prior example, Doug's annual tax liability on the same $35,000 withdrawal would be 20% rather than Debbie's 12.86%.

The exclusion ratio can be advantageous to even very wealthy variable annuity owners as the next example demonstrates.

Example #3
John, who is 72, has a retirement income of $300,000 from his previous employer. He has four variable annuities worth $500,000 each issued by different companies. John's investment in each variable annuity is $300,000. John recently annuitized one of his annuities for a $60,000 annual payment guaranteed for 10 years. Although John is in the 33% tax bracket, he can obtain 16.5% taxation on the annual stream of income provided by the variable annuity. Based on an investment of $300,000 and an expected payout of $600,000 ($60,000 x 10 years), John's exclusion ratio would be 50%. Half of each $60,000 payment would be taxed at 33% while the other half of each annuity payment would not be subject to taxation because it is a return of John's investment principal. Because John elected to annuitize his annuity, he will pay the equivalent of 16.5% in income taxes on his annual variable annuity income stream even though he is in a 33% income tax bracket.

---

[4] Once Doug withdraws all of his growth, further withdrawals will be made on a tax-free basis.

[5] It is assumed that the annuity is guaranteed for 20 years. The actual payment would most likely exceed $35,000. Doug and Debbie will eventually pay the same total tax to the IRS over time.

§1004. COMMUTATION

Many people do not like the idea of annuitizing their annuities because such an election is usually irrevocable and requires one to part with control of an asset they have spent years accumulating. Today, many annuity companies offer commutated or revocable annuitization. A variable annuity owner can annuitize his annuity and take advantage of the exclusion ratio while maintaining the right to reverse his annuitization election, fully or partially, in the future if he so chooses. (See §608 above on this topic).

§1005. VARIABLE ANNUITIZATION

Another factor causing reluctance to annuitize is the fact that once the fixed payments are set, inflation may have an impact on future payments. To solve this problem many major annuity issuers provide variable annuitization which guarantees a minimum fixed payment that can increase over time as the stock market rises. Such annuitization provides protection against inflation for those individuals who will receive annuity payments over a long period of time.

§1006. PROPOSED LEGISLATION

At press time there was a bill before Congress that would make a portion of any annuitized income from a non-qualified variable annuity available to the recipient on a tax-free basis.

§1007. THE OVERLOOKED BENEFIT OF VARIABLE ANNUITY TAX DEFERRAL

Most people believe that the only benefit of tax deferral is that an investment can grow without current taxation and therefore will grow to a larger amount than a taxable investment. Many people believe the tax deferral offered by variable annuities is not that big of a benefit because once the variable annuity is taxed at ordinary income tax rates its after-tax value is not significantly different than the after-tax value of a taxable investment like a mutual fund which receives capital gains treatment. Hopefully, Chapter 9 pointed out that in most cases the tax deferral provided by a variable annuity will result in a larger net gain than a similar investment in a mutual fund that is not tax-deferred. The real benefit of tax in deferral lies in the economic concept of opportunity cost. This economic concept holds that money not used to pay taxes on a tax deferred investment that would have been paid with a taxable investment can be invested and obtain a return that must be factored into the net ending value of a variable annuity. This concept is discussed in Chapter 10B.

§1008. CONCLUSION

This chapter demonstrates that withdrawals taken from a variable annuity in retirement will rarely generate an income tax of more than 15%. By using annuitization and taking advantage of the exclusion ratio even this 15% tax can be reduced. This chapter also pointed out that investments that grow tax-deferred (i.e. variable annuities) will grow to much larger sums than similar investments that are subject to income taxes each year (i.e. mutual funds).

- CHAPTER 10B -

VARIABLE ANNUITY TAX DEFERRAL AND TIME VALUE OF MONEY

§10B01. INTRODUCTION

The owner of a mutual fund typically pays income taxes that his mutual fund generates out of his pocket rather than paying this tax obligation out of his funds. A variable annuity owner, because he has no annual tax liability, can invest the same amount of money that a mutual fund owner uses each year to pay his income taxes. This benefit is an application of the economic concept of time value of money. The ability to invest deferred tax payments is actually one of the biggest and most commonly overlooked benefits arising from the tax deferral advantage provided by variable annuities. This chapter discusses this concept.

§10B02. MUTUAL FUND VERSES VARIABLE ANNUITY INVESTMENT – TIME VALUE OF MONEY CONSIDERED

When mutual fund owners pay annual federal income taxes on their funds from sources other than their mutual funds, that money is not available for further investment elsewhere. A variable annuity owner can invest such funds each year because he does not have to pay annual taxes on his variable annuity. The gain on this money *must* be factored into any decision to buy mutual funds or variable annuities. The following hypothetical illustrates the concept of time value of money:

Hypothetical
Dave and Donna are 55 year-old twins. Dave wants to invest $50,000 in a mutual fund for ten years. The fund has annual ownership expenses of 2.2% a year.[1] The commission to buy the fund is 4%. Annual distributions will be half realized and half unrealized. Annual taxes on realized gains will be half long-term capital gains taxed at 15% and half short-term capital gains of 25% for an average income tax of 20%. Unrealized gains will be taxed ten years from now at 20%.[2] The mutual fund will have a gross return of 10% a year. Donna will invest her $50,000 in a variable annuity. Annual non-tax costs of owning the variable annuity will be 2.7%. The variable annuity will also have a gross return of 10% a year. Annual income taxes are deferred, but will be paid at 25% when Donna sells her annuity ten years from now.[3] Dave and Donna both have $90,000 taxable incomes today that will drop to $70,000 in retirement.

Table #1 summarized Dave's mutual fund investment over the next ten years based on the facts set out in the above hypothetical.

---

[1] Trading costs of 0.7%, 12b-1 fees of 0.25% and annual expense ratio of 1.25% = 2.2%.

[2] The 15% long-term capital gains rate increases to 20% after December 31, 2010.

[3] Donna's gain of $48,633 (see Table #8 below) plus her $70,000 retirement income and the value of her separate investment account (see Tabe #8 below) will not exceed the 25% tax rate.

TABLE #1: $50,000 MUTUAL FUND INVESTMENT RETURNING 10% ANNUALLY WITH A 20% TAX LOSS ON REALIZED GAINS

END OF YEAR[4]	BEGIN. VALUE OF MF	10% GAIN ON MF	LESS 2.2% COSTS	AFTER COST MF VALUE	AFTER COST GAIN	REAL-IZED GAIN	UNREAL-IZED GAIN	ANN. TAX LIAB.
1	$48,000	$52,800	$1,162	$51,638	$3,638	$1,819	$1,819	$364
2	$51,638	$56,802	$1,250	$55,552	$3,914	$1,957	$1,957	$391
3	$55,552	$61,107	$1,344	$59,763	$4,211	$2,105	$2,106	$421
4	$59,763	$65,739	$1,446	$64,293	$4,530	$2,265	$2,265	$453
5	$64,293	$70,722	$1,556	$69,166	$4,873	$2,436	$2,437	$487
6	$69,166	$76,083	$1,674	$74,409	$5,243	$2,622	$2,621	$524
7	$74,409	$81,850	$1,801	$80,049	$5,640	$2,820	$2,820	$564
8	$80,049	$88,054	$1,937	$86,117	$6,068	$3,034	$3,034	$607
9	$86,117	$94,728	$2,084	$92,644	$6,527	$3,264	$3,263	$653
10	$92,644	$101,908	$2,242	$99,666	$7,022	$3,511	$3,511	$702
TOTALS				**$99,668**	**$51,666**	**$25,833**	**$25,833**	**$5,166**

Based on the information set out in Table #1, after ten years, Dave's mutual fund would be worth $99,668. His income tax liability on realized and unrealized gains of $51,666 ($25,833 x 2) at 20% would be $10,344 ($5,166 unrealized and $5,166 realized), thus reducing Dave's mutual fund gain to $89,335 after *all* taxes and ownership costs are factored in.[5]

Table #2 examines Donna's variable annuity investment of $50,000 for ten years.

---

[4] To make calculations simpler it will be assumed Donna's variable annuity was initially purchased on April 15 and that taxes are due ten years later.

[5] See note 2 above and facts of the hypothetical.

TABLE #2: $50,000 VARIABLE ANNUITY INVESTMENT RETURNING 10% ANNUALLY WITH INCOME TAX DEFERRAL

END OF YEAR[6]	BEGINNING VALUE OF VARIABLE ANNUITY	10% GAIN ON VARIABLE ANNUITY	2.7% ANNUAL COSTS	AFTER COST VALUE	MUTUAL FUND TAX MONEY INVESTED	SEPARATE INVESTMENT ACCOUNT VALUE
1	$50,000	$55,000	$1,485	$53,515	$364	$671[7]
2	$53,515	$58,867	$1,589	$57,278	$391	$673
3	$57,278	$63,005	$1,701	$61,304	$421	$677
4	$61,304	$67,434	$1,821	$65,613	$453	$681
5	$65,613	$72,174	$1,949	$70,225	$487	$684
6	$70,225	$77,248	$2,086	$75,162	$524	$688
7	$75,162	$82,678	$2,232	$80,446	$564	$691
8	$80,446	$88,490	$2,389	$86,101	$607	$695
9	$86,101	$94,711	$2,557	$92,154	$653	$699
10	$92,154	$101,369	$2,737	$98,633	$702	$702
TOTALS				**$98,633**	**$5,166**	**$6,861**

From Table #2 it can be determined that Donna's variable annuity would be worth $98,633 after ten years. Of this amount, $48,633 is gain and when taxed at 25%,[8] reduces Donna's variable annuity value by $12,158 to $86,475. This is slightly less than Dave's after-cost, after-tax mutual fund value of $89,335. The conclusion that the mutual fund would have been the better investment would not be accurate because time value of money was not considered. Donna could have invested the same amount each year that Dave used to pay his annual mutual fund income taxes with. As the last column in Table #2 demonstrates, the separate investment account (representing time value of money) contained $6,861 after ten years of growth. Of this amount, $5,166 was principal and $1,695 was gain. If the gain is reduced by 25%,[9] the separate

---

[6] To make calculations simpler it will be assumed Donna's variable annuity was initially purchased on April 15 and that taxes are due ten years later.

[7] $364 x 9 years x 7.03% = $671. Each successive investment is reduced by one year.

[8] See Footnote 3 above.

[9] See Footnote 3.

investment account drops in value to $6,437. When this account is added to the $86,475 after-tax, after-cost value of Donna's variable annuity, her total net economic variable annuity value increases to $92,912, which is $3,577 more than Dave was able to obtain with his mutual fund investment.

§10B03. INCOME TAXES PAID FROM A MUTUAL FUND

A question often raised is whether time value of money applies in a situation where a mutual fund owner pays the annual income tax owed on his mutual fund from the mutual fund. In such a case, time value of money would not apply because the mutual fund owner is not paying income taxes from a source other than his mutual funds and therefore a variable annuity owner would have nothing to invest in a separate (time value of money) investment account. However, when the income taxes are paid from a mutual fund each year, the value of the mutual fund decreases. This would not happen where income taxes are paid from some source other than the mutual fund. If annual income taxes are paid from a mutual fund and *all* costs and taxes are considered, the net ending value of the mutual fund and variable annuity will be very close. The example below demonstrates this.

> **Example**
> Mary, who is 52 is considering a mutual fund purchase of $30,000 for 8 years. The mutual fund is assumed to yield a gross annual return of 10 %. The fund charges a 5% commission. Mary's annual income tax liability will be 20% on net gain and the fund considered charges a 1.5 % management fee (including 12b-1 fees) and has trading costs of 0.7%. Eight years from now Mary's mutual fund portfolio's net value would be $44,750.[10] This assumes the same mutual fund is held for eight years. Mary is also considering a variable annuity purchase of $30,000. She assumes the annuity will gross 10% annually. She will buy her variable annuity from a financial professional. Mary's tax rate when the variable annuity is sold will be 25%. Her annual expenses are 2.2% and trading costs are 0.5%. Eight years from now Mary's variable annuity would have an after-tax value of $46,246.[11] This assumes the variable annuity is liquidated all at one time. Even so, the variable annuity will yield nearly $1,500 more than the mutual fund over eight years on a net basis.

§10B04. CONCLUSION

The income tax liability of mutual funds and variable annuities are often compared based solely

---

[10] $30,000 - 5% commission = $28,500 + 10% = $31,350 - 2.2% costs = $30,666 - $28,500 = $2,160.30 - 20% tax = $1,728.24 ÷ $28,500 = 6.064%. 6.064% x 8 x $28,500 = $45,444.54 - $30,000 = $15,444.54 gain. 30% of this gain ($4,694) is long-term gain taxed at 15%. 15% of $4,633 = $695. $45,444.54 - $695 = $44,750.

[11] $30,000 + 10% = $33,000 - 2.7% costs = $32,109 - $30,000 = $2,109 ÷ $30,000 = 7.03%. 7.03% x $30,000 x 8 years = $51,661 less $30,000 = $21,661 in gain taxed at 25% = $16,246 + $30,000 = $46,246.

on the assumption that if a variable annuity is taxed at a higher rate than a mutual fund, the mutual fund is the more tax efficient investment. Such comparisons are faulty because they ignore the major advantage of tax deferral – namely, time value of money. When this economic concept is factored into the comparison of the income tax liability of owning mutual funds and variable annuities, it often provides the variable annuity owner with a larger economic benefit than they could obtain from a similar mutual fund investment.

For more information on tax deferral and time value of money, please see Report #1 titled "Variable Annuity Tax Deferral and Time Value of Money." This report is available by calling Parker-Thompson Publishing at (919) 832-2687.

- CHAPTER 11 -

MAKING AN INFORMED INVESTMENT DECISION

§1101. INTRODUCTION

Once investors understand how tax laws impact the long-term return received by mutual funds and variable annuities, they will be in a better position to make informed long-term investment decisions.

§1102. REVIEW

The material presented in Chapters 8-10 demonstrated the following:

- In many cases, mutual fund investors will pay annual federal income taxes on their funds that exceed the 15% long-term capital gains rates that many of these investors have been led to believe they would pay.

- Studies have shown that annual federal income taxes reduce total annual net mutual fund returns by 20% a year or more. [This book will use the lower 20% figure]. Investors should calculate and use their *actual* tax loss figure when comparing mutual funds to variable annuities.

- The great majority of couples are in a marginal tax bracket of 25% or less. Those couples in a 25% marginal tax bracket often pay an average federal income tax of 15% or less on their income even if their annual gross income is as much as $100,000. This is true regardless of whether their income is from pensions, Social Security, variable annuity withdrawals or other sources.

- Money invested in a tax-deferred investment (i.e variable annuities) will always grow to a much larger sum than money invested in a similar taxable investments (i.e. mutual funds) held for the same period of time.

- The after-tax income generated from a variable annuity will frequently be greater than the after-tax income generated from a taxable investment such as a mutual fund.

§1103. INFORMED DECISION-MAKING

Once long-term investors understand the basic facts set out above, they will be in a better position to make investment decisions that could have a dramatic impact on their retirement or other long-range financial goals. The following statement set out below is one of the most common statements made by so-called financial professionals who advise people to avoid variable annuities:

> Long-term investments should be made in mutual funds because these funds are taxed annually at long-term capital gains rates of 15%. Variable annuities should be avoided because withdrawals from these annuities are subject to ordinary income taxes. If you're in a 25% marginal tax bracket, you'll pay 25% in income taxes on your variable annuity withdrawals.

The statement set out above is misleading for several reasons:

- The claim that mutual fund investors receive 15% long-term capital gains tax treatment on their annual mutual fund gains is misleading. (See Chapter 8).

- The statement ignores the negative impact that annual income taxes have on mutual fund returns. (See Chapter 8).

- The statement ignores the advantage of the income tax deferral provided by variable annuities. (See Chapter 9 and 10B).

- The statement falsely implies that people in a 25% marginal tax bracket pay 25% in ordinary income taxes on withdrawals taken from their variable annuities. (See Chapter 10).

Although such misleading statements are commonly made, they are highly misleading and often cause investors who rely on such statements to make investment decisions that will cost them thousands of dollars in lost gains. Such inaccurate statements exist because when made, they sound logical and authoritative. However, such statements begin to fall apart when examined closely. The deceptive nature of such statements becomes apparent to anyone who takes the time to learn the truth about variable annuities.

§1104. ANALYSIS

The best way to demonstrate to investors the misleading nature of anti-variable annuity statements such as the one discussed in the previous section is to use a simple example comparing a potential long-term investment in mutual funds with one made in a variable annuity.

FACTS:

John and Mary Brown are 43 years old. They have just finished paying for the college education of their twin sons. They want to retire in 20 years. John and Mary want to invest $20,000 a year in a mutual fund or variable annuity. John has been talking to a fee-only financial planner who has suggested mutual funds as a retirement investment for John and Mary. In suggesting mutual funds, the planner made a statement similar to the one discussed in the previous section to dissuade John and Mary from buying a variable annuity. Mary did some reading on retirement investing that fairly compared variable annuities and mutual funds and was impressed with the long-term benefits provided by variable annuities. John and Mary have discussed what each of them learned and decided to "crunch the numbers" on their computer to see which investment would provide a better retirement nest egg.

ALTERNATIVE #1 - MUTUAL FUND INVESTMENT:

If John and Mary invest a total of $20,000 a year for 20 years in a mutual fund providing an average annual return of 10%, they will have $709,283 after accounting for income taxes, trading costs, annual mutual fund expenses, and fees.[1] The fee-only financial planner advising John and Mary charges a 1% annual management fee. In retirement, John and Mary estimate they will need to withdraw 10% from their investment nest egg to supplement other retirement income they have. Assuming these annual $70,928 payments will come from mutual fund distributions each year and these distributions are taxed at a maximum capital gains tax of 15%, John and Mary will *net* $60,289 a year in income from their funds.

ALTERNATIVE # 2 - THE VARIABLE ANNUITY INVESTMENT:

If John and Mary put $20,000 a year into a variable annuity, their annuity will grow tax-deferred to $880,430 if invested at a net return of 7.03%[2] (see §709). John and Mary plan to withdraw 10% a year from their variable annuity in retirement. This will provide them with $88,043 in gross income per year. Assuming all of this income is subject to a somewhat high ordinary income tax of 25%, John and Mary will net $66,032[3] a year in retirement.

John and Mary will receive $5,742 ($66,032 - $60,289) more in retirement income if they invest in the variable annuity. In addition, if John and Mary elect to invest in a variable annuity, their retirement nest egg will contain $171,147 more in it than if they choose to invest in mutual funds.[4] This is because the mutual fund investment would grow to only $709,283 while the variable annuity would grow to $880,430 due to tax deferral. Based on their research, John

---

[1] $20,000 per year + 10% = $22,000 - 3.2% (1.0% annual management fee less annual expenses of 1.5% and less trading costs of 0.7%) = $21,296 - $20,000 = $1,296 - 20% tax = $1,037 ÷ $20,000 = 5.184% on $20,000 / year for 20 years = $709,283.

[2] $20,000 + 10% = $22,000 - 2.7% in expenses = 7.03% x 20 years x $20,000/yr = $880,430.

[3] $88,043 x .75 = $66,032.

[4] $880,430 - $709,283 = $171,474.

and Mary have decided to put their money in a variable annuity. Because John and Mary sought to learn more about investing in mutual funds and variable annuities, they learned that long-term investing in a variable annuity would provide them with greater financial security in retirement than a similar investment in a mutual fund. Put another way, had John and Mary relied on the anti-variable annuity statement made by the planner they talked with, they would have failed to maximize their retirement income. It is important to note that if John and Mary wanted to take a lump sum and pay all taxes due, they would only net $695,365 with the mutual fund portfolio[5] but $741,971 with the variable annuity.[6]

§1105. CONCLUSION

Once investors understand the basic rules regarding taxation of mutual funds and variable annuities, they should begin to realize that many of the negative statements they hear about variable annuities are really inaccurate misstatements that can lead them to make costly investment decisions. Investors who want the best return on their investment over the long-term must be willing to take the time to analyze the returns provided by mutual funds and variable annuities over the long-term. The result will almost always demonstrate that a long-term investment in a variable annuity will be a better choice than a similar investment in a mutual fund.

---

[5] $709,283 - $400,000 = $309,283 gain x .3 = $92,785 x .15 = $13,918. $709,283 - $13,918 = $695,365.
[6] $880,430 - $400,000 = $480,430 gain - $138,459 in income taxes (2010) = $741,971.

- CHAPTER 12 -

THE LATE-YEAR PURCHASE TRAP

§1201. INTRODUCTION

Purchasing mutual funds late in the year can result in a significant income tax loss that does not occur when variable annuities are purchased.

§1202. LATE-YEAR PURCHASES

Mutual funds must distribute realized gains to fund owners each year in order that these distributions can be reported for income tax purposes by the funds' owners. Mutual fund companies usually make distributions to fund owners of record in November or December. Distributions are broken down into dividends (qualified or not), long-term capital gains and short-term capital gains. These distributions are reported on IRS 1099-DIV forms which are usually sent to investors with other information concerning the distribution. For the uninformed, the purchase of a mutual fund late in the year just before a fund makes a distribution can result in a significant tax disadvantage. The following example demonstrates this problem:

> **Example**
> Judy recently inherited $400,000. She wanted to invest the money for her retirement. In late November, after much research, she selected an aggressive Internet mutual fund with a track record of returning 25% a year. Judy invested her $400,000 by purchasing 20,000 shares of the fund at $20 per share. Two weeks later, Judy received a distribution notice from the fund company for $5 per share or $100,000. This $5 represented the per share growth in the Internet fund for the *entire* year. Half of the distribution was ordinary income and half was long-term capital gain. The price of the fund was adjusted downward by the amount of the distribution. Thus, the fund's market value fell from $20 to $15 per share. After the distribution, Judy owned 20,000 shares of the fund worth $300,000 ($15 x 20,000) plus a cash distribution of $100,000 (20,000 x $5) for a total investment value of $400,000. Although Judy reinvested the distribution, she had to report the $100,000 distribution as income. She paid $25,000 in income taxes on the distribution. After paying her taxes, Judy's net fund investment stood at $375,000, reflecting an immediate $25,000 income tax loss even though her mutual fund did nothing more than make a required distribution. Had Judy put her $400,000 inheritance into similar investments within a variable annuity, she would not have suffered a $25,000 tax loss.

§1203. A PARTIALLY CLOSED MARKET

Many mutual fund investors are aware of the distribution tax trap discussed in the example in the previous section and attempt to avoid this trap by not buying funds late in the year. However, by doing so, these investors may only be able to invest ten months out of the year while annuity investors can invest all year long. In short, mutual fund investors may reduce by 17% their opportunity to enter the stock market than variable annuity investors do.

§1204. ARE TAX-EFFICIENT FUNDS THE SOLUTION?

As discussed in §806 above, tax-efficient funds are rarely the answer to the tax burden confronted by mutual fund owners. A fund that is tax-efficient today, by its very nature, becomes tax-inefficient as time passes. As a general rule, tax efficiency usually comes with a cost-reduced return.

§1205. WAITING DOESN'T HELP

Waiting until year-end distributions are made by mutual fund companies before investing in such funds may not be the solution for mutual fund investors because of the embedded gain problem discussed in the next chapter.

§1206. CONCLUSION

Purchasing mutual funds late in the year can result in a significant income tax disadvantage for the unwary mutual fund purchaser. Variable annuity purchasers are not exposed to this potential income tax problem.

- CHAPTER 13 -

THE EMBEDDED GAINS TAX TRAP

§1301. INTRODUCTION

For mutual fund companies, if the redemption or sale of their shares is not offset by an equal amount of share purchases, the realized capital gains, dividends, etc. that must be reported each year by the mutual fund company are divided among a smaller group of mutual fund owners. This can present serious tax consequences to non-redeeming mutual fund owners. Variable annuity owners are protected against this tax trap.

§1302. THE REDEMPTION TRAP

There are many occurrences that will cause mutual fund owners to sell or redeem their fund shares. A poor performing stock market, the departure of a popular fund manager or general poor fund performance are some examples. When redemptions increase, fund managers frequently must sell stocks to generate the needed cash to meet these increased redemptions. This, in turn, increases realized gains for the fund. As mentioned earlier, mutual fund companies must distribute all dividends and realized capital gains (both long- and short-term) late in the year to those fund owners who continue to hold the mutual fund. When fund owners begin redeeming their shares and leaving a fund, dividend income and realized capital gains must be distributed to fewer fund owners, thus increasing each owner's share of the distributed gains. These increases result in the remaining fund owners paying higher income taxes. To compound things, increased redemptions are frequently a result of a declining stock market or declining fund share prices. This can put a remaining fund owner in the unpleasant position of owning a mutual fund that is *losing* money while still having to pay a large income tax bill.[1] The embedded gain problem is discussed in the following example:

> **Example**
> Mary was interested in buying XYZ Fund. The fund bought mostly value stocks. It had a long track record of doing very well. XYZ Fund historically held stocks for long periods. Its low turnover ratio resulted in small annual distributions which, in turn, translated into lower income taxes for fund owners. Because Mary was averse to paying unnecessary income taxes, she chose not to buy XYZ Fund late in the year. By doing so, she was able to avoid the distribution tax trap that strikes those who buy funds late in the year. In January, the stock market began to fall. By February, the market had dropped 20% and XYZ Fund had dropped from a high of $30 per share to $24 per share. The financial media reported unusually

---

[1] *Bloomburg Wealth Manager* discussed this problem in their lead article in their July/August 1999 issue.

large mutual fund redemptions. XYZ Fund was faced with such redemptions and sold stock to meet the redemption demand. At $24 per share, Mary believed that XYZ Fund was a bargain and purchased 20,000 shares at $24 for a total of $480,000. Redemptions remained high and XYZ Fund fell to $20 a share and stayed at that level for several months. In the following December, Mary received a distribution of $8.00 per share, requiring her to report $160,000 on her income tax return. Between capital gains and ordinary income, Mary paid $30,000 in income taxes on her fund even though the fund was down $80,000 from where she purchased it. The reason Mary got hit with a large tax bill while holding a losing mutual fund is that redemptions by other fund owners wanting to sell XYZ Fund forced the fund's managers to sell stocks and generate gains even though the fund was losing value due to a general market decline. The selling activity by the fund managers "embedded" these gains in the fund that ultimately became a tax trap for investors like Mary who chose not to redeem her shares.

Variable annuity owners are never exposed to the embedded gains problem discussed above because variable annuities are held in separate accounts for each investor. If one variable annuity owner sells funds he holds in a variable annuity, it will have no impact on the tax liability of other variable annuity owners who choose not to redeem their shares.

§1303. THE 100% INCOME TAX

When embedded gains are distributed in a year when the distributing fund company has gone down in value, it can set up one of the harshest income tax traps that can befall a mutual fund owner. If caught in this tax trap, a mutual fund owner can see his income tax hit triple digits! Mutual fund owners are the only investors who are exposed to paying income taxes on their investments that can exceed the highest marginal tax bracket of 35%. It is not unusual for mutual fund owners to face income taxes of 100% or more as the following example demonstrates:

Example
In January, Barb followed her financial advisor's suggestion and invested a recent inheritance of $250,000 in a portfolio of mutual funds. By year's end, the portfolio was down $50,000 or 20%. Shortly after that, Barb received a $50,000 distribution based on embedded gains. Barb did not reinvest the distribution. The distribution required Barb to pay $10,000 in income taxes to the IRS. Barb's advisor consoled her by telling Barb that things would "even out when the market moved up again." The following year, Barb's fund moved up to $260,000. Barb felt lucky to be up $10,000 in her mutual fund. What Barb didn't realize was that an income tax of $10,000 on a profit of $10,000 is a 100% income tax!

§1304. CONCLUSION

Buying mutual funds late in the year can create a nasty tax liability for investors who do not understand how mutual funds are taxed. Staying in or buying a mutual fund during a period of net redemptions can increase a mutual fund owner's income taxes significantly. The purchase of variable annuities presents no such tax problems.

- CHAPTER 14 -

COSTLY TAX TRAPS

§1401. INTRODUCTION

Mutual fund ownership is fraught with costly income tax traps that the owners of variable annuities do not have to confront. The potential cost of getting caught in such tax traps must be considered when one contemplates the purchase of a mutual fund.

§1402. MUTUAL FUND TAX TRAPS

The taxation of mutual funds is extremely complex. Basic tax guides often devote a chapter or more attempting to explain the tax laws that govern the ownership of mutual funds. Not fully understanding these tax laws can be costly to mutual fund owners as the following example demonstrates:

Example

Lisa recently sold one of her mutual funds for a gain of $50,000. She was concerned that the income tax on this $50,000 gain could be $10,000 or more. Lisa's brother suggested that she review her portfolio and find an investment or two that had total paper losses of $50,000. By selling such investments by year's end, Lisa could offset her $50,000 gain and avoid a large tax. Lisa found a mutual fund in her portfolio that had a $50,000 paper loss and sold it on December 28 to offset the $50,000 gain she had on the mutual fund she sold earlier in the year. In the first week of January of the following year, Lisa repurchased the mutual fund she sold in December for just about what she sold it for. Lisa reported the two offsetting mutual fund sales on her income tax return in April. She was audited by the IRS and told that the sale that took place in December could not offset her gain on the mutual fund she sold earlier. The IRS explained that Lisa had violated the wash sale rule.[1] With penalties and interest, Lisa owed the IRS more than $12,000. Had Lisa owned a variable annuity, she could have sold any of her sub-accounts for a profit and not worried about the tax ramifications because variable annuities are not subject to the wash sale rule when sub-accounts are sold, bought or exchanged within a variable annuity because such transactions do not generate any tax liability.

§1403. THE FIFO TRAP

Another common trap mutual fund owners face is known as the FIFO trap.[2] This is a rule the IRS applies to the sale of mutual funds. (FIFO stands for first in, first out). The rule states that if a mutual fund owner has purchased the same mutual fund on more than one occasion, and less than all of the fund is later sold, the IRS assumes, for tax purposes, that the

---

[1] IRC §1091.

[2] FIFO stands for first-in-first-out.

first shares of the mutual fund bought are shares that are sold. This rule sets up a potentially costly trap for mutual fund owners as the next example demonstrates:

Example

Several months ago, Paul purchased 5,000 shares of Zenith Fund at $10 a share. Recently, Zenith was selling for $30. Paul bought another 5,000 shares of Zenith Fund at $30 a share. Later, Paul needed some money and decided to sell 5,000 shares of the Zenith Fund he owned. Zenith was currently selling for $31 a share. Paul thought his gain on his sale would be the difference between $30 and $31 a share, or $1 per share. Paul was not aware of the FIFO rule used by the IRS. Because of this rule, Paul was deemed to have sold the Zenith Fund he first purchased at $10. Therefore, Paul's gain is $21 per share for 5,000 shares, or $105,000. The tax on this mutual fund sale will exceed $15,000.

§1404. CONCLUSION

The taxation of mutual funds is so complex that many mutual fund owners lose money unnecessarily each year by falling into the tax traps related to mutual fund ownership. Some mutual fund owners retain tax professionals to avoid these traps. Either way, a cost is exacted from the mutual fund owner. Variable annuities do not present similar tax traps.

- CHAPTER 15 -

MUTUAL FUND TAXATION IN A DECLINING STOCK MARKET

§1501. INTRODUCTION

As prior chapters pointed out, income taxes exact a huge price for owning mutual funds. The annual income taxes imposed on mutual funds greatly reduce their rate of return. Income taxation of mutual funds in a declining stock market can make the ownership of mutual funds even more costly.

§1502. VARIABLE ANNUITIES AND TAXATION IN A DECLINING STOCK MARKET

Because variable annuities do not pay income taxes on a current basis, a decline in the value of a variable annuity is not exacerbated by the payment of income taxes.

§1503. MUTUAL FUNDS AND TAXATION IN A DECLINING STOCK MARKET

Mutual funds are the only investment where income taxes are paid when the investment is losing value in a declining stock market. Because of this negative feature of mutual funds, a declining stock market can have a much more dramatic impact on a mutual fund owner. The following examples demonstrate the tax problem mutual fund owners face when the stock market is declining. Variable annuities do not present the same problem.

Example
Edna purchased a variable annuity for $100,000 two years ago. In the first year, her variable annuity went up 20% in value. The next year, it went down 16%. Edna's variable annuity is currently worth $100,800.

Example
Frank purchased a mutual fund for $100,000 two years ago. In the first year, his mutual fund went up 20%. The next year, the fund went down 16%. In each year, Frank paid $3,000 in income taxes on his mutual fund portfolio. At the end of the first year, Frank's mutual fund was worth $117,000 ($120,000 - $3,000). The second year, the fund was worth $95,280 ($117,000 - 16% - $3,000). This is $5,520 less than Edna's variable annuity account value.

The above examples demonstrate the impact that a single bad year in the stock market can have on a mutual fund. Although Edna and Frank made identical investments, Frank's mutual fund investment is worth $5,520 less than Edna's variable annuity a year later. In the third year of ownership, Frank will need to obtain a return in excess of 8% to get him back to his fund's original cost of $100,000.[1] If Edna, the variable annuity owner, receives an 8% return, her variable annuity will be worth nearly $109,000.[2] This will put Edna nearly $9,000 ahead of

---

[1] $95,280 x 8.102% = $103,000 - $3,000 in taxes.
[2] $100,800 x 8% = $108,864.

Frank. Even if Edna were to pay a 33% income tax on her gain, her annuity would still be worth $6,000 more than Frank's mutual fund.

§1504. CONCLUSION

The tax burden faced by mutual fund owners is heavy even in strong markets. In weak markets, the tax burden on mutual fund owners can become onerous.

- CHAPTER 16 -
THE DREADED ALTERNATIVE MINIMUM TAX

§1601. INTRODUCTION

Mutual fund owners are exposed to a potential increase in their income taxes due to the IRS's Alternative Minimum Tax (AMT). Variable annuity owners are never exposed to the AMT rule based on the fact that they own variable annuities.

§1602. THE ALTERNATIVE MINIMUM TAX (AMT)

The AMT is very complex and results in an increased income tax burden when taxpayers claim certain deductions or receive tax favored income. One of the situations that may cause one to have to pay increased income taxes under the AMT is receiving large capital gains distributions from mutual funds. The following example demonstrates this tax trap:

Example

Jack is a retired businessman who works part time as a teacher at a local community college. His salary is $40,000. His taxable income is $26,250. He has a large portfolio of mutual funds he purchased over the years. Recently, Jack received a distribution from his mutual funds of nearly $200,000. This distribution resulted in an additional income tax of just over $42,000. Not only did the tax on the distribution wipe out his teaching income, but instead of paying less than 15% on his taxable income, the AMT required Jack to pay nearly double this amount. To add insult to injury, the mutual funds Jack owned went down in value by 23% for the tax year.

As the above example points out, the AMT is a tax trap that often snares unsuspecting mutual fund owners. The AMT *cannot* be triggered by the ownership of variable annuities because these annuities, unlike mutual funds, do not make involuntary income distributions.

§1603. CONCLUSION

People who build up large portfolios of mutual funds may be setting themselves up for a significant income tax increase by exposing themselves to the Alternative Minimum Tax (AMT). People who build up large variable annuity portfolios are never subject to the AMT because ownership of variable annuities cannot trigger the dreaded AMT. The AMT increases the 15% long-term capital gains rate to an effective tax rate of $22\frac{1}{2}\%$.

- CHAPTER 17-
THE BREAK-EVEN POINT

§1701. INTRODUCTION

All investors know that an investment that grows tax-deferred (i.e. a variable annuity) will grow to a larger amount than one that is taxed on an annual basis (i.e. a mutual fund). By the same measure, a long-term investor in a tax-deferred investment, after all income taxes are paid, will usually net more income than an investor who invests in an annually taxed investment. Mutual fund proponents counter this basic rule of finance by pointing out that variable annuity purchasers may have to pay surrender fees or IRS penalties if they don't hold their annuities for the long-term. These same mutual fund proponents claim such fees and penalties greatly reduce the advantage of tax deferral that comes with variable annuity investing. As with much of what the proponents of mutual funds say, this argument is misleading.

§1702. SURRENDER CHARGES

Because variable annuities are intended to be long-term investments, many variable annuity issuers will impose a surrender fee if a variable annuity is treated as a short-term investment. Surrender charges may be imposed on the initial investment or account value for full surrenders. Surrender charges for partial withdrawals are usually based on the amount withdrawn. A common surrender fee charged by many variable annuity companies today imposes a 7% surrender fee on the value of a variable annuity if the annuity is surrendered within a year of its purchase. This fee drops to 6% in the second year, 5% in the third year and so on. After seven years, the surrender fee disappears.[1] Most variable annuities allow withdrawals of 10% to 15% of an annuity's value each year without imposing a surrender fee.[2] Long-term investors in variable annuities should not be concerned with surrender fees because they disappear after seven years in most cases. Most variable annuity investors usually plan on holding their variable annuities for at least seven years. It is interesting to note that many investors who choose to invest in mutual funds rather than variable annuities because of surrender penalties frequently buy their mutual funds in the B-share form which also impose a surrender penalty similar to that of variable annuities.

---

[1] The surrender fee discussed in this section will be the one used in the examples in this book. Investors should keep in mind that some surrender fees can run for longer or shorter periods or can be larger or smaller in amount. Many variable annuities are sold without surrender fees.

[2] The penalty-free withdrawal may still be subject to the 10% IRS penalty discussed in the next section. Surrender fees are waived by many variable annuity companies when an owner becomes unemployed, terminally ill or must enter a nursing home.

§1703. THE 10% IRS PENALTY

Because variable annuities are long-term investments that enjoy tax-deferred growth, the IRS imposes a 10% penalty, in addition to ordinary income taxes, on the growth (i.e. untaxed) portion of a variable annuity if this growth is withdrawn from the annuity before the owner is 59½ years old. Most long-term variable annuity purchasers are saving for retirement and realize they will most likely never be subject to this 10% IRS penalty.

§1704. THE BREAK-EVEN POINT

There is a point in time when tax-deferred investing in variable annuities will provide a larger net account value than a similar investment made in a mutual fund even if surrender fees and IRS penalties are taken into consideration. Financial professionals refer to this time period as the break-even point. If one plans to invest for a period longer than the break-even point, he should consider an investment in a variable annuity. If one plans to invest for a period of time that is less than the break-even point, he should consider a mutual fund investment. The following simple problem and solution demonstrates the concept of the break-even point:

Problem

Adam, who is 49, just inherited $25,000 and wants to invest it for his retirement ten years from now. He is considering an aggressive mutual fund suggested by his stockbroker. Adam is also looking at a similar investment available through a variable annuity. Adam expects a 10% return and realizes that he will lose 20% of his net return each year to income taxes if he selects the mutual fund. Both the mutual fund and the variable annuity impose non-tax expenses. Adam realizes a variable annuity investment may result in the imposition of surrender fee and a possible IRS penalty if he does not hold his annuity for the long-term. Which investment would be best for Adam?

Solution

If Adam buys the mutual fund he is considering, the fund will be worth $41,989 in ten years.[3] If he buys the variable annuity, it will be worth $49,317 in ten years.[4] After reducing the variable annuity's growth by the 10% IRS penalty and income taxes at 20%, the variable annuity will still be worth $42,022, or $33 more than the mutual fund.[5]

The above problem demonstrates that if Adam plans to stay invested for at least ten years, he will be better off investing in the variable annuity rather that the mutual fund. The reason for

---

[3] $25,000 x 10% reduced by typical costs, commissions and income taxes (see §709) = 6.064% x $23,750 x 10 years = $42,790. 30% of the $17,774 gain or $5,337 is taxed at 15% = $801. $42,790 - $801 = $41,989.

[4] $25,000 + 10% = $27,500 - 2.7% = $26,758 - $25,000 = $1757.50. $1757.50 ÷ $25,000 = 7.03%. $25,000 x 7.03% x 10 years = $49,317.

[5] $49,317 - $25,000 = $24,317 in gain. An average income tax rate of 20% and a 10% IRS penalty reduce this amount to $42,022. There would be no surrender penalty because the variable annuity was held for more than seven years.

this is at anytime after ten years, Adam can liquidate his variable annuity, pay all income taxes, surrender fees and IRS penalties and still have more than had he invested in a mutual fund. For every day beyond the ten years, Adam will be progressively better off financially than had he invested in a mutual fund. It is important to realize that in the problem discussed above, Adam was 59 when he liquidated his variable annuity. Had he waited six more months before selling his annuity, he could have avoided the 10% IRS penalty and would have been able to increase his net sale proceeds from $42,022 to $44,454.

It is important to note in the above problem that it was assumed that Adam would hold his mutual fund for ten years. Statistics shows that most mutual fund investors hold their mutual funds for about three years before selling them. If Adam did trade in his mutual fund account, he could face new commissions fees, transaction costs and possibly additional income taxes. This would have the effect of reducing the previously calculated break-even point to something less than ten years. (The concept of opportunity cost, as discussed in Chapter 10B, is ignored. If it were considered, the variable annuity's ending value would be greater.)

In most cases, long-term investors plan to invest at least to age $59^1/_2$ or at least not withdraw money from their retirement savings until $59^1/_2$.

§1705. AVOIDING THE 10% IRS PENALTY

The 10% IRS penalty mentioned above is not imposed on withdrawal from variable annuities after the owner turns $59^1/_2$. The IRS penalty imposed on withdrawals prior to age $59^1/_2$ can be avoided if the withdrawals are taken in a "series of equal periodic payments" based on the life expectancy of the annuity owner. This exception to the 10% IRS penalty, found in IRC §72, can be important to investors considering a potential investment in a variable annuity or mutual fund as the following example demonstrates:

Example
Jack, who is $48^1/_2$ wants to invest $170,000. Six years from now, he will need to withdraw approximately $10,000 annually as he enters early retirement. His stockbroker suggested an A-share mutual fund rather than a variable annuity because the variable annuity would impose both a surrender fee and a 10% IRS penalty if Jack made withdrawals as planned. Jack talked to a financial planner who determined that in six years, a $170,000 investment in a variable annuity returning 10% would grow to $255,554.[6] Jack could withdraw 4% of his variable annuity or approximately $10,222 at age $54^1/_2$ until he reached age $59^1/_2$ without any 10% IRS penalty because such withdrawals would qualify under IRC§72 as a series of substantially equal periodic payments. After age $59^1/_2$, the 10% penalty

---

[6] $170,000 x 7.03% x 6 years = $255,554.

would not apply. Jack would not pay a surrender fee because his withdrawals are less than 10% of his variable annuity account value. As mentioned, most variable annuity issuers do not impose surrender fees on withdrawals of 10% to 15% of an owner's variable annuity account value.

The above example demonstrates that surrender fees and IRS penalties can be circumvented. Whenever one can invest in a tax-deferred variable annuity and avoid surrender fees and IRS penalties, they will almost always be better off with the variable annuity than if they had invested in an annually taxed investment such as a mutual fund.

§1706. SURRENDER FEES AND IRS PENALTIES DETER WITHDRAWALS

Surrender fees and IRS penalties almost always carry a negative connotation. However, many investors, in order to avoid surrender fees and IRS penalties, will take withdrawals from their variable annuity only as a last resort. In the long run, this helps variable annuities to grow and create financial security. Mutual funds generally do not have surrender fees[7] and are not subject to the 10% pre-age $59^1/_2$ IRS penalty unless held in qualified plan or retirement account such as a IRA. For this reason, many investors will withdraw money from a mutual fund before considering withdrawals from variable annuities.

§1707. SURRENDER FEES AND IRS PENALTIES CAN BE ELIMINATED BY THE TAX DEFERRAL PROVIDED BY VARIABLE ANNUITIES

Section 1704 contains an explanation and example of how surrender fees and IRS penalties can be offset by tax deferral.

§1708. SURRENDER PENALTY FREE VARIABLE ANNUITIES

Most variable annuity issuers today make available variable annuities that have no surrender penalties for a modest additional cost.

§1709. CONCLUSION

Before an investment is made in either a mutual fund or a variable annuity, an investor must fully understand the impact of annual taxes, tax deferral, surrender fees, transaction costs, (i.e. commissions) and IRS penalties. Only after fully considering these issues can an intelligent investment decision be made. In nearly all cases, an investment in a variable annuity will reach a point in time (i.e. the break-even point) where an investor will be better off financially by investing in the variable annuity than a mutual fund. This can even be true where surrender fees and IRS penalties may be imposed on the variable annuity investor.

---

[7] B-shares do have surrender charges.

- CHAPTER 18 -

ELIMINATION OF ESTATE AND INCOME TAXES

§1801. INTRODUCTION

Financial planners have discovered several ways to cleanse variable annuities of both estate and income taxes. Accomplishing the same tax savings with mutual fund portfolios is generally not possible.

§1802. SIMPLE TAX PLANNING WITH VARIABLE ANNUITIES PROVIDES ESTATE AND INCOME TAX SAVINGS NOT AVAILABLE TO MUTUAL FUND OWNERS

As the following example demonstrates, estate planning with variable annuities frequently results in a greater estate tax reduction than can be accomplished with mutual funds.

Example

Jack and his wife, both 68, have an estate worth $11,000,000. One million dollars of this estate is a variable annuity of which half consists of contributions and half is growth. The remainder of the estate, which consists of a house, vacation property, investments, car, etc., is worth $10,000,000. Jack and his wife each own half of these assets. Each has a will contains portability language. Jack and his wife need $55,000 a year to supplement their other retirement income. At their death, Jack and his wife want their entire estate to pass to their three children without estate taxes if possible. Jack and his wife are also concerned that their children will have to pay income taxes on his annuity. They want to prevent this. The solution for these concerns is relatively simple. Jack should have his children purchase (and own) a $1,000,000 second-to-die life insurance policy on the lives of Jack and his wife. The annual premium for such a policy should be about $30,000. After the policy is in place, Jack should exchange his variable annuity for an immediate joint lifetime annuity (i.e. no guarantee other than lifetime payments). The immediate annuity will pay Jack and his wife approximately $85,000 a year for as long as either lives. Jack can give $30,000 to his children gift tax-free each year to enable them to pay the premiums on the life insurance they purchased. This leaves Jack and his wife with the $55,000 income supplement they need each year. The exclusion ratio will provide a major income tax advantage to Jack and his wife as they receive their $85,000 annuity payments (the exclusion ratio stops once all principal is recovered). If either spouse dies tomorrow the annuity will continue to pay the surviving spouse for his or her lifetime. At the second spouse's death the estate's value of $10,000,000 and will pass to the children estate tax free by applying the current $5,000,000 federal estate tax exemption together with the portability feature of the unified credit. The joint immediate annuity is valued at zero because it is a lifetime annuity that ceases to have any value at the second spouse's death. In addition, the children will receive $1,000,000 estate and income tax free from the insurance company in the form of insurance proceeds. In short, a combination of annuitization, basic tax planning and asset substitution will allow the children to inherit an $11,000,000 estate free of all death and income taxes.[1] Had Jack owned mutual funds instead, he may have held them until death in order to preserve a step-up in basis for his children. This would result in estate taxes of $350,000. In addition, the $85,000 in annual income from the immediate annuity would have been forfeited.

> For more information on estate tax planning with variable annuities, please see Report #9 titled "Eliminating Estate and Income Taxes from Retirement Accounts – An Opportunity for Financial Professionals." This report is available by calling Parker-Thompson Publishing at (919) 832-2687.

Chapter 25 discusses the concept of the stepped-up basis as it relates to mutual funds and variable annuities.

§1803. CONCLUSION

Investors need to understand that avoiding both estate and income taxes on a variable annuity is a simple matter.[2] The same tax savings with a similar mutual fund portfolio may not be possible.

---

[1] This example is very basic. By using systematic withdrawals, purchasing variable universal life insurance, purchasing a variable immediate annuity, purchasing earnings enhancement riders, etc. the benefit of this type of financial planning can be enhanced.

[2] Chapter 48 discusses another method for withdrawing money from a variable annuity while avoiding income taxes on the withdrawals.

- CHAPTER 19 -
LOST INCOME TAX EXEMPTIONS

§1901. INTRODUCTION

Involuntary distributions from mutual funds may cause fund owners to lose some of their income tax exemptions. The reason for this is higher incomes subject taxpayers to phaseout rules that reduce exemptions. Whenever a taxpayer loses tax exemptions due to the involuntary distributions generated by their mutual funds, it results in an increased income tax that must be attributed to ownership of the mutual funds. The owners of variable annuities are never exposed to losing income tax exemptions and thus having to pay higher taxes because variable annuities are tax-deferred and do not make involuntary annual distributions that can cause one to lose tax exemptions.

Phaseouts for personal exemptions were eliminated for 2010. However, these phaseouts are scheduled to be added to the tax law in the future. For this reason, examples of how phaseouts applied in 2009 are included in this chapter so readers can begin to understand how these phaseouts might work in the future.

§1902. LOSS OF INCOME TAX EXEMPTIONS

Taxpayers and their dependents are given a $3,650 income tax deduction for each personal exemption they claim (2009). Personal exemptions are usually claimed for the taxpayer, his spouse, minor children and other dependents. If a taxpayer's adjusted gross income exceeds a certain level ($250,200 for 2009), the ability to fully deduct personal exemptions is reduced. This, in effect, raises income taxes. The loss of personal exemptions can occur as the result of mutual fund ownership but not as the result of variable annuity ownership, as the next two examples demonstrate. An example of a 2009 personal exemption phaseout is set out below:

> **Example #1**
> Jack and Lisa have four minor children. Their adjusted gross income (AGI) for 2009 is $250,200. They own a variable annuity worth $600,000. Jack and Lisa claim six personal exemptions for themselves and their four children for total exemptions of $21,900. At year's end, Jack and Lisa learned their variable annuity had gone up in value by $60,000. Because Jack and Lisa have an AGI of $250,200, they will lose none of their personal exemptions. At a 33% marginal tax rate, these exemptions save $7,227 in taxes for Jack and Lisa. In addition, Jack and Lisa do not have to report their $60,000 annuity gain to the IRS or pay taxes on it currently.

Example #2

George and Helen have four minor children. Their adjusted gross income (AGI) for 2009 is $250,200. They own a mutual fund portfolio worth $600,000. George and Helen claim six personal exemptions for themselves and their four children for total exemptions of $21,900. Late in the year, George and Helen received a distribution from their mutual fund of $60,000. This increased their AGI to $310,200. This increase will result in a reduction of $3,504 in the $21,900 in personal exemptions to which George and Helen were entitled.[1] The $3,504 tax loss is a result of owning mutual funds and has the impact of increasing income taxes. A tax exemption loss of $3,504 on a mutual fund distribution of $60,000 is, assuming a marginal tax rate of 33%, the equivalent of an additional tax of $1,156 or 1.92% of the mutual fund's distribution. Assuming, conservatively, that the $60,000 distribution itself will be taxed to George and Helen at 19%, the loss of $3,504 in personal exemptions increases that 19% tax on the mutual fund distribution to 20.92%.

From the above examples it can be determined that George and Helen not only had to pay taxes on their $60,000 mutual fund distribution, but lost valuable tax exemptions due to the mutual fund distribution they received. On the other hand, Jack and Lisa paid no taxes on their variable annuity gain and did not have their income taxes increased due to a loss of any personal exemptions.

§1903. CONCLUSION

Mutual fund owners not only must pay taxes on their realized mutual fund gains each year, but may also lose valuable tax exemptions resulting from their mutual fund distributions. This, in turn, can result in increased income taxes for the mutual fund owners, thereby reducing overall rate of return they receive on their funds. Variable annuity owners are not exposed to similar tax increases or exemption losses due to the ownership of their variable annuities.

---

[1] $310,200 - $250,200 = $60,000 ÷ $2,500 = 24 x 2% = 48% x $21,900 = $10,512 x $^1/_3$ = $3,504.

- CHAPTER 20 -
LOST INCOME TAX DEDUCTIONS

§2001. INTRODUCTION

Involuntary distributions from mutual funds may cause fund owners to lose some of their itemized income tax deductions. Whenever a taxpayer loses income tax deductions due to the ownership of a mutual fund it results in an increased tax that must be attributed to mutual fund ownership. The owners of variable annuities are never exposed to losing income tax deductions due to variable annuity ownership because such annuities are tax-deferred and do not make involuntary annual distributions. Phaseouts for itemized deductions were eliminated for 2010. However, their phaseouts are scheduled to be added to the tax law in the future. For this reason, an example of a phaseout for itemized deductions for 2009 is set out below so the reader can understand the possible impact these phaseouts might have if reinstituted in the future.

§2002. LOSS OF INCOME TAX DEDUCTIONS

Married taxpayers who have adjusted gross incomes above $166,800 in 2009 are required to reduce many of their itemized income tax deductions including their home mortgage interest deduction. Involuntary distributions from mutual funds, over which a fund owner has no control, can increase a fund owner's adjusted gross income (AGI) enough to cause partial loss of many important income tax-reducing deductions. The loss of income tax deductions can be significant. The loss or reduction of these deductions can result in a taxpayer having to pay a larger income tax than normal. On the other hand, any growth in the investments held in a variable annuity are not reportable as taxable income until withdrawn and therefore protect annuity owners from losing any part of their income tax deductions. An example of a phaseout of itemized deductions in 2009 is discussed in the following examples:

> **Example #1**
> Bill and Judy Marshall, both 66 years old, are retired. They each currently own a variable annuity. Due to a strong market, Bill and Judy enjoyed a combined $60,000 gain in the value of their annuities. For 2009, Bill and Judy have an adjusted gross income (AGI) of $166,800. Their $60,000 annuity gain is deferred income and does not have to be currently reported. Their combined personal exemptions of $7,300 for 2009 and $25,000 in itemized deductions for home interest, state taxes and charitable contributions reduce their adjusted gross income to a taxable income of $134,500 resulting in an income tax of $26,000. Based on these facts:
>
> - The Marshalls' taxable income was not increased by the growth in their variable annuities.

- No itemized deductions were lost or reduced.

- Their marginal tax bracket remained at 25%.

- Their average tax bracket remained at 19.33%.

- Their variable annuity gain was not taxed.

- No additional taxes were incurred due to their variable annuity ownership.

Example #2

Jack and Betty Kelly, both 66 years old, are retired. Each has a mutual fund portfolio. Jack and Betty both received distribution notices (i.e. Form 1099-DIVs) for $30,000 each, reflecting a combined $60,000 gain made in their mutual funds. Not counting their mutual fund gains, Jack and Betty had an adjusted gross income (AGI) of $166,800 for 2009. They had combined personal exemptions of $7,300 in 2009 and $25,000 in itemized deductions for home mortgage interest, state taxes and charitable contributions. This results in a taxable income of $134,500. The mutual fund distribution, which could not be controlled by Jack and Betty, increased their adjusted gross income to $226,800 and their taxable income to $194,500. Half of the distribution was long-term capital gains and half was short-term capital gains. Because Jack and Betty's AGI is $60,000 above the $166,800 limit, they must reduce their itemized deductions by 1% of this amount. A reduction of 1% of $60,000 is $600 for 2009. Jack and Betty's $226,800 AGI is now reduced by $7,300 in personal exemptions and itemized deductions of $24,400 to $195,100. Their income tax liability will be $38,992.[1] As a result of owning mutual funds, Jack and Betty had the following tax consequences:

- The mutual fund distributions involuntarily increased the Kelly's taxable income by $60,000.

- The mutual fund distributions increased the Kelly's marginal tax bracket from 25% to 28%.

- The mutual fund distributions increased the Kellys' average tax rate.

- The Kellys had to pay $12,992 more than the Marshalls in additional income taxes due to their mutual fund distribution.

- The Kellys had their taxable income increased by an additional $600 due to having their itemized deductions reduced by this amount.

Example #3

Don and Judy have an adjusted gross income (AGI) of $82,500. In addition to personal exemptions and itemized deductions of $17,000, Don and Judy have an $11,750 personal use casualty loss deduction. Casualty deductions are limited

---

[1] $195,100 less $30,000 long-term capital gains = $165,100 which will generate a tax of $34,492 + $4,500 (15% of the $30,000 in long-term capital gains) = $38,992.

[2] $82,500 x 10% = $8,250. $11,750 - $500 = $11,250 - $8,250 = $3,000.

to amounts above 10% of AGI after a $500 floor deduction. Normally, Don and Judy would be entitled to a $3,000 casualty loss deduction.[2] However, they received an involuntary mutual fund distribution of $30,000 which raised their AGI to $112,500. This made them ineligible for any casualty deduction. In effect, the distribution caused Don and Judy to lose a $3,000 deduction. At a 25% marginal tax rate, this lost deduction would cost Don and Judy $750. This loss would not have occurred if Don and Judy had invested in a variable annuity instead of a mutual fund. In addition, Don and Judy must pay income taxes on the $30,000 mutual fund distribution. This tax burden could exceed $4,500.

§2003. CONCLUSION

The ownership of mutual funds not only results in direct taxes on realized gains involuntarily distributed by the fund, but creates increased indirect taxes by reducing tax deductions. Owners of variable annuities do not face similar negative tax repercussions from owning variable annuities.

- CHAPTER 21 -

LOST INCOME TAX CREDITS

§2101. INTRODUCTION

Distributions from a mutual fund may cause fund owners to lose one of their income tax credits due to IRS phaseout rules. Whenever a taxpayer loses income tax credits due to the ownership of a mutual fund, it results in an increased income tax that must be attributed to mutual fund ownership. The owners of variable annuities are never exposed to losing income tax credits due to variable annuity ownership because such annuities are tax-deferred and do not make involuntary annual distributions. Although most phaseouts were eliminated for 2010, the phaseout for the child tax credit and other credits was not.

§2102. LOSS OF INCOME TAX CREDITS

Taxpayers with minor children are entitled to certain credits which reduce their income tax liability. This credit is referred to as the child tax credit. The child tax credit for 2010 allows a $1,000 credit for each dependent child under age 17. This credit is reduced or lost if a taxpayer's adjusted gross income (AGI) exceeds certain levels. For every $1,000 above an adjusted gross income of $110,000 (2010), $50 of the child tax credit is lost. Involuntary distributions from mutual funds may result in the partial or total loss of this credit. The loss or reduction of any tax credit can result in an increase in income taxes. Variable annuity ownership, because of tax deferral, does not create the potential for the reduction or loss of tax credits or the resulting increase in taxation as does the ownership of mutual funds. The following examples demonstrate this.

> **Example #1**
> Dave and Ellen have three children between the ages of four and 16. Their adjusted gross income (AGI) for 2010 is $110,000. Dave and Ellen have an annuity that went up in value by $60,000. This increase is not currently reportable as income and therefore, Dave and Ellen's AGI remains at $110,000. Dave and Ellen are able to claim a $1,000 child tax credit for each of their three children, giving them a total credit of $3,000, which is used to reduce their tax liability to the IRS.

> **Example #2**
> Frank and Gina have three children between the ages of four and 16. Their adjusted gross income (AGI) for 2010 is $110,000. Frank and Gina are entitled to $3,000 in child tax credits (3 x $1,000). Frank and Gina have a mutual fund that recently made a distribution of $60,000 for the year 2010. This distribution raised Frank and Gina's AGI to $170,000. This increase will result in the complete loss of the $3,000 child tax credit. The loss of this credit increases the taxable income

of Frank and Gina by $3,000 and increases their tax burden by $840 at a 28% tax rate. Assuming conservatively that the tax on the mutual fund gain will be $7,200 or 12%, the loss of $3,000 in child tax credits increases this tax from $7,200 to $10,200 or from 12% to 17%. Mutual fund distributions can reduce the child care credit in much the same manner as they reduce the child tax credit discussed above.

§2103. OTHER CHILD-RELATED TAX CREDITS

There are other tax credits available to offset dependent care expenses, adoption costs, child education expenses, etc. These credits can be lost or greatly reduced when a taxpayer's income is increased by a mutual fund distribution.

§2104. OTHER TAX CREDITS

There are other tax credits not related to children that can be lost or reduced due to a mutual fund distribution. Included are:

- The Lifetime Learning Credit
- American Opportunity Credit

§2105. CONCLUSION

Mutual fund owners not only must pay taxes on their mutual fund gains each year but may also lose valuable income tax credits due to their mutual fund ownership. This, in turn, can result in increased income taxes for the mutual fund owners thereby reducing the overall rate of return they receive on their funds. Variable annuity owners are not exposed to similar tax increases due to the tax deferral feature of variable annuities.

- CHAPTER 22 -
A NATIONAL SALES TAX

§2201. INTRODUCTION

The current income tax structure in the United States is under attack by politicians and taxpayers alike. One possible alternative to our current income tax code would be to replace it with a national sales tax or consumption tax. If such a tax is adopted in the future, variable annuity owners will benefit greatly while mutual fund owners will suffer.

§2202. A NATIONAL SALES TAX

Tax reform is one of the major election issues concerning both politicians and voters alike. It is quite possible that our current income tax system could be replaced with a sales or consumption tax sometime in the future. Variable annuity owners will reap a huge windfall if this occurs. Variable annuity owners who have deferred income taxes for many years may completely avoid income taxes in retirement if the current income tax structure is indeed replaced by a sales or consumption tax. On the other hand, mutual fund owners who are currently paying income taxes each year on their portfolios will be the big losers if a sales or consumption tax replaces our current income tax structure.

Congress has already embraced the idea of tax-free retirement income. Except for persons with large retirement incomes, Social Security is a form of tax-free retirement income. The newly created Roth IRA allows people to save for retirement and ultimately receive tax-free retirement income. Moving to a non-income based tax structure and allowing retired persons to make income tax-free withdrawals from 401(k)s, 403(b)s and variable annuities may be the next step in this process. Current tax law provides for Roth 401(k)s and Roth 403(b)s that would provide tax-free retirement income much like the Roth IRA does currently.

§2203. CONCLUSION

Once investors understand that there is some possibility that our current income tax structure could be eliminated in the future, they might find it more prudent to defer paying income taxes today by investing in variable annuities rather than investing in mutual funds which require the payment of income taxes on an annual basis.

- CHAPTER 23 -

A FLAT TAX

§2301. INTRODUCTION

Complaints about the complexity of the U.S. income tax code are growing daily. The most often suggested solution for the complexity of our tax code is the creation of a simple flat tax. Such a tax would benefit variable annuity owners but not mutual fund owners.

§2302. A FLAT TAX

It seems almost certain that the income tax code of the United States will have to be simplified. Voters are demanding simplification and Congress is promising it. Most proposals to simplify our current income tax code involve the imposition of some form of a flat tax. Flat tax rates ranging from 10% to 17% have been proposed by our representatives in Congress. If a flat tax of 17% is adopted, both mutual fund owners and variable annuity owners will be subject to the same income tax burden at retirement. A mutual fund owner may well question whether it was worth paying 20% or more in income taxes on his mutual fund holdings over the years only to find himself in a 17% tax bracket at retirement, especially if his neighbor who deferred all income taxes with variable annuities winds up in the same 17% tax bracket.

§2303. CONCLUSION

Investors need to understand that if the U.S. tax structure is simplified by the adoption of a flat tax, long-term variable annuity owners will benefit greatly while mutual fund owners will suffer.

- CHAPTER 24 -

CAPITAL GAINS RATES AND HOLDING PERIODS

§2401. INTRODUCTION

Capital gains rates and the holding periods for obtaining these rates are subject to change. If capital gains rates go up or the capital gains holding period is lengthened, the tax burden of mutual fund owners will increase.

§2402. WHAT IF CAPITAL GAINS RATES RISE OR HOLDING PERIODS ARE INCREASED?

Mutual fund proponents treat the existence of the temporary long-term capital gains rates of 15% and the holding period of twelve months to obtain these rates as if they were permanently etched in stone by Congress. Nothing could be further from the truth. History has shown that the capital gains rates and the holding periods to obtain favorable capital gains treatment have fluctuated with some regularity over time. In the past twenty years, Congress has changed this tax rate seven times. Currently, capital gains rates are at historic lows. The capital gains holding period of one year is the shortest such period on record. A future increase in the temporary long-term capital gains rates to 20% or more would make the tax advantage of purchasing variable annuities instead mutual funds much more pronounced than it is today. Current income tax law increases the 15% long-term capital gains rate to 20% after December 31, 2012. Many long-term mutual fund owners have paid as much as 30% capital gains rates on their mutual funds in years past, and from 15% to 20% in recent years. If these mutual fund owners learn just before retirement that these rates will be increased, it will surely raise the question of why they didn't purchase a variable annuity instead of mutual funds. In addition to Congress raising the current 15% long-term capital gains tax to 20% in 2013, it is also quite possible that they could, some time in the future, adjust the holding period necessary to obtain this tax rate. An adjustment from a twelve-month holding period to an eighteen-month period could result in many mutual fund companies making distributions to fund owners that would not qualify for long-term capital gains.

The deficit in the U.S. is growing daily. In the future, if additional revenues are needed, an increase in the capital gains rate or its holding period is a possibility. The war effort in Iraq and the need for health care benefits will force the U.S. deficit higher. Homeland security costs will continue for many years, as will the cost of the credit crisis of 2008-2009. An increase in taxes may be needed to fund all of these efforts. Capital gains rates may be one of the first areas from which additional tax revenues can be raised. As of late December of 2010, Congress has refused to make permanent the 15% capital gains. The Democrats do not like the current capital gains rate and will most likely push to increase it at the first opportunity.

§2403. CONCLUSION

Investors need to understand that the temporary capital gains rates and the holding period to obtain these rates could increase in the future. Should this happen, mutual fund owners will be saddled with ever increasing taxes while the variable annuity owner will continue to realize the full benefits of tax deferral.

- CHAPTER 25 -
THE STEP-UP IN BASIS RULE

§2501. INTRODUCTION

Proponents of mutual funds claim that the step-up in cost basis that mutual funds receive at an owner's death is a major reason for investors to buy mutual funds. These same proponents claim that variable annuities do not receive a similar stepped-up basis. As with most of the claims made by mutual fund advocates, the claims regarding the step-up in cost basis is, at best, misleading.

§2502. THE STEPPED-UP BASIS – GENERAL

For the past several years, the Internal Revenue Code has provided an unlimited step-up in the cost basis of mutual funds to beneficiaries who inherited them.[1] The same step-up in cost basis rule is not available to beneficiaries who receive variable annuity proceeds from a *deceased* annuity owner.[2] Cost basis, or more simply basis, refers to the original cost of a mutual fund or variable annuity together with any upward or downward adjustments in such cost. The concept of a stepped-up cost basis allows beneficiaries who inherit mutual funds purchased with *non-qualified* money to treat such funds as if they purchased them on the decedent's date of death for their fair market value on that date.[3] When beneficiaries later sell these mutual funds, they will pay long-term capital gains taxes only on the difference between the sale price and the fair market value of the funds on the date the transferring decedent died. This is true even though the decedent may have paid much less (or much more) for the funds. The following examples demonstrate application of the stepped-up basis rule where a mutual fund and variable annuity owner have died:

> **Example**
> Abel purchased a mutual fund for $20,000 a little over 12 years ago. At his death, the fund was worth $40,000. Abel left the fund by will to his daughter Betty. Shortly after receiving the mutual fund, Betty sold it for $40,000. Betty will not incur any income tax liability on the sale of the fund because she is allowed to treat the inherited mutual fund as if she purchased it for its $40,000 fair market value determined as of the date of her father's death. Stated another way, Betty's

---

[1] IRC §1014 and §1015. This benefit was limited by Economic Growth and Tax Relief Reconciliation Act of 2001 (EGTRRA), See note 9.

[2] Variable annuity proceeds are considered income in respect of a decedent under IRC §691. Income in respect of a decedent is not eligible for a step-up in basis at the owner's death, but any income tax due can be largely offset by an IRC §691 income tax deduction. Variable annuities purchased or added to prior to October 20, 1979 receive a step-up in basis at the owner's death.

[3] The alternate valuation date, which is six months after death may also be used. See IRC §2032. Variable annuities, qualified plans and accounts (e.g., IRAs) do not get a step-up in basis at an owner's death.

basis in her inherited mutual fund for income tax purposes would be stepped-up from her father's basis of $20,000 to the $40,000 date of death value.[4] If the fund were sold by Betty for more than $40,000, she would be responsible for paying long-term capital gain taxes only on those sale proceeds that exceeded $20,000.[5]

Example

Carla purchased a variable annuity for $20,000 a little over 12 years ago. At Carla's death, the variable annuity, due to tax deferral, was worth $47,220 and passed to her son Dave who was named as the beneficiary of the variable annuity. Dave will be required to pay ordinary income taxes on those proceeds he receives that exceed his mother's initial $20,000 purchase price for the variable annuity.[6] This is true whether the variable annuity is sold or held by Dave. This tax liability arises because Dave is not entitled to a step-up in the $20,000 original cost or basis of the annuity purchased by his mother. In short, Carla's $20,000 purchase price for her variable annuity is carried over or transferred to Dave.[7]

The perceived benefit of a step-up in basis to those who inherit mutual funds has frequently been cited as a major reason for investing in mutual funds rather than variable annuities. However, a close analysis of the stepped-up basis rule, especially following the recent tax law changes,[8] indicates that this rule is not nearly as beneficial as investors and their families have been led to believe. The following sections discuss this issue.

§2503. TAX LEGISLATION MAY ERODE THE BENEFIT OF THE STEPPED-UP BASIS RULE

Congress passed legislation that eliminated the unlimited step-up in basis rule and replaced it with a reduced stepped-up basis rule for 2010.[9] Many mutual fund owners who purchased funds years ago relying on the unlimited stepped-up basis rule to provide their beneficiaries with an income tax benefit may be surprised to learn that this benefit could again come under legislative attack. The following example demonstrates what happened in 2010 when a step-up in basis rule was modified for inherited mutual funds.

---

[4] The $20,000 original basis may have changed somewhat due to reinvestment of distributions, etc. The fund's value could be set at the alternate valuation date (six months after the owner's death) if this date were elected for estate tax purposes. (See IRC §2032).

[5] If the funds were sold for less than $40,000, resulting in a loss, Betty would owe no income taxes. However, she would not be able to take any income tax deduction for the loss. Betty would not owe any income taxes on any gain from her basis up to $40,000. Betty could keep the mutual fund portfolio to avoid income taxes and might be able to pass it on to her beneficiaries with a stepped-up basis at her death. The sale of assets that receive a stepped-up basis as a result of an owner's death are always taxed at long-term capital gains rates regardless of how long a beneficiary holds the inherited funds.

[6] Annuitization or spreading out payments from the variable annuity over time would reduce the impact of the income taxes owed.

[7] If the variable annuity were worth less than $20,000 at Carla's death, a deduction on her final income tax return would be allowed.

[8] On an after-tax basis, Carla's son would receive more than Abel's daughter. (Assumes a 25% tax on gain).

[9] See IRC §1022. This code section will only be in effect for 2010 unless extended or made permanent.

Example:

Ed, who is an 80-year old widower, has real estate and stocks worth $1,300,000. He also has a mutual fund portfolio he recently purchased for $500,000. These assets had doubled in value by 2010 when Ed died. Ed's heirs would have to pay income taxes on the difference between $3.1 million ($1.8 million [basis] + $1.3 million [2010 step-up]) and $3.6 million ($1.8 million doubled) or $500,000. Their income tax liability would be based on capital gains rates of 15% (2010) resulting in a potential tax of $75,000.[10]

The new step-up in basis rule applied only for 2010. This modified rule has been repealed for 2011 and beyond, but it demonstrates that Congress is willing to adjust the step-up in basis rules if necessary.

§2504. THE STEPPED-UP BASIS – AN ILLUSION

The assumption that a mutual fund portfolio, because it receives a step-up in basis, will provide beneficiaries with a larger inheritance than a variable annuity is not always true. In many instances, the opposite proves to be the case. The reason for this is that the tax-deferred growth provided by a variable annuity will, in many cases, offset or exceed the tax savings provided by the step-up in basis received by beneficiaries who inherit mutual funds at an owner's death. The following two examples demonstrate this:[11]

Example

Sixteen years ago, Ellen invested $100,000 in a mutual fund portfolio that grew at 10% annually. Each year taxes on her distributions reduced Ellen's rate of return by 20%.[12] The annual cost of owning the mutual fund was 1.5% and trading costs were 0.7%.[13] The commission paid by Ellen was 2^1/2%. These expenses reduced Ellen's net rate of return to 6.064%.[14] Ellen recently died and left her mutual fund, now worth $250,088,[15] to her four young grandchildren. Ellen had no other assets. The fund was sold soon thereafter for $250,088. The grandchildren avoided capital gains taxes on the fund's unrealized gains because the cost basis of the mutual fund in their hands was stepped-up to $250,088. In short, the grandchildren received the full $250,088 value of the inherited mutual fund unreduced by capital gains taxes.

---

[10] In 2010, Ed's heirs or beneficiaries will receive a maximum step-up in basis of $1,300,000 which is added to the $1.8 million original basis.

[11] This paper compares mutual funds and variable annuities that are sold by financial professionals. If no load mutual funds or variable annuities are involved, adjustments for commissions paid and other costs of ownership must be made.

[12] The average mutual fund loses approximately 2% of its total annual gain to income taxes according to studies done by Lipper, Inc. and others.

[13] The average A-share mutual fund has an annual expense ratio of 1.5% and trading costs of 0.7%.

[14] $100,000 - $2,500 = $97,500 + 10% = $107,250 - 2.2% = $104,891 - $97,500 = $7,391 x -20% = $5,912 ÷ $97,500 = 6.064%.

[15] 6.064% x $97,500 x 16 years = $250,088.

105

Example

Sixteen years ago, Frank purchased a variable annuity for $100,000. The annuity grew at the net rate of 10% but due to annual expenses and trading costs of 2.7% associated with owning the annuity, Frank's net rate of return was reduced to 7.03%.[16] Frank recently died leaving his annuity, now worth $296,543,[17] to his four young grandchildren. Frank had no other assets. The annuity proceeds paid out to the grandchildren were subject to a total of $28,176 in *ordinary* income taxes on the annuity's growth of $196,543, thus reducing their inheritance from $296,543 to $272,043.[18] This is $21,955 more than in the first example where a stepped-up basis was obtained.

As the examples above indicate, beneficiaries of variable annuities are frequently better off financially than beneficiaries who receive mutual funds from a decedent even after factoring in the claimed income tax advantage of the step-up in basis available to those who inherit mutual funds.

§2505. THE TAX SAVINGS MUTUAL FUND OWNERS MIGHT OBTAIN FROM A STEP-UP IN BASIS IS NOT THAT LARGE

Many mutual fund owners measure the gain in their mutual fund by subtracting the original cost of the fund from the current market value. Doing so distorts the potential tax savings that a step-up in basis actually provides. The following example demonstrates this:

Example

Ten years ago Jack purchased a mutual fund for $10,000. Today it is worth $22,500. Jack needs some money but is reluctant to sell his mutual fund. He believes there is $12,500 in gain in the fund and he wants to pass this gain to his children income tax-free by taking advantage of the step-up in basis rule. What Jack does not realize is that by paying taxes each year on his mutual fund and reinvesting his mutual fund distributions, which most mutual fund investors do, his original $10,000 cost basis is adjusted upwardly annually to reflect the taxes Jack paid each year on these reinvested distributions. Jack's current *upwardly adjusted* basis in his mutual fund could be as much as $20,000. This means that if Jack died, any potential tax liability owed by his beneficiaries would be imposed on $2,500, not $12,500. The income tax Jack would save his beneficiaries on this $2,500 by providing a step-up in basis would, at best, amount to a few hundred dollars.

---

[16] Annual ownership costs are 2.2% and trading costs are 0.5%. $100,000 + 10% = $110,000 - 2.7% = $107,030 - $100,000 = $7,030 ÷ $100,000 = 7.03%.

[17] $100,000 x 7.03% x 16 years = $296,543.

[18] $296,543 - $100,000 = $196,543 ÷ 4 = $49,136 per grandchild. Less $5,700 for each grandchild's single standard deduction for 2010 = $43,436 less a personal exemption of $3,650 = $39,786. The tax tables for 2010 show the tax on $39,786 is $6,125 for a single person. The four grandchildren will pay a total tax of $24,500 (4 x $6,125), leaving a net inheritance of $272,043 ($296,543 - $24,500).

Very few mutual fund owners really understand how little income tax they actually save their beneficiaries when mutual funds are inherited. The following example demonstrates this:

Example:

Quinn, a widower, purchased a conservative mutual fund several years ago for $100,000 and it grew to $200,000 by 2007. It has remained at this $200,000 value for the last several years. Quinn considered giving the fund to his daughter but decided not to sell the fund because he wanted to pass the mutual fund to his daughter and provide her with a step-up in basis. Including the mutual fund, Quinn's net estate is valued at just under $5,000,000. If Quinn dies in 2011 while his fund is worth $200,000, he will only have saved his daughter the income taxes that would have been due had Quinn given his daughter the fund while he was alive. Assuming Quinn had paid income taxes every year on his mutual fund distributions and these distributions were reinvested, any tax liability would be based only on the *unrealized* capital gains that have built up inside of Quinn's mutual fund. Assuming the unrealized gain in Quinn's mutual fund amounts to 30% of the gain, the tax liability on the fund would be calculated by applying the 15% long-term capital gains rate to $30,000 (30% of $100,000 in growth) yielding a total tax of $4,500.[19] In short, the benefit that the step-up in basis would provide Quinn's daughter on a $200,000 bequest would amount to a mere $4,500. If given the choice of receiving $195,500 ($200,000 - $4,500) in 2007 or letting $200,000 sit in a stagnate conservative bond fund for several years, most people would take the $195,500 and forego the "benefit" of a stepped-up basis. (No estate taxes would be due).

§2506. THE STEP-UP IN BASIS - THE TRUE INCOME TAX COST

The step-up in basis rule states that when a beneficiary inherits mutual funds from a deceased owner, any income tax liability owed on the mutual fund's gain up to the fund's value on the owner's date of death is eliminated regardless of how much gain has built up in the fund. This rule does not in any way limit the income taxes that the owner had to pay prior to his death. Simply stated, income taxes are paid on mutual funds by their owners prior to death so their beneficiaries can inherit these funds without an income tax liability when the owner dies. Variable annuities are not subject to income taxes while the owner his alive, but places the burden of paying income taxes on the beneficiaries who inherit them. This raises an interesting question – is it better to inherit a mutual fund without an income tax liability because the deceased owner paid income taxes on the funds while he was alive, or inherit a variable annuity with an income tax burden because the deceased owner did not have to pay income taxes while owning the variable annuity? As the following examples demonstrate, the latter choice often proves to be the best:

---

[19] The daughter can use her father's eight-year holding period to obtain long-term capital gains treatment.

Example

Don purchased a mutual fund for $50,000 twenty years ago. He paid a commission of 4%. Annual expenses and trading costs for the fund were 2.2%. The fund grew at an average of 10% a year but lost 20% of its net value on average each year to annual income taxes. Don's net rate of return was 6.064%.[20] Don recently died. His mutual fund was worth $155,812 at his death. Don's daughter Ellen inherited the fund and sold it for $155,812.[21] Due to the step-up in basis rule, she paid no income taxes on the $155,812. However, Ellen calculated that her father paid $51,109 in income taxes while he owned the mutual fund.[22]

Example

Judy purchased a variable annuity for $50,000 twenty years ago. The annuity had combined annual costs and trading costs of 2.7%. The variable annuity grew at 10% a year. Judy's net rate of return was 7.03%.[23] Judy recently died with her variable annuity worth $194,572.[24] She left the variable annuity to her son Ed. The variable annuity had $144,572 in gain in it. Ed liquidated the variable annuity for $194,572 and paid 21% in income taxes or $30,360 on the annuity's gain. He netted $164,212 from the sale. This $164,212 is $8,400 more than Ellen received in the prior example. It is interesting to note that the IRS received $51,109 in income taxes from Don on the mutual fund portfolio in the prior example, but only $30,360 from Ed on his variable annuity inheritance.

What the above example demonstrates is that the tax-deferral provided to beneficiaries of variable annuities can be much more valuable than the step-up in basis provided to those who inherit mutual funds.

§2507. MUTUAL FUNDS, UNLIKE VARIABLE ANNUITIES, ARE SUBJECT TO A STEP-DOWN IN BASIS

Mutual fund owners rarely consider that their beneficiaries are subject to a step-*down* in basis when mutual funds lose value prior to an owner's death. This cannot happen with variable annuities. As the following examples demonstrate, the variable annuity is a superior investment relative to mutual funds when a step-down in basis occurs:

Example

Jim, age 83, purchased a mutual fund portfolio several years ago. He invested $100,000 in the fund. During a recent stock market correction, the value of Jim's fund portfolio dropped to $75,000. Shortly thereafter he died. Jim's 53-year old daughter was the beneficiary of his portfolio. At Jim's death, the daughter had

---

[20] $50,000 - $2,000 = $48,000 + 10% = $52,800 - 2.2% = $51,638 - $48,000 = $3,638 -20% = $2,910 ÷ $48,000 = 6.064%.

[21] 6.064% x 20 years x $48,000 = $155,812.

[22] $50,000 - $2,000 = $48,000 + 10% = $52,800 - 2.2% = $51,638 - $48,000 = $3,638 ÷ $48,000 = 7.5792% x 20 years x $48,000 = $206,921 (ignoring income taxes) - $155,812 = $51,109.

[23] $50,000 + 10% = $55,000 - 2.7% = $53,515 - $50,000 = $3,515 ÷ $50,000 = 7.03%.

[24] 7.03% x 20 years x $50,000 = $194,572.

to take the portfolio at the *stepped-down* value of $75,000. The daughter sold the portfolio and reinvested the $75,000 in an index fund. Seven year later, her portfolio doubled in value to $150,000. The daughter then sold the index fund and paid 15% in long-term capital gains taxes ($11,250) on her index fund's increased value of $75,000, netting her $138,750 ($150,000 - $11,250).

Example

Judy, age 83, purchased a variable annuity several years ago. She invested $100,000 in the annuity. During a recent stock market correction, the value of her annuity dropped to $75,000. Shortly thereafter Judy died. Her 53-year old son was the beneficiary of Judy's annuity and received a check for $100,000 from the annuity issuer as a death benefit. No income taxes were due at this time because there was no gain in the annuity. Judy's son took the $100,000 and purchased a new variable annuity in his name. He invested the proceeds in an index fund within the new annuity. Seven years later his variable annuity doubled in value to $200,000. Judy's son then sold the annuity and paid 25% or $25,000 in income taxes on his $100,000 gain netting him $175,000 ($200,000 - $25,000). This is $36,250 more than Jim's daughter received in the prior example on essentially identical facts. The under-performance of the mutual fund is a direct result of the step-down in basis attributed to the mutual fund.

§2508. VARIABLE ANNUITIES PROVIDE ECONOMICAL RIDERS THAT WILL PAY INCOME TAXES OWED BY BENEFICIARIES

Today, many variable annuity issuers provide riders that will pay the income taxes owed on a decedent's variable annuity when proceeds of the annuity are paid to a beneficiary. This benefit is commonly referred to as an earnings enhancement benefit, or EEB. In short, a variable annuity purchaser may buy a step-up in basis for his beneficiaries if he desires. In the majority of cases, such riders provide a better benefit to the beneficiaries of variable annuities than the step-up in basis rule provides to those who inherit mutual funds. The following examples demonstrate this:

Example

Andy purchased a mutual fund for $100,000. Andy paid $2,000 in commissions to buy his mutual fund. Ten years later Andy died and left the mutual fund to his son. Andy's gross annual rate of return was 10%. Annual expenses (1.5%) and trading costs (0.7%) totaled 2.2% and income taxes reduced Andy's net mutual fund gain by 20%. Andy's net rate of return was 6.064%. When he died, Andy's mutual fund was worth $176,566.[25] A significant portion of this $176,566 was unrealized capital gains. The son received a step-up in basis and therefore did not have to pay any income taxes on the unrealized gain in the mutual fund.

---

[25] $100,000 - $2,000 = $98,000 + 10% = $107,800 - 2.2% = $105,428 - $98,000 = $7,428 - 20% = $5,943 ÷ $98,000 = 6.064%. $98,000 x 6.064% x 10 years = $176,566.

Example

Betty purchased a variable annuity for $100,000. She paid 40 basis points or 4/10% of her annuity's value each year for an earnings enhancement benefit (EEB) rider that would increase the gain in her variable annuity by 25% to help pay income taxes if Betty died and the proceeds of the annuity were paid to her daughter. Betty's rate of return was 10%. Annual expenses (2.2%), trading costs (0.5%) and the EEB rider (0.4%) totaled 3.1%. Betty's net rate of return was 6.590%. Ten years later, Betty died and left her variable annuity to her daughter. At her death, Betty's variable annuity was worth $189,306.[26] Of this amount, $89,306 was gain. The rider Betty purchased added 25% of this gain to the value of her variable annuity at death providing Betty's daughter with $211,633 in total proceeds rather than the original $189,306.[27] Betty's daughter had to pay income taxes of 25% on the variable annuity's growth of $111,633 which amounted to $27,908. After paying this tax, Betty's daughter received $183,725. This is $7,159 more than Andy's son received in the prior example even though Andy's son received a stepped-up basis in the mutual funds he inherited.

The above examples demonstrate that for investors who want to pass their mutual funds to beneficiaries without saddling them with income taxes, the earnings enhancement benefit provided by many variable annuity issuers may do a better job of this than buying mutual funds and hoping that a stepped-up basis will be available in the future (which does not appear to be the case) to shelter beneficiaries from income taxes on inherited mutual funds. The benefit of earnings enhancement riders are dramatically increased when coupled with the spousal continuation benefit that many variable annuity companies provide when a spouse dies (This unique benefit is discussed in the next section). Variable annuity owners need to keep in mind that the earnings enhancement rider may also be coupled with the deduction allowed by IRC §691 (discussed below in §2512) if estate taxes are involved. Two other points should be mentioned. An EEB can be used to pay income *or* estate taxes. A step-up in basis for mutual funds can only reduce income taxes. If an EEB is not needed to pay income or estate taxes it is paid out to beneficiaries in cash. If a step-up in basis for mutual funds is not used to reduce income taxes, it does *not* provide a cash benefit to anyone.

§2509. THE SPOUSAL CONTINUATION BENEFIT OFFERED BY MANY VARIABLE ANNUITY ISSUERS IS BETTER THAN A STEP-UP IN BASIS

Most variable annuity companies allow surviving spouses to take over a deceased spouse's variable annuity and continue the tax-deferred growth of the variable annuity. This

---

[26] $100,000 + 10% = $110,000 - 3.1% = $106,590 - $100,000 = $6,590 ÷ $100,000 = 6.59%. $100,000 x 6.590% x 10 years = $189,306.

[27] One fourth of $89,306 = $22,327 + $189,306 = $211,633.

benefit is referred to as spousal continuation. Although a spouse who inherits a mutual fund from a deceased spouse may receive a step-up in basis, the spousal continuation benefit provided by variable annuities will frequently prove to be of greater economic benefit than the step-up in basis obtained when mutual funds are inherited. The following examples demonstrate this:

Example

Ed purchased a mutual fund for $50,000 and held it for five years. Ed paid $2,000 to buy the fund. Ed's rate of return was 10%. Annual expenses were 2.2% (1.5% annual expense ratio and trading costs of 0.7%). Income taxes reduced the net gain on Ed's mutual fund by 20%. Ed's net rate of return was 6.064%.[28] During this five-year period, the mutual fund grew in value to $64,429.[29] At this point, Ed died and his wife Fran inherited the mutual fund with a stepped-up basis of $64,429. Although the fund contained unrealized gains, the stepped-up basis rule allowed Fran to avoid having to pay any income taxes on any of the gain. Fran held the fund for an additional five years and the fund grew to $86,481 before she sold it.[30]

Example

Henry purchased a variable annuity for $50,000 and kept it for five years before he died. Henry's rate of return was 10%. Annual expenses were 2.7% (2.2% annual expense ratio and trading costs of 0.5%). Henry's net rate of return was 7.03%.[31] Because spousal continuation was available, Henry's wife Jan was able to continue the variable annuity in her name just as if she purchased the annuity. For this reason, Jan would not have to pay any income taxes on the variable annuity's gain at Henry's death. After electing spousal continuation, Jan held the variable annuity for five more years. At the end of the second five-year period, the variable annuity was worth $98,634.[32] If the gain in the variable annuity of $48,634 were taxed at this time at an average tax rate of 22%, Jan would net $87,935 from the variable annuity.[33] This is $1,454 more than Fran obtained in the prior example even though Fran received a stepped-up basis in the mutual funds she inherited at her husband's death.[34] It is also important to note that Fran's $86,481 net mutual fund portfolio value does not include a reduction for the income taxes that would be due on unrealized gains she made following her husband's death.

What the above examples demonstrate is that the tax deferral provided by spousal continuation of a variable annuity can be financially more advantageous than the step-up in basis

---

[28] $50,000 - $2,000 = $48,000 + 10% = $52,800 - 2.2% = $51,638 - $48,000 = $3,638 - 20% = $2,910 ÷ $48,000 = 6.064%.

[29] $48,000 x 5 years x 6.064% = $64,429.

[30] $64,429 x 6.064% x 5 years = $86,481.

[31] $50,000 + 10% = $55,000 - 2.7% = $53,515 - $50,000 = $3,515 ÷ $50,000 = 7.03%.

[32] $50,000 x 7.03% x 10 years = $98,634.

[33] $48,634 x 0.22 = $10,699. $98,634 - $10,699 = $87,935.

[34] $87,935 - $86,481 = $1,454.

received when mutual funds are inherited by spouses. When spousal continuation is combined with the earnings enhancement rider (discussed in the previous section) the economic benefit to the surviving spouse can be greatly increased.

§2510. ANNUITIZATION IS A BETTER ALTERNATIVE TO A STEP-UP IN BASIS

Annuitization of a variable annuity by a beneficiary often provides more income than a mutual fund can generate for a beneficiary even if the inherited fund receives a step-up in basis. The following examples demonstrate this.

Example

Jane, age 65, purchased a variable annuity 20 years ago for $63,850. Jane's gross average rate of return was 10%. Annual expenses were 2.7% (2.2% annual expense ratio and trading costs of 0.5%). Jane's net rate of return was 7.03%.[35] The annuity is now worth $248,469.[36] Jane recently died. Her husband Roy is the beneficiary of her annuity. Roy, who is 65, needs at least $14,700 *after taxes* for rest of his life from Jane's annuity to supplement his other income. Roy elected to annuitize Jane's annuity so that it would provide him with an income stream for his lifetime. It is assumed Roy's life expectancy is 20 years. The annuity company agreed to pay Roy $17,580 a year for his lifetime.[37] At an average income tax rate of 20% and an exclusion ratio of 18.16%, Roy will net $14,703 a year for life.[38] This is a little more than what Roy needs. These annuity payments are guaranteed for Roy's life and are also guaranteed to be paid for a minimum of 20 years. If Roy should die before 20 years, the $17,580 annuity payments will continue to be paid to his beneficiaries. In short, the variable annuity will provide a *guaranteed* income in excess of Roy's needs for the rest of his life.

Example

Bob, age 65, purchased a mutual fund 20 years ago for $63,850. The commission to buy the fund was $2,500. Bob's rate of return was 10%. Annual expenses were 2.2% (1.5% annual expense ratio and trading costs of 0.7%). Income taxes reduced the net gain on Bob's mutual fund by 20%. Bob's net rate of return was 6.064%.[39] Over 20 years this mutual fund grew in value to $199,147.[40] Bob recently died. His wife, Rita, who is 65, inherited Bob's mutual fund and received a step-up in basis to $199,147. Rita needed at least $14,700 *after taxes* from the inherited fund to supplement her other income. Rita's tax rate is 20%. It is assumed Rita's life expectancy is 20 years. Rita was interested in avoiding risk and wanted to obtain a lifetime stream of income and therefore contacted a financial advisor. The

---

[35] $63,850 + 10% = $70,235 - 2.7% = $68,339 - $63,850 = $4,489 ÷ $63,850 = 7.03%.

[36] 7.03% x 20 years x $63,850 = $248,469.

[37] A life expectancy of 20 years is assumed. The annuity is guaranteed to pay for 20 years. The interest rate the annuity company is using is 4%. An immediate annuity of $248,469 will pay $17,580 for 20 years before taxes.

[38] $17,580 and an exclusion ratio of 18.16% ($63,850 ÷ [$17,580 x 20]) less 20% tax = $14,703.

[39] $63,850 - $2,500 = $61,350 + 10% = $67,485 - 2.2% = $66,000 - $61,350 = $4,650 - 20% = $3,720 ÷ $61,350 = 6.064%.

[40] 6.064% x $61,350 x 20 years = $199,147.

advisor told Rita that she could receive $14,700 a year income tax-free from a municipal bond fund portfolio if the portfolio earned a consistent return of 4.54% a year.[41] The advisor told Rita that a 4.54% rate of return on a municipal bond fund portfolio for 20 years was not something she should count on. This could cause Rita to outlive her nest egg. He suggested Rita consider buying a 4% lifetime annuity with her $199,147 but soon realized that such an annuity would:

- Provide an annual *after-tax* income of only $13,264 for Rita's lifetime;[42] or

- Provide *after-tax* income of $14,695 for less than 17 years.[43]

What the two examples above demonstrate is that annuitization of a variable annuity will often provide a larger *after-tax, after-expense* stream of income than a mutual fund will even though the mutual fund provides a step-up in basis to beneficiaries who inherit such funds.

§2511. THE RATCHETING DEATH BENEFIT PROVIDED BY VARIABLE ANNUITIES MAY OUTPERFORM A MUTUAL FUND'S STEP-UP IN BASIS

Many variable annuities allow investors to select a death benefit that ratchets up over time at a stated rate that is usually between 5% and 7% or the market rate of return if higher. Mutual funds have no similar benefit. In many cases the ratcheting death benefit may result in beneficiaries receiving significantly more from a decedent who owned a variable annuity rather than a mutual fund. This is true even though the mutual fund, unlike the variable annuity, would receive a step-up in basis at the owner's death. The following examples demonstrate this:

Example
Ben purchased a mutual fund for $200,000 when he was 60. Ben wanted his daughter to inherit the fund. Due to a poor market, Ben's net annual rate of return was 4.89%. At Ben's death at age 77, his mutual fund was worth $450,000. Ben paid income taxes on the fund annually when he owned it. Ben's daughter inherited the fund and did not have to pay any further income taxes because of the step-up in basis rule.

Example
Sara purchased a variable annuity for $200,000 when she was 60. Sara wanted her son to inherit the annuity. The annuity had a 7% ratcheting death benefit. Due to a poor market, Sara's net annual rate of return was 4.2%. When Sara died at age 77, her variable annuity was worth $402,000, but because of the ratcheting death benefit, Sara's son received a check for $631,763. Sara's son paid 30% income tax on the $431,763 gain in the variable annuity. This reduced his net inheritance to

---

[41] $199,147 x 4.54% x 20 years = $14,700 annual tax free payments for twenty years.

[42] $199,147 x 4% x 20 years = $14,090. With an exclusion ratio of 70.7% ($199,147 ÷ $281,800) and a 20% tax rate, Rita would receive only $13,264 of the $14,700 she needs to live on. ($14,090 x 29.3% (1 - 70.7%) = $4,128 x .20 = $826. $14,090 - $826 = $13,264).

[43] $199,147 x 4% and withdrawing $15,886 in payments per year would provide after-tax payments of $14,700 for just under 17 years if a 20% tax rate is combined with an exclusion ratio of 62.68%.

$502,234. This is $52,234 more than Ben's daughter received in the prior example even though she received a step-up in basis.

§2512. THE USE OF IRC §1035 WITH A VARIABLE ANNUITY MAY OUTPERFORM A MUTUAL FUND'S STEP-UP IN BASIS

Owners of variable annuities, unlike mutual fund owners, may take advantage of IRC §1035. IRC§1035 allows the tax-free exchange of one variable annuity for another. The appropriate use of this IRS Code provision can result in beneficiaries receiving significantly more from a decedent who owned a variable annuity rather than a mutual fund. This is true even though the mutual fund, unlike the variable annuity, would receive a step-up in basis at an owner's death. The following examples demonstrate this:

Example

Dana, a widow, purchased a mutual fund for $350,000 when she was 55. Dana is now 70 and in poor health. Dana wants her son to inherit her mutual fund. Dana's mutual fund went up in value to a high of $700,000 two years ago, but when Dana died her mutual fund was only worth $500,000. At her death, Dana's son inherited the mutual fund. Due to the step-up in basis, Dana's son did not have to pay income taxes on the mutual fund's gain and therefore received the full $500,000 value of his mother's mutual fund.

Example

Steve, a widower, purchased a variable annuity for $350,000 when he was 55. Steve is now 70 and in poor health. Steve wants his daughter to inherit his variable annuity. His annuity increased in value to $700,000 two years ago. At that time, Steve's financial advisor suggested that Steve take advantage of IRC§1035 and transfer his variable annuity to another similar variable annuity. This could be accomplished without costs or income taxes. The benefit of the transfer would be that Steve's original death benefit of $300,000 provided by his first annuity would increase to $700,000 with the new variable annuity. This would guarantee that Steve's daughter would never receive less than $700,000 at Steve's death. Steve followed his advisor's suggestion. When Steve died his variable annuity had gone down in value to $500,000. Steve's daughter received a check from the annuity company for $700,000. She had to pay 35% in taxes on the $350,000 in gain in the variable annuity which left her with a net (after-tax) inheritance of $577,000. This is $77,000 more than Dana left her son in the prior example even though the son received a step-up in basis. [Note: The fact that Dana would most likely have paid income taxes on her fund during ownership was ignored in these examples].

§2513. LIFETIME TRANSFERS OF VARIABLE ANNUITIES RECEIVE A STEP-UP IN BASIS

One of the major benefits of owning a variable annuity is that if an owner gives his annuity away during his lifetime, his donee receives a stepped-up basis, whereas a similar lifetime gift of a mutual fund does not provide the donee with a stepped-up basis.[44] In order to obtain this benefit, the donor of a variable annuity need only report any gain in the variable annuity given away on his income tax return for the year of the gift. For example, Ann, who is 60, bought a variable annuity for $100,000 and gave it to her son seven years later when it was worth $120,000. By reporting the $20,000 gain on her income tax return for the year of the gift, Ann's son would get a step-up in basis in the annuity to $120,000. He could sell the variable annuity for $120,000 without having to pay any income taxes, IRS penalties or surrender charges regardless of his age. Ann's son would be responsible for paying future income taxes only on withdrawals or sale proceeds from the annuity that exceeded $120,000. If Ann gave mutual funds worth $120,000 to her son during her lifetime for which she paid $100,000, her son would not receive a stepped-up basis, but rather a carryover in basis. The son's basis would be $100,000. The son would have to pay long-term capital gains taxes on all proceeds above $100,000 when the fund was sold. Knowledge of this beneficial tax treatment of variable annuities allows lifetime gifts of annuities to be made under conditions that are more advantageous tax-wise than where mutual funds are passed to beneficiaries with a stepped-up basis at the owner's death. The following examples demonstrate this:

Example:
Andy bought a mutual fund portfolio seven and a half years ago for $900,000 and it has increased in value to $1,400,000.[45] Andy and his second wife Betty are both 70 years old. Andy has six children who are Betty's step-children. Andy also has fourteen grandchildren. Andy wants his $1,400,000 mutual fund portfolio to pass to his children and grandchildren at his death with a step-up in basis. To ensure a step-up in basis for his children and grandchildren, Andy decided to leave the $1,400,000 portfolio to them in his will. Andy has $5,000,000 in other assets he plans on leaving to his wife. Andy also has $4,100,000 in an investment account he wants to leave his children and grandchildren. Assuming Andy dies in 2011, the $1,400,000 mutual fund portfolio and the $4,100,000 investment account passing to his children and grandchildren will be subject to an *estate* tax of $175,000,[46] netting them $5,325,000.[47] No *income taxes* will be due on the mutual fund portfolio at Andy's death due to application of the step-up in basis rule. The remaining assets would pass to Andy's wife without any *estate tax* by applying the unlimited marital deduction.

---

[44] IRC §72(e)(4)(c)(i) governs the step-up in basis for lifetime gifts of variable annuities. Donees of lifetime transfers (i.e., gifts) of mutual funds receive a carryover basis rather than a step-up in basis.

[45] See Chapter 7 above.

[46] $5,500,000 - $5,000,000 = $500,000 x .35 = $175,000..

[47] $5,500,000 - $175,000 = $5,325,000.

Example

Bob bought a variable annuity years ago for $900,000 and it has increased in value to $1,498,000.[48] Bob and his second wife April are 70 years old. Bob has six children who are April's step-children. Bob also has fourteen grandchildren. Bob wants his children and grandchildren to receive his annuity. Bob also has $5,000,000 in other assets he wants to leave to his wife. Bob has an investment account containing $4,100,000 that he also wants to pass to his children and grandchildren if possible. In late 2010, Bob and his wife decided to give the $1,498,000 annuity to their 20 children and grandchildren. Bob and his wife will report the $598,000 gain in the transferred annuity on their 2010 income tax return and will pay 35% in ordinary income taxes, or $209,300, on this gain. This tax will be paid from the $4,100,000 investment account. After making the gift, the children and grandchildren will receive a stepped-up basis of $1,498,000 in the annuity. The 10% IRS penalty would not apply because the annuity has no gain on which to impose the penalty due to the step-up in basis. There will be no gift taxes on this transaction. Of the $1,498,000 gift, $520,000 is untaxed because of the split gifts made by Bob and his wife to their children and grandchildren (i.e. $26,000 x 20 = $520,000). The $978,000 excess gift is untaxed because it is more than covered by the exemption amount available for gifts made in 2010. Assuming Bob dies in 2011, his remaining assets would pass to his wife without estate taxes by applying the unlimited marital deduction. The children and grandchildren would receive $5,388,700 (the $1,498,000 variable annuity plus the remaining $3,890,700 balance in the investment account). This $5,388,700 transfer would not be subject to estate taxes (The taxable gift of $1,498,000 plus the $3,890,700 investment account balance are less than the 2011 federal estate tax exemption amount of $5,000,000). By giving the variable annuity away during life, Bob and his wife were able to pass $5,388,700 to Bob's children and grandchildren. This is $63,700 more than Andy passed to his children and grandchildren in the previous example even though Andy's children and grandchildren received a step-up in basis in Andy's mutual fund portfolio.[49]

It is important to note that in the examples discussed above the owners of the mutual funds would have saved their beneficiaries a significant amount in estate or income taxes (or both) by giving their mutual funds away during their lifetime. The major problem with this is that investors have been told that a step-up in basis for mutual funds is available only if they die with the fund's in their estate. These investors rarely seek advice regarding lifetime transfers of their funds. When the issue of lifetime transfers of mutual funds is discussed, many financial advisors advise against such transfers by pointing out that they will often generate income taxes and will result in forfeiture of the step-up in basis offered by mutual funds. All of this raises an

---

[48] See Chapter 7 above.

[49] $5,388,700 - $5,325,000 = $63,700. If the estates in the two examples above were non-taxable, the variable annuity would still pass more to the next generation. This can be proven by reducing the investment account from $4,100,000 to $3,500,000 in each example.

interesting question – if maximum tax savings can be obtained, in most cases, by giving variable annuities and mutual funds away during an owner's lifetime, is the step-up in basis touted by mutual fund proponents a real benefit?

In the above examples, all of the beneficiaries received a step-up in basis in the mutual funds and variable annuities they received. However, the beneficiaries of the variable annuity were subject to a smaller *total* tax burden than the recipients of the mutual fund portfolio. More importantly, to pass a stepped-up basis to beneficiaries with mutual funds, the owner of the funds must die first and therefore will never have the opportunity to see the benefit the bequest of his mutual funds might provide. With a variable annuity, a step-up in basis can be provided to donees by way of a *lifetime* gift made by the variable annuity owner. Not only does the lifetime transfer of a variable annuity save taxes, but it allows the donor to see the benefits provided by his gift (e.g., houses being bought, grandchildren being educated, etc.). In short, variable annuity ownership allows an owner to choose when to make a gift of his annuity, when to pass a step-up in basis to his beneficiaries and when to make available those benefits that will flow from making such a transfer. The owner of a mutual fund has none of this flexibility. As a general rule, the longer a mutual fund owner lives, the less benefit his beneficiaries will derive from a mutual fund inheritance. For example, if the owner of a mutual fund portfolio lives to 90, his children could be in their late sixties. An inheritance received by one who is in his late sixties is not nearly as useful as a gift received by one who is in his forties.

Another advantage of transferring a variable annuity during life is that ordinary investment losses may be used to offset any gain in the variable annuity. This can't be done with mutual funds as the following two examples demonstrate:

Example
Jack, who is 60, had an annuity worth $15,000 for which he paid $12,000 seven years ago. Jack gave the annuity to his daughter and reported the $3,000 gain on his tax return. Jack also had a $3,000 ordinary (short-term) loss from the sale of some stock. Jack used the $3,000 loss to offset the gain in the annuity given to his daughter. This kept Jack from paying any taxes on the transfer of the annuity. Not only was Jack able to avoid a potential income tax liability, but Jack's daughter would still receive a step-up in basis in the annuity to $15,000. The daughter could sell the annuity for $15,000 and have no taxable gain. She would not have to pay the standard 10% IRS penalty even if she was under age $59^{1}/_{2}$ because this penalty is only imposed on investment *gain*. A variable annuity transfer provides a stepped-up basis and therefore generates no gain on which to impose a 10% penalty. All surrender charges have expired.

Example

Tara, who is 60, had a mutual fund worth $15,000 for which she paid $12,000 seven years ago. Tara transferred the fund to her son. Tara also had a $3,000 short-term stock market loss. The son would not get a stepped-up basis in the transferred mutual fund and Tara could not use her $3,000 stock market loss to offset the $3,000 gain in the mutual fund she transferred to her son. If the son sells the fund in the future he will have to pay income taxes on all proceeds received from a sale of the fund that exceed $12,000.[50]

§2514. THE INCOME IN RESPECT OF A DECEDENT DEDUCTION (IRC §691)

Although non-qualified mutual funds qualify for a step-up in basis when inherited by beneficiaries, they cannot take advantage of IRC §691. This code provision is referred to as the income in respect of a decedent or IRD provision. Unlike non-qualified mutual funds, this IRS code provision is available only to those who inherit non-qualified variable annuities from a decedent. (Those who inherit *qualified* mutual funds and variable annuities can use §691 but the mutual fund beneficiaries lose the step-up in basis benefit). The IRD provision allows an income tax deduction for any portion of a variable annuity that must be reported by beneficiaries as income. The deduction is equal to the estate taxes generated by that portion of a variable annuity that will have to be reported as income by the beneficiaries who receive the variable annuity. This income tax deduction, in conjunction with income tax deferral, can be quite large in some cases and can often provide the beneficiaries of a variable annuity with a larger net inheritance than mutual funds can, even though mutual funds provide a step-up in basis. The following two examples demonstrate the positive impact the IRD deduction has on net variable annuity proceeds received from a decedent:

Example

Jim purchased a $50,000 mutual fund ten years ago. The commission to buy the mutual fund was $2,000. Jim's gross annual rate of return was 10%. Annual expenses were 2.2% (1.5% annual expense ratio and trading costs of 0.7%). Income taxes reduced the net gain on Jim's mutual fund by 20%. Jim's net rate of return was 6.064%.[51] Jim's mutual fund has a current value of $86,481.[52] Jim had other assets worth $5,000,000. Jim died in 2011 and left his mutual funds to his four grandchildren. His total net estate was valued at $5,086,481 and was subject to an

---

[50] Tara could sell the mutual fund and offset the $3,000 gain with her $3,000 loss. She could then give the $15,000 in proceeds to her son to purchase the fund she sold. This would put her son in the same position as Jack's daughter in the prior example. The difference would be that Tara and her son would most likely incur transaction costs and gift taxes not incurred by Jack and his daughter.

[51] $50,000 - $2,000 = $48,000 + 10% = $52,800 - 2.2% = $51,638 - $48,000 = $3,638 -20% = $2,911 ÷ $48,000 = 6.064%.

[52] $48,000 x 6.064% x 10 years = $86,481.

estate tax of $30,268.[53] This left a net value of $5,056,213 to Jim's grandchildren. Because of the step-up in basis there were no income taxes on the mutual fund portfolio.

Example:

Donna purchased a $50,000 variable annuity ten years ago. Donna's gross annual rate of return was 10%. Annual expenses were 2.7% (2.2% annual expense ratio and trading costs of 0.5%). Donna's net rate of return was 7.03%.[54] Donna died in 2011. The beneficiaries of the variable annuity were Donna's four grandchildren. Her variable annuity was valued at $98,634 at the time of her death.[55] The rest of Donna's estate was worth $5,000,000 making Donna's net estate worth $5,098,634. Estate taxes were $34,522 reducing Donna's estate to $5,064,112.[56] There was a $48,634 gain in the variable annuity that, at an unrealistically high 20% income tax rate, will reduce the net value received by Donna's grandchildren by $9,726 to $5,054,386. This is $1,876 *less* than Jim's grandchildren received when they inherited Jim's mutual funds ($5,056,213 - $5,054,336). This difference is attributed to the step-up in basis received by Jim's beneficiaries. However, the above comparison does not consider the IRC §691 income in respect of a decedent (IRD) deduction available to beneficiaries who inherit non-qualified variable annuities but not to beneficiaries inheriting similar mutual funds. In short, Donna's grandchildren would not pay income taxes at 20% on the variable annuity gain of $48,634 but would be allowed an income tax deduction for that portion of the estate tax paid attributable to the portion of Donna's annuity that was subject to income taxes. Estate taxes on the variable annuity's full $98,634 value were $34,522.[57] Of the $98,634, $48,634 is the portion of the variable annuity subject to income taxes ($98,634 - $50,000). This $48,634 represents 49.308% of the $98,634 full value. Therefore, 49.308% of the estate tax of $34,522, or $17,022, is the §691 IRD *income* tax deduction available to Donna's grandchildren. Donna's grandchildren would pay income taxes on $31,612 ($48,634 - $17,022), not $48,634. Even at a 20% tax rate, Donna's beneficiaries would have an income tax liability of $6,322 (20% of $31,612), not $9,726. By adjusting for the IRD deduction, Donna's grandchildren will receive a net estate of $5,057,790,[58] which is more than Jim's grandchildren received (in the prior example) even though they received a step-up in basis.

What the above examples demonstrate is that a combination of the IRD deduction, lower annual ownership costs and the income tax-deferral available to beneficiaries who receive variable annuities from a deceased owner can be more valuable than the step-up in basis available to beneficiaries who inherit mutual funds from a decedent. The reason for this is that

---

[53] $86,481 x 0.35 = $30,268. (five million dollar exemption for 2011)

[54] $50,000 + 10% = $55,000 - 2.7% = $53,515 - $50,000 = $3,515 ÷ $50,000 = 7.03%.

[55] $50,000 x 7.03% x 10 years = $98,634.

[56] $98,634 x 0.35 = $34,522. $5,098,634 - $34,522 = $5,064,112.

[57] $98,634 x 0.35 = $34,522.

[58] $5,098,634 - $34,522 - $6,322 = $5,057,790.

the mutual fund owner had to pay annual income taxes during the ownership of his fund and his beneficiaries could not take advantage of IRC §691.

§2515. HOLDING A MUTUAL FUND IN AN ESTATE IN ORDER TO OBTAIN A STEP-UP IN BASIS IS OFTEN A COSTLY MISTAKE

It is critical for investors to understand that the "benefit" of a step-up in basis for mutual funds can *only* be obtained by dying and passing these funds to beneficiaries. By keeping such funds in one's estate to obtain a stepped-up basis for beneficiaries, mutual fund owners frequently generate estate taxes that more than negate any perceived income tax benefit from providing a stepped-up basis to beneficiaries. The following examples demonstrate this.

Example

Sam, who is 60 years old, purchased a variable annuity five years ago for $65,000. In 2010 when the variable annuity was worth $91,000,[59] he gave it to his daughter Paula. He used a split gift with his wife. Sam paid 20% in income taxes, or $5,200 on the $26,000 growth in the annuity. Sam died in early 2011 with a $5,000,000 estate. Sam's estate tax obligation would be $22,750.[60] Sam's income and estate tax burden together would be $27,950 (i.e., $5,200 + $22,750). Assuming Paula sold the variable annuity for $100,000 and paid income taxes on the annuity's $9,000 growth since she received it, she would owe $1,800 in income taxes using a 20% average tax rate.[61] The total tax burden for Sam and his daughter would be $29,750 (i.e., $27,950 + $1,800).

Example:

Betty, who is 60 years old, purchased a mutual fund five years ago for $65,000. In 2010, when the fund was worth $87,250,[62] she contemplated giving it to her son Jack, but decided against the gift because it would result in Jack not receiving a stepped-up basis. Without a step-up in basis, Jack would have to pay income taxes on any sale proceeds representing gain. Betty decided to keep the fund and pass it to Jack at her death, thus providing Jack with a step-up in basis. Betty died in 2011 with $5,000,000 in assets in addition to the mutual fund which had grown to $100,000. Her $5,100,000 estate was left to Jack. If Jack, as the beneficiary of the mutual fund, sold the fund for $100,000, he would owe no income taxes because he would have received a stepped-up basis in the fund. However, the estate tax burden on Betty's $5,100,000 estate would be $35,000.[63] This is $5,250 more in taxes than those paid by Sam and his daughter in the previous example.

---

[59] See Chapter 7 above.

[60] $91,000 gift - $26,000 annual exclusion (2010) = $65,000 (Sam's net gift to his daughter that must be included on his death tax return to determine the death tax). When this $65,000 is added to his current estate value of $5,000,000 it will equal $5,065,000. The estate tax on $65,000 above the five million dollar exemption for 2011 is $22,750 (35% of $65,000).

[61] $100,000 - $91,000 = $9,000 x 20% = $1,800.

[62] See Chapter 7 above.

[63] $5,100,000 - $5,000,000 exemption = $100,000 x 0.35 = $35,000.

Holding on to mutual funds for the possibility that they might be passed to beneficiaries with a step-up in basis can result in increasing estate taxes by more than any potential income tax benefit a step-up in basis might provide to beneficiaries. It must also be remembered that Congress may reduce any benefit currently provided by the step-up in basis rule in the future.

§2516. COMPLETE REPEAL OF THE FEDERAL ESTATE TAX WOULD BENEFIT VARIABLE ANNUITY OWNERS

Congress has repeatedly promised to end the federal estate tax. Most tax experts believe that estate taxes could be repealed in the near future for all but the very wealthy. Any repeal, whether partial or full, would most likely result in the elimination of the stepped-up basis rule for those who inherit mutual funds. Variable annuity owners will not be affected because annuities do not currently receive a step-up in basis at an owner's death. The following examples compare a mutual fund investment with a variable annuity investment as if both estate taxes and the step-up in basis rule have been repealed.

Example

Twelve years ago, Ed invested $75,000 in a mutual fund. Ed's gross annual rate of return was 10%. Annual expense were 2.2% (1.5% annual expense ratio and trading costs of 0.7%). Income taxes reduced the net gain on Ed's mutual fund by 20%. Ed paid $2,000 to purchase his fund.[64] Ed's net rate of return was 6.064%.[65] Ed recently died and left his mutual fund, now worth $147,958, to his four grandchildren.[66] Of the $72,958 in gain, $23,104 was unrealized. Ed had no other assets. The fund was sold soon thereafter and the grandchildren had to pay total long-term capital gains taxes of $3,466 on the inherited funds because their was no step-up in basis.[67] The net amount passing to the grandchildren was $144,942.

Example

Twelve years ago, Fran purchased a variable annuity for $75,000. Fran's rate of return was 10%. Annual expenses were 2.7% (2.2% annual expense ratio and trading costs of 0.5%). Fran's net rate of return was 7.03%.[68] Fran died in 2010 leaving her annuity, now worth $169,484,[69] to her four grandchildren. Fran had no other assets. The $169,484 in annuity proceeds paid out to the grandchildren were subject to a total of $9,080 in *ordinary* income taxes on the annuity's growth of $94,484, thus reducing their inheritance from $169,484 to

---

[64] Actual commissions could be 3%.

[65] $75,000 - $2,000 = $73,000 + 10% = $80,300 - 2.2% = $78,533 - $73,000 = $5,533 - 20% = $4,427 ÷ $73,000 = 6.064%.

[66] $73,000 x 12 years x 6.064% = $147,958.

[67] The unrealized gain of $23,104 ($77,012 x .3 x .15) was taxed at 15% long-term capital gains rates. This tax would be $3,466.

[68] $75,000 + 10% = $82,500 - 2.7% = $80,273 - $75,000 = $5,273 ÷ $75,000 = 7.03%.

[69] $75,000 x 7.03% x 12 years = $169,484.

$162,592.[70] This is $17,650 more than Ed's grandchildren got in the previous example.

What the above examples demonstrate is that if a repeal of the estate tax occurs, the variable annuity may prove to be a better investment than mutual funds for long term investors. [NOTE: The estate tax was eliminated for 2010, but estates could elect to use 2011 tax laws.]

§2517. VARIABLE ANNUITIES CAN BE EASILY STRIPPED OF ALL POTENTIAL ESTATE AND INCOME TAXES

The supposed benefit of a step-up in basis with a mutual fund is that beneficiaries can inherit such funds without paying income taxes if the funds are sold for no more than their inherited value which is set at the decedent's date of death. To obtain a step-up in basis with a mutual fund portfolio one may expose the full value of the funds to estate taxes. Often, these taxes can be greater than any income taxes saved by those who inherit the funds. As was discussed in Chapter 18, variable annuities lend themselves to being easily stripped of all potential income taxes beneficiaries may have to pay as well as all potential estate taxes. In light of this characteristic, it becomes a moot issue as to whether or not a variable annuity can receive a stepped-up basis at an owner's death. The following example demonstrates how variable annuities can be stripped of all potential estate and income taxes:

Example

Jack, age 67, a widower, has an estate worth $6,000,000. One million dollars of his estate is a variable annuity of which half consists of his contributions and half is growth. If Jack died in 2011, his estate taxes would be $350,000. Income taxes owed by beneficiaries on the variable annuity could reach $175,000. Combined, these taxes could exceed $500,000.[71] The $5,000,000 non-annuity portion of Jack's estate consists of his house, car, etc. Jack wants to retire but needs to supplement his pension by at least $50,000 (after taxes) each year in order to do so. Jack wants his entire estate to pass to his three adult children without death or income taxes if possible. The solution for all of Jack's concerns can be resolved easily. Jack should have his children purchase (and own) a $1,000,000 life insurance policy on Jack's life. The premiums on this policy will be approximately $27,000 a year. After the policy is in place, Jack should convert his variable annuity to an immediate straight life annuity (i.e., no guarantee other than lifetime payments). The immediate annuity will pay Jack approximately $90,000 a year for his lifetime (assumed to be 15 years). The exclusion ratio will shelter 37% of this income from taxation

---

[70] $169,484 - $75,000 = $94,484 ÷ 4 = $23,621 per grandchild. Less $5,700 for each grandchild's single standard deduction for 2010 = $17,921 less $3,650 personal exemption = $14,271. The tax tables for 2010 show the tax on $14,271 is $1,723 for a single person. The four grandchildren will pay a total tax of $6,892 (4 x $1,723), leaving a net inheritance of $162,592 ($169,484 - $6,892).

[71] $375,000 + $175,000 = $550,000.

for several years.[72] Jack is in a 20% average tax bracket. The after-tax annuity payment Jack will receive will be $78,660.[73] Jack can give his children $27,000 each year to pay the premiums on the life insurance they purchased. (No gift taxes would be due because of the $13,000 annual per person exclusion). This leaves Jack with more than the $50,000 in additional income he needs each year. If Jack died in 2011, his estate will be worth $5,000,000 and will pass to his children estate tax free due to the $5,000,000 estate tax exemption applicable in 2011. The immediate annuity would be valued at zero because it is a straight life annuity that ceases to have any value at death. In addition, the children will receive $1,000,000 estate and income tax free from the insurance company. (Estate taxes are avoided because the insurance is not in Jack's estate. In addition, insurance proceeds are not subject to income taxation.) In short, a combination of annuitization and asset substitution eliminates all estate and income taxes for Jack's children and enables them to inherit Jack's entire $6,000,000 estate and income tax-free. If Jack lived beyond 2011, he would receive $90,000 a year from the immediate annuity.

If a mutual fund investor died in 2011 with a $6,000,000 net estate ($1,000,000 in mutual funds and $5,000,000 in other assets) his estate taxes alone would be $350,000.

§2518. NON-SPOUSAL SYSTEMATIC WITHDRAWALS AND ANNUITIZATION

All of the examples discussed above had the beneficiaries of a variable annuity liquidating the annuity on receipt and paying all income taxes due at one time. In reality, this would be a very rare scenario. Beneficiaries of variable annuities have several options for paying income taxes other than in a lump sum upon receipt of the annuity. One option is to take withdrawals based on the beneficiary's life expectancy. Another option is to annuitize the annuity and take lifetime payments. This option provides three benefits:

- Income taxes are reduced (because payments are received over time);
- The exclusion ratio can be used;
- A lifetime stream of income is guaranteed.

A mutual fund beneficiary may liquidate his inherited mutual fund and annuitize the proceeds but is unlikely to generate a net (after-tax) income as large as the variable annuity will produce. The following two examples demonstrate this:

Example:
Ed invested $10,000 a year in a mutual fund portfolio for 25 years starting at age 60. Ed's gross average rate of return was 10%. His annual tax loss was 20% of his mutual fund's net gain. Annual expenses and trading costs totaled 2.2%.

---

[72] $500,000 ÷ [$90,000 x 15] = 37%.
[73] $90,000 x 0.63 = $56,700 x 0.20 = $11,340. $90,000 - $11,340 = $78,660.

Commissions were 5%. Ed's net return was 6.064%.[74] At his death in 2011, at age 85, Ed's fund portfolio was worth $557,828.[75] Ed's 65-year-old daughter Betty inherited the fund. Betty's taxable retirement income from other sources is $82,250 (2011). The step-up in basis rule eliminated any income taxes on the inherited fund portfolio. Ed did not have a taxable estate for estate tax purposes.

Example
Jane invested $10,000 a year in a variable annuity for 25 years starting at age 60. Jane's gross average rate of return was 10%. Annual cost to own the annuity were 2.7%. Jane's net return was 7.03%.[76] Jane died in 2011 at age 85 with her variable annuity worth $679,877.[77] Jane's 65-year old son Sal inherited the annuity. Sal's taxable retirement income from other sources is $82,250 (2011). Jane did not have a taxable estate for estate tax purposes. Sal would have to pay income taxes on the gain in his mother's variable annuity in the amount of $140,178 (2011) resulting in an after-tax value of $539,699.[748] This amount is less than the $557,828 mutual fund value Betty received in the previous example.

The real likelihood that Sal would elect to pay income taxes all at one time at the highest possible tax rate upon receiving Jane's variable annuity is unlikely. If Sal wanted to, he could annuitize the annuity and receive annual payments of $48,102[79] for his life expectancy of 20 years. His exclusion ratio would be 26%.[80] Based on this, Sal's after-tax annual payment from the variable annuity would be $39,203.[81] Betty, in the previous example, could annuitize her $557,827 for her 20 year life expectancy. Betty would receive $39,467 a year in pre-tax income.[82] Her exclusion ratio would be 70.67%.[83] Based on this, Betty would receive $36,573[84] in after-tax annual income or $2,630[85] a year *less* than Sal would receive. This provides Sal with over $52,000 more in income over 20 years compared to Betty's income over the same period.

Many investors do not like to annuitize assets. In this case, such investors may want to elect to take annual payments (i.e., systematic withdrawals) from an inherited annuity based on

---

[74] $10,000 - 5% = $9,500 + 10% = $10,450 - 2.2% = $10,220 - $9,500 = $720 -20% = $576 ÷ $9,500 = 6.064%.

[75] 6.064% x 25 years x $9,500 annual investment = $557,828.

[76] $10,000 + 10% = $11,000 - 2.7% = $10,703 - $10,000 = $703 ÷ $10,000 = 7.03%.

[77] 7.03% x 25 years x $10,000 annual investment = $679,877.

[78] $679,877 - $250,000 investment + $82,250 taxable income = $512,127 - $373,650 = $138,477 x .35 = $48,467 + $101,086 = $149,553 - $12,925 (tax on $82,250) = $136,628. $679,877 - $136,628 = $543,249.

[79] $679,877 for 20 years at 4% = $48,102/year.

[80] $250,000 ÷ $962,040 ($48,102 x 20 years) = 26%.

[81] $48,102 - 26% = $35,595. The income tax on the $35,595 would be $8,899 at 25%. $48,102 - $8,899 = $39,203. If payments were made for more than 20 years the exclusion ratio would not be available after that and the entire $48,102 annual payment would be taxable.

[82] $557,828 x 4% x 20 years = $39,467.

[83] $557,828 ÷ $789,345 ($39,467 x 20) = 70.67%.

[84] Of $39,467 only 29.33% or $11,575 would be taxed. The tax on $11,575 at 25% = $2,894, netting Betty $36,573.

[85] $39,203 - $35,573 = $2,630.

their life expectancy. This election provides an alternative way to avoid having to pay income taxes in a lump sum on an inherited variable annuity at the highest tax rates.

§2519. OBTAINING CAPITAL GAINS TREATMENT ON VARIABLE ANNUITIES

Owners of variable annuities can convert these annuities to capital assets and obtain capital gains treatment on their variable annuity gains. Chapter 48 discusses this topic.

§2520. CONCLUSION

In many cases the net amount received by donees or beneficiaries who receive variable annuities as gifts or inheritances may be larger than that provided by the step-up in basis when mutual funds are inherited. In many cases the step-up in basis provided by lifetime transfers of variable annuities may be more tax efficient than the step-up in basis provided by mutual funds. Many IRS code provisions available only to variable annuity owners are of greater benefit than the step-up in basis provided by mutual funds. The ability of variable annuity owners to eliminate all potential estate *and* income taxes, in many cases, may eliminate the need to be concerned about a step-up in basis rule available to those who inherit mutual funds.

- CHAPTER 26 -

RETIREMENT ACCOUNT RESTRICTIONS

§2601. INTRODUCTION

The ownership of mutual funds can negatively impact an owner's ability to take advantage of tax reducing measures made available through retirement accounts. The ownership of variable annuities does not pose similar problems.

§2602. IRA AND ROTH IRA CONTRIBUTION LIMITATIONS

Mutual fund ownership may disqualify taxpayers from taking advantage of the tax benefits that come with contributing to a traditional IRA to a Roth IRA. The ability to fund an IRA or a Roth IRA and obtain a valuable tax deduction can be lost to the owners of mutual funds. The ownership of variable annuities does not result in a similar loss of tax advantages. The following examples demonstrate how mutual fund ownership can cause the forfeiture of tax benefits made available by funding IRAs and Roth IRAs:

> **Example #1**
> Jack and Betty work for companies that have retirement programs. Their combined adjusted gross income for 2010 was $89,000. At this level of income they can contribute $5,000 to their IRAs. This $10,000 will reduce their income taxes by about $2,500. For 2010, Jack and Betty received a mutual fund distribution of over $10,000. This made them ineligible to make an IRA contribution. Because of the mutual fund distribution they lost almost $2,500 in a reduction of their income taxes and had to pay additional taxes on the mutual fund distribution. Variable annuities, because they do not generate involuntary income, would not have carried the same negative tax consequences.

> **Example #2**
> Sam and Sara, who are both 47 years old, are both school teachers and are covered by their employer's pension plan. Their adjusted gross income (AGI), is $167,000 for 2010. In 2010, they received a $10,000 mutual fund distribution which made them ineligible to contribute $10,000 to their Roth IRA and obtain an $10,000 income tax deduction that would save them $2,800. Had they owned their funds within a variable annuity, they would not have lost this important tax benefit. Sam and Sara can sell off their mutual funds so next year they may be eligible to take advantage of a Roth IRA but they may incur commissions and taxes in doing so.

§2603. CONCLUSION

The ownership of mutual funds can result in the loss of one's ability to fund traditional or Roth IRAs as well as prohibit the conversion of a traditional IRA to a Roth IRA. These limitations result in the loss of tax benefits provided by these retirement accounts. These important tax saving elections are not lost when variable annuities are owned.

- CHAPTER 27 -

TAXATION OF SOCIAL SECURITY

§2701. INTRODUCTION

Social Security retirement income is not subject to income taxation unless a recipient reports other income that causes his total income to exceed certain limits. Most retired people in their mid-60s receive Social Security checks as part of their retirement income. For many retired people, Social Security can make up a large portion of their retirement income. Mutual fund distributions frequently raise income levels for retired people resulting in the taxation of their Social Security income. Because variable annuities do not make distributions, the mere ownership of a variable annuity cannot cause an owner's Social Security to be taxed.

§2702. SOCIAL SECURITY TAXATION

Single taxpayers who have provisional incomes of $25,000 or more and married couples who have provisional incomes of in excess $44,000 are subject to having from 50% to as much as 85% of their Social Security retirement income subject to ordinary income taxes.[1] This additional tax burden can be a major problem for retired persons who own mutual fund portfolios. The following example demonstrates this problem:

> **Example #1**
> Jack is 65 years old and has pension income of $24,000 a year. He has a mutual fund portfolio worth $150,000. He and his wife receive $20,000 a year in combined Social Security retirement income. Jack and his wife do not have a need for any income above his pension and their Social Security. Although Jack and his wife do not have a need for any money, Jack's mutual fund annually distributes $15,000 in capital gains to him. This mutual fund distribution increases the annual income of Jack and his wife to $59,000. Because of this, a large part of the Social Security income paid to Jack and his wife will be subject to ordinary income taxes.

§2703. SOCIAL SECURITY AND VARIABLE ANNUITIES

In the above example, had Jack held his mutual funds within a variable annuity, none of the Social Security retirement income he and his wife received would be subject to income taxes. The reason for this is that gains made within variable annuities are tax-deferred and do not count in determining whether Social Security retirement income will be taxed. Retired persons who find themselves in a situation like that of Jack and his wife frequently ask if shifting their mutual funds to a tax-free bond fund would solve their problem. The answer is no. The reason

---

[1] Provisional income is gross income plus tax-free income plus one-half of total Social Security retirement income.

for this is that, unlike tax-deferred income, tax-free income must be taken into consideration when determining whether Social Security retirement income will be subject to income taxes. One of the best ways for retired persons to protect their Social Security retirement income from taxation would be to convert their mutual fund portfolio to a variable annuity. The problem with this is that commissions and income taxes due on the sale of mutual funds could be quite large. Preparing for retirement by owning variable annuities instead of mutual funds in the first place eliminates this problem.

§2704. CONCLUSION

Recipients of Social Security retirement income should understand that even minimal mutual fund distributions could cause their Social Security income to be taxed. This negative tax result is not possible with these annuities because these annuities do not make involuntary distributions and therefore, a variable annuity owner will not have any additional income to report. This is one of the major advantages of tax deferral.

- CHAPTER 28 -
THE TAX DEDUCTIBILITY OF VARIABLE ANNUITY LOSSES

§2801. INTRODUCTION

The owners of non-qualified variable annuities, like the owners of stocks and mutual funds, can suffer losses due to a stock market decline. The owners of variable annuities who have losses in their annuities often seek guidance on how these losses should be treated for income tax purposes. This chapter examines this issue.

§2802. BACKGROUND

The activity of the stock market over the past few years has generated losses for the owners of both mutual funds and stocks. When such investments are sold at a loss, their owners can deduct some or all of these capital losses by reporting them on Schedule D of their personal income tax returns. There are numerous sources available to assist taxpayers in properly deducting these losses.

The owners of non-qualified variable annuities that have losses may also deduct these losses. However, the guidance provided by the IRS regarding the tax treatment of losses incurred when non-qualified variable annuities are sold is basic at best. For this reason, tax professionals have reached vastly different conclusions regarding this important tax issue. Some tax practitioners have taken the position that losses resulting from the sale of non-qualified variable annuities are not deductible under any circumstances. Other financial entities that have examined this issue have concluded that such losses are fully deductible without limitation. Many financial professionals believe the proper deductibility of variable annuity losses lies somewhere between these two extremes.

This chapter reviews IRS Revenue Rulings, tax court cases, tax code provisions, government publications and other related materials to the extent such sources provide guidance regarding the deductibility of variable annuity losses. By combining this data, the author hopes to forecast how the IRS, the courts or Congress will ultimately rule on this important tax issue.

§2803. PROFIT MOTIVE REQUIREMENT

The starting point in the determination of whether the loss resulting from the sale of a non-qualified variable annuity is deductible or not requires an examination into the motive for ones purchase of a variable annuity. The IRS has taken the position that the loss resulting from the sale of a non-qualified variable annuity, for deductibility purposes, must have arisen in the conduct of a trade or business or in some transaction entered into with a profit motive although not necessarily connected with a trade or business. Because most non-qualified variable annuities are not purchased as part of a trade or business, the author will limit his examination to those variable annuities purchased by individuals as personal investments. Most variable annuities are purchased with the intent that such annuities will produce a profit for their buyers at some point in the future. For this reason, demonstrating a profit motive regarding a variable annuity purchase is not difficult to do in most cases. However, in some cases the IRS has been successful in showing that a variable annuity was not purchased with a profit motive. When such a determination is made, it will result in the non-deductibility of any loss resulting from the sale of such a variable annuity.[1]

§2804. IRS MESSAGE #1052060

Whenever the IRS responds in writing to taxpayer questions, the response is referred to as an IRS Message. An example of an IRS Message responding to a taxpayer's question concerning the deductibility of variable annuity losses is IRS Message #1052060 issued in December of 2001. The hypothetical facts supplied by the taxpayer on which IRS Message #1052062 was issued appear below:

> My annuity is described as a deferred variable annuity by the prospectus. I invested $100,000 three years ago. Since the decline in the [stock] market it is currently valued at $68,000. The funds invested were [non-qualified] funds. If I request a liquidation of my contract, may I deduct the loss incurred which is the difference [between] the original investment and the net [amount] received from the liquidation on my [tax] return up to my current income for the year?

In response to this question, the IRS held that the taxpayer's $32,000 loss was fully deductible as a miscellaneous itemized deduction to the extent the loss exceeded 2% of the taxpayer's adjusted gross income (AGI). Based on the facts set out above, if the taxpayers adjusted gross income (AGI) was $100,000, his loss deduction would be limited to $30,000 ($32,000 less 2% of $100,000 = $30,000). The cost basis for calculating losses on variable annuities is the total *after-tax dollar* contributions made to the variable annuity.[2] The amount received upon surrender is subtracted from the cost basis to determine the loss. Any prior withdrawals must also be taken into consideration. For example, Ben paid $30,000 for a non-qualified variable annuity he recently surrendered for $18,000. Ben's basis of $30,000 would be reduced by the surrender proceeds of $18,000 yielding a $12,000 miscellaneous itemized deduction subject, according

---

[1] Cases discussing this issue are *Early v. Atkinson*, 175 F.2ᵈ 118 (1949), *Industrial Trust v. Broderick*, 94 F.2ᵈ 927 (1938), *Cohan v. Comm.*, 11 B.T.A. 743 (1928). Also see IRC§165(c)(2).

[2] IRC §1011.

132

to the IRS, to a further reduction of 2% of Ben's AGI. If prior to surrendering his variable annuity, Ben withdrew $2,000 from the annuity, this withdrawal would have to be reflected in a downward adjustment of his cost basis from $30,000 to $28,000. Assuming the account balance upon surrender was $18,000 and Sam's basis of $30,000 is reduced to $28,000, this would yield a $10,000 loss.[3]

§2805. IRS PUBLICATION 575

IRS Message #1052060 concedes that there are no IRS publications directly addressing the deductibility of variable annuity losses, but indicates that IRS Publication 575 (*Pension and Annuity Income*) may provide, by analogy, some guidance on this issue.[4] Publication 575 addresses losses from lump sum distributions (i.e. surrenders) from *qualified plans* by stating that if a participant obtains a lump sum distribution from his *qualified plan* that is less than the participant's cost basis, the resulting loss is deductible. IRS Message #1052060 points out that Publication 575, which the IRS cites for support of the deductibility of losses resulting from the complete surrender of a non-qualified annuity, requires such deduction be treated as a miscellaneous itemized deduction. In addition, the deduction, according to the IRS, may be taken only to the extent it exceeds 2% of the taxpayer's adjusted gross income (AGI) for the year of the distribution.

> ### Example
> Over the past several years Mike contributed $70,000 in *after-tax dollars* to a *qualified* plan at his place of employment. He recently resigned from his job and elected to take a lump sum distribution from his plan. Upon surrendering his annuity, Mike received $40,000. On these facts the IRS, in accord with IRS Publication 575, would allow Mike a $30,000 miscellaneous itemized deduction subject to the 2% AGI threshold.

IRS Message #1052060 states that there should be no distinction made between losses resulting from lump sum distribution of a *qualified plan* and a loss resulting from the complete surrender of a *non-qualified* variable annuity. It is important to understand that a loss deduction for a variable annuity is realized only upon a *complete surrender*. Nothing less will do. For example, a §1035 tax-free exchange of one variable annuity for another is *not* a complete surrender and no deduction would be allowed if the first annuity showed a loss at the time of the exchange.

---

[3] Rev. Rul. 61-201 C.B. 1961-2, 46 would seem to include surrender fees as part of the loss just as surrender fees with bank CDs and B-share mutual funds are includable as part of a loss deduction.

[4] Recently the courts have held that §691 does provide an income tax deduction for variable annuity beneficiaries.

§2806. IRS PUBLICATION 590

IRS Publication 590 (*Individual Retirement Arrangements*) discusses the tax treatment of losses resulting from the liquidation of traditional and Roth IRAs. This publication holds that losses resulting from the surrender of such IRAs are deductible as miscellaneous itemized deductions subject to the 2% AGI threshold where *after-tax* dollars have been used to fund these IRAs.

Example
Oscar has several deductible and non-deductible IRAs. He recently liquidated all of these IRAs. The amount he received was $40,000 less than the *after-tax* dollar (i.e. non-deductible) contributions he made to these IRAs. The IRS would hold that Oscar is entitled to a miscellaneous itemized deduction of $40,000 subject to the 2% AGI threshold.

Example
Nora contributed $16,000 to her only Roth IRA. She recently liquidated it for $10,000. The IRS would allow Nora a $6,000 miscellaneous itemized deduction subject to the 2% AGI threshold.

§2807. THE 2% ADJUSTED GROSS INCOME THRESHOLD

The real controversy regarding variable annuity losses does not involve the general issue of the deductibility of these losses. Such deductibility is clearly allowed by the IRS and used by taxpayers. The real question seems to center on the narrower issue of how these losses are to be reported to the IRS. As mentioned earlier, many tax professionals, as well as the IRS, have taken the position that the loss incurred on the sale of a variable annuity is treated as a miscellaneous deduction that must be itemized and reported on line 22 of Schedule A of Form 1040. Additionally, this deduction is limited to the amount the deduction exceeds 2% of a taxpayer's adjusted gross income (AGI).

Example:
Sara purchased a non-qualified variable annuity for $100,000. She recently sold it for $65,000. Sara's adjusted gross income (AGI) is $150,000. Sara's loss is deductible only if she itemizes her deductions. Additionally, Sara's deduction, according to the IRS, would be limited to the amount $35,000 exceeds 2% of her AGI (i.e. $3,000). In other words, Sara's net deduction would be limited to $32,000.

§2808. IRC §67(b)

Proponents of the proposition that variable annuity losses are subject to the 2% AGI threshold frequently cite IRC §67(b) to support their position. This section sets out those losses that are exempt from the 2% AGI threshold. Of the dozen exemptions, none relates directly to variable annuity losses. This argument would be more persuasive if it could be demonstrated that the exemptions listed in IRC §67(b) were intended to be a complete list. However, it appears that the exemptions listed in IRC §67(b) were not intended to be exhaustive. For example, gambling losses, to the extent of gambling gains, are a miscellaneous itemized deduction *not* subject to the 2% AGI threshold, but, just as with variable annuity losses, IRC §67(b) does not make reference to gambling loss deductions.

§2809. IRS PUBLICATION 529

Many tax professionals argue that variable annuity losses are deductible without regard to the 2% AGI threshold. They support their position by citing IRS Publication 529 titled *Miscellaneous Deductions*[5] and Revenue Ruling 61-201 (also see Rev. Rul. 72-193). Publication 529 sets out two exhaustive lists relating to those miscellaneous itemized deductions that are and are *not* subject to the 2% AGI threshold.[6] The first list contains forty-one miscellaneous itemized deductions that are subject to the 2% AGI threshold. Each deduction is listed and discussed fully. None of the miscellaneous itemized deductions on this list remotely deals with variable annuity losses. On a second list, seven miscellaneous itemized deductions are listed as *not* being subject to the 2% AGI threshold. Included in this second list is the loss resulting from the "[u]nrecovered investment in an annuity." The example provided in IRS Publication 529 of such a loss involves a taxpayer who died and did not fully recover the total contributions he paid into an annuitized annuity. On these facts the decedent's estate was entitled to a miscellaneous itemized deduction on the decedent's final income tax return for the unrecovered portion of his investment in his annuity. This deduction is taken on Line 28 of Schedule A (1040) for 2010 and would *not* be subject to the 2% AGI threshold. It would seem logical that if a taxpayer sells an annuity for a $10,000 loss, this loss would qualify as an "unrecovered investment in an annuity" and should receive the same tax treatment as a decedent who dies before fully recovering his investment in an annuity he owned. Logic aside, many tax professionals, citing the above example, argue that the miscellaneous deduction provided for in IRS Publication 529 for the "unrecovered investment in an annuity" only applies to *deceased* taxpayers who die with annuitized annuities.

Revenue Ruling 61-201 has been interpreted by its supporters as stating that variable annuity losses are ordinary losses that may be deducted "above the line" (i.e., itemization is not

---

[5] IRS Publication 529 (Cat No 150560) 2001.

[6] IRS Publication 529, p.10 *et seq*.

required). Also pointed out by supporters of this ruling is the fact that nothing is said in the ruling about taxpayers having to meet any adjusted gross income threshold. Those tax professionals who believe variable annuity losses are deductible without regard to the 2% AGI threshold report taking this loss deduction on Line 14 of the 2010 1040 Form (supported with a Form 4797) or entering a negative figure on Line 21 of the 1040 Form. The determination of whether a variable annuity loss is subject to the 2% AGI threshold is important. As discussed below, a variable annuity loss deduction taken on the 1040 Form itself, rather than on a Schedule A, is not subject to the 2% AGI threshold and will not trigger the alternative minimum tax (AMT).

Some tax practitioners make the distinction between the *sale* of a variable annuity to a third person for a loss and *surrendering* the variable annuity to the issuing company for a loss. In the first case, it is argued that the deduction clearly would not be subject to the 2% AGI threshold.

The author believes that the issue of whether or not variable annuity losses are subject to the 2% AGI threshold will have to be decided by the courts. For taxpayers with large variable annuity losses and relatively small adjusted gross incomes this issue may be moot. However, for taxpayers with small variable annuity losses and larger adjusted gross incomes, the 2% AGI threshold could prove to be costly.

> **Example**
> Bill has a $70,000 non-qualified variable annuity loss this year. His adjusted gross income (AGI) is $150,000. If he takes a miscellaneous itemized deduction for his variable annuity loss and applies the 2% AGI threshold to the deduction, he will be entitled to a $67,000 net deduction. If Bill's variable annuity loss was only $5,000 and his AGI was $250,000, he would receive no deduction at all for his variable annuity loss after application of the 2% AGI threshold.

§2810. OTHER IMPORTANT CONSIDERATIONS

There are other issues that an annuity owner should consider if he must sell his annuity for a loss. The advice of a tax professional is strongly urged if such a sale is contemplated for the following reasons:

- Depending on whether the proceeds from the sale will be used to purchase another annuity, the seller may forfeit all or a large portion of his existing death benefit;

- If the variable annuity generates an unusually large miscellaneous itemized deduction, taking such a deduction may trigger an IRS audit;

- If the proceeds from the sale of the variable annuity will be used to purchase the same annuity after realizing a loss from such a sale, the repurchase may constitute a wash sale that could negate the loss deduction;

- The sale of the variable annuity may result in the imposition of surrender charges that may make such a sale less beneficial; and

- The sale of a variable annuity resulting in a large miscellaneous itemized deduction may trigger the alternative minimum tax (AMT).

- Large miscellaneous itemized deductions may be partially phased out depending on the taxpayer's income level.

- The current variable annuity may have come about as the result of an IRC §1035 transfer and may show a "phantom loss."

Each of these topics is discussed below.

§2811. LOSS OR REDUCTION IN THE DEATH BENEFIT

The sale of a variable annuity reduces to zero any death benefit once provided by the annuity. Even if a new variable annuity is purchased with the sale proceeds, the new death benefit will usually be for a lesser amount.

Example

Betty purchased a variable annuity for $100,000 several years ago. The annuity provided a $100,000 death benefit. Betty decided to sell her variable annuity for $60,000 to obtain a $40,000 miscellaneous itemized deduction on her tax return. A short while later Betty purchased a new variable annuity with the $60,000 in sale proceeds. Her new death benefit would be $60,000. Had Betty decided not to buy another variable annuity, she would have lost her entire death benefit.

The loss or reduction in the value of the death benefit provided by a variable annuity must always be weighed against the benefit received from any tax deduction resulting from the sale of the annuity. An investor's age, health and number of dependents are some of the factors that should be considered before selling a variable annuity if such a sale will result in the loss or reduction of an existing death benefit. If avoiding the potential loss or reduction in the value of a death benefit is important, the annuity owner might consider adding additional funds to the purchase of a new variable annuity. For example, if an annuity originally purchased for $100,000 is sold for $60,000, the owner could add $40,000 to the $60,000 in sale proceeds to purchase a $100,000 variable annuity with a new $100,000 death benefit. Doing so would still generate a tax loss of $40,000 while preserving the $100,000 death benefit. There are a few variable annuity issuers who will provide a variable annuity owner with the same death benefit the owner had in a prior annuity if all sale proceeds are reinvested in their annuity. For example, if $70,000 is received from the sale of a variable annuity originally costing $100,000 and the $70,000 in proceeds are reinvested in the variable annuities of certain companies, these companies will issue a variable annuity with an account value of $70,000 and a death benefit of $100,000. A reduction in a death benefit may, in many cases, be cured by purchasing term life insurance as the next example demonstrates:

Example

Zeb, who is 56, owns a variable annuity he purchased for $100,000. It is worth $80,000 today. He wants to sell the variable annuity to realize a $20,000 deductible loss and reinvest the $80,000 into another variable annuity. He is hesitant to do this because his current death benefit is $100,000. His new annuity will provide a death benefit that will only cover his $80,000 purchase price. The death benefit in the new variable annuity ratchets up at 7% a year. In 3.3 years the death benefit in the new variable annuity will be $100,000. Zeb could buy a $20,000 term insurance policy for $150 that will provide a $20,000 death benefit to him for the next 3.3 years. When the term policy expires, his death benefit in his new variable annuity will be $100,000. By doing so Zeb obtains, without losing any death benefit, a $20,000 income tax deduction that will provide him with a cash benefit of $2,000 to $7,000 depending on his tax bracket.

§2812. INCREASED AUDIT RISK

Anytime a deduction is taken that falls outside of statistical parameters set by the IRS, it can trigger an IRS audit. For example, a taxpayer with an adjusted gross income of $100,000 who takes a miscellaneous itemized deduction of $40,000 would most likely be the target of an IRS audit. As a general rule, if a deduction is proper and provable, the possibility of an audit, standing alone, should not be a reason for not taking the deduction.

§2813. WASH SALE VIOLATION

If an annuity is sold and the *same* annuity repurchased within thirty days, the IRS might successfully argue, by analogy, that the transaction was the equivalent of a wash sale thus negating any loss deduction resulting from such a sale. Prudence would dictate a different variable annuity be purchased or different subaccounts selected following any sale and repurchase. Waiting for more than 30 days before buying a new variable annuity might also be a solution for this problem.

§2814. POTENTIAL SURRENDER CHARGES

The sale of a variable annuity that generates a loss deduction may not be advantageous after factoring in the surrender charges that may be due at the time of sale.

Example

Jack purchased a variable annuity for $100,000. He recently sold the annuity for $90,000. Of the $10,000 loss, $5,000 was a surrender penalty charged by the variable annuity issuer. Jack's AGI was $100,000. Based on these facts, Jack could only deduct $8,000 of the $10,000 loss. Because Jack is in a 25% average tax bracket this deduction will reduce Jack's tax liability to the IRS by $2,000. The $90,000 in proceeds together with the $2,000 tax benefit nets Jack $92,000 from the sale of his variable annuity. Prior to the sale, Jack's variable annuity was worth $95,000. The premature sale of the variable annuity actually decreased the net value of the annuity by $3,000. Jack might consider waiting to sell his variable annuity until some time in the future when he will not have to pay any surrender charges.

It is also important to understand that if a second variable annuity is purchased with proceeds from the sale of a prior variable annuity, a new, and possibly longer, surrender period may be imposed on the owner.

§2815. THE ALTERNATIVE MINIMUM TAX

Taking large miscellaneous itemized deductions is one of the things that will trigger the alternative minimum tax (AMT). In light of this, the possible sale of a variable annuity to obtain a loss deduction should be weighed against the possible adjustment in income tax liability that may result if the annuity owner is required to pay alternative minimum tax rates rather than his regular (and usually lower) income tax rates. For example, a variable annuity loss deduction of $100,000 for a taxpayer with an adjusted gross income of $100,000 will not necessarily result in no income taxes. The AMT could impose a stiff income tax on these facts by eliminating nearly all of the variable annuity loss deduction. There are ways to reduce or eliminate the adverse impact of the AMT where large variable annuity losses are involved. For example, instead of taking a $100,000 in one year, the variable annuity can be broken up into five smaller $20,000 variable annuities by making partial §1035 transfers. Over five years each of the five new variable annuities could be surrendered to yield a $20,000 deduction for each of the five years. The following example demonstrates this point:

> **Example**
> Dr. Jones, who is 60, purchased a variable annuity for $160,000, recently it was worth $80,000. If the annuity is sold, the $80,000 loss could trigger the AMT and in effect, eliminate most of this deduction. Dr. Jones, following his advisor's advice, used IRC §1035 to make partial transfers of his annuity to four other annuities that had no surrender penalties. He now has four variable annuities each with a cost basis of $40,000. Each variable annuity has a value of $20,000 and a loss of $20,000. Dr. Jones could take the $20,000 loss on each variable annuity over the next four years with much less chance of triggering the alternative minimum tax (AMT).

§2816. PHASEOUTS

Under current tax law some credits are reduced when taxpayers have adjusted gross incomes above certain levels. These levels are reset each year by the IRS. For example, a portion of a couple's child tax credit may be lost where married taxpayers have an AGI in excess of a specified income level. [Many phaseouts could reappear after 2010]. Prior to 2011, some deductions and exemptions were reduced when a taxpayer's income reached a certain level.

§2817. ITEMIZATION REQUIRED

If the loss on a variable annuity is taken on Schedule A of the 1040 Form, itemization is required. If the deduction is taken on line 14 or 21 on the front of the 1040 Form (2010), itemization is not required. This is also true if the loss is deducted on Schedule D of the 1040. This may be a consideration to a taxpayer contemplating the deduction of a variable annuity loss.

§2818. PHANTOM LOSSES

If a variable annuity appears to have a loss, it will be important to determine if the ownership of the current variable annuity resulted from an IRC §1035 transfer. If so, the loss in the current variable annuity may actually be a gain.

Example
Joe purchased a variable annuity for $100,000. When it was worth $125,000 he transferred it to a new annuity by using IRC §1035. Later Joe sold the second variable annuity for $115,000 claiming he had a loss of $10,000. In actuality, he had a gain of $15,000. His $100,000 original purchase price (i.e., cost basis) was transferred or carried over to the second variable annuity. Therefore when the second annuity was sold for $115,000, a gain of $15,000 resulted rather than the $10,000 loss Joe assumed.

§2819. DEDUCTIBILITY OF VARIABLE UNIVERSAL LIFE INSURANCE LOSSES

Many investors have purchased variable universal life (VUL) insurance policies over the past several years. VUL is a combination of an investment plus permanent life insurance. A question has arisen as to whether a loss in a VUL policy is deductible in the same manner as a variable annuity. The basic answer is no. The IRS has taken the position that a VUL is a personal insurance policy and therefore any loss on such a policy would not be deductible. However, many tax professionals have had success in transferring a VUL to a variable annuity by using IRC §1035. Such a transfer carries over the VUL's basis and account value. For this reason, any loss in a VUL will be reflected in the new variable annuity. Once the transfer has been made, any loss resulting from the sale of the variable annuity in the future should be deductible. Until then, gain in the variable annuity above the transferred account value up to the transferred basis is not subject to income taxes. The qualifications for deductibility of a variable annuity and the considerations discussed above should be reviewed if such a transfer is made to obtain deductibility for a VUL that has lost value. The requirement that the variable annuity be purchased with a profit motive (§2803) would most likely require the variable annuity be held for some reasonable period of time. An immediate sale of the variable annuity shortly after the VUL exchange has occurred may raise questions as to whether the variable annuity was purchased with a profit motive in mind. Permanent life insurance, other than VUL, could also be exchanged for a variable annuity by using §1035. Tax transactions such as the one discussed above should not be recommended to a client without a tax professional's input and advice. (Chapter 46 discusses this issue also).

§2820. CONCLUSION

Although the IRS clearly recognizes the deductibility of losses resulting from the sale of *non-qualified* variable annuities, the issue of whether these deductions are subject to the 2% AGI threshold is still in controversy. The author believes that regulations will be issued in the near future that will address this issue. If such regulations are not forthcoming, the courts or Congress may have to resolve this issue. It is interesting to note that variable annuities are the only investment the IRS argues are subject to the 2% AGI threshold. Until this occurs, the decision to sell a non-qualified variable annuity at a loss and deduct this loss for income tax purposes should not be done without the advice of a tax professional.

- CHAPTER 29 -

ESTIMATED TAXES

§2901. INTRODUCTION

Distributions from mutual funds will often result in the owner of the funds having to pay estimated taxes. The ownership of variable annuities does not trigger this tax burden.

§2902. ESTIMATED TAX BURDEN

A mutual fund distribution can cause the owner of the fund to pay estimated taxes. The following example demonstrates this potential tax problem:

Example #1
Charles owned a mutual fund portfolio worth $200,000. In August, Charles received a $20,000 distribution from the fund although it had gone down in value by $23,500. Charles learned from his CPA that he would have to pay $5,000 in estimated taxes to the IRS by mid-September and another $1,000 estimated tax payment to the state tax collector. Had Charles owned his funds in the form of a variable annuity, he would not have had to pay estimated taxes. This is true because variable annuities do not make taxable distributions like mutual funds.

§2903. CONCLUSION

The ownership of mutual funds, unlike the ownership of variable annuities, may require the owner of such funds to pay estimated taxes to the federal and state tax collectors. This requirement can apply even if the funds held have lost value.

- CHAPTER 30 -
STATE AND LOCAL TAXES

§3001. INTRODUCTION

As earlier chapters have demonstrated, mutual funds are subject to annual income taxes at the federal level. What many mutual fund owners don't realize is that in many jurisdictions state and local taxes must also be paid on mutual funds whenever mutual fund distributions are made. Because variable annuities are tax-deferred, state and local taxes do not negatively impact variable annuity owners in the same way as mutual fund owners.

§3002. STATE INCOME TAXES

As mentioned in Chapter 8, mutual fund owners can lose up to half of the net annual gain on their mutual funds to federal income taxes. This book uses a more conservative tax loss figure of 20%. Few mutual fund owners consider the tax impact state income taxes may have on their mutual fund portfolio. One reason for this is that state income taxes are usually deductible on the federal income tax return and therefore many mutual fund owners ignore the impact of these taxes. By doing so these mutual fund owners fail to realize how much state income taxes add to the cost of mutual fund ownership. The problem with state income taxes is that they still exact a cost on mutual fund portfolios even if fully deductible on the federal income tax returns. The following example demonstrates this.

> **Example**
> Sam purchased a mutual fund for $100,000 and a year later received a taxable distribution of $10,000. Half of this distribution was a long-term gain and half short-term. Sam's average federal income tax bracket is 30% requiring Sam to pay $2,250 in federal income taxes on the distribution. Sam had to report the same $10,000 distribution for state tax purposes. Sam's average state income tax bracket was 6.7%. Based on this, Sam paid $670 in state income taxes on his mutual fund distribution. By deducting this $670 on his federal income tax return, Sam will save only 30% of $670 or $201, thus increasing his total average federal and state tax burden on his mutual funds from 2.25% to over 2.7%.[1]

A mutual fund owner who does not itemize deductions is not able to deduct state income taxes on his federal tax return. In such cases, the state income tax must be added onto the federal tax burden. The next example demonstrates the impact of non-deductible state income taxes on long-term mutual fund ownership. Although most mutual fund investors ignore the impact that state income taxes have on their mutual fund portfolios, this can be a costly mistake.

---

[1] $2,250 + $469 = $2,719 ÷ $100,000 = 2.7%. Some states don't recognize the concept of capital gains and tax mutual fund distributions as ordinary income.

Example

Sara purchased a mutual fund for $25,000 twenty-five years ago. The costs and taxes associated with the purchase were standard (see §709). Sara's fund returned 10% a year (gross). At the end of the twenty-five-year holding period, Sara expected to have $103,384.[2] However, her mutual fund was only worth $94,735.[3] Sara was concerned about the $8,649 differential and contacted her CPA who informed Sara that she forget to factor in state income taxes. State income taxes were 5% and, because Sara did not itemize deductions, they increased the annual tax burden on her mutual funds from 2% to 2.5%. The $8,649 loss suffered by Sara was a direct result of having to pay state income taxes.

§3003. MISCELLANEOUS STATE TAXES

Many states collect taxes on intangibles such as stocks, bonds and mutual funds. Intangible taxes are rarely imposed on insurance or insurance products like variable annuities. A typical intangibles tax of $.25 per $100 of value may seem insignificant, but on an $800,000 mutual fund portfolio, this tax can amount to $2,000 a year. Some states impose taxes on variable annuity premiums but the tax is usually not due at sale but upon withdrawal. In many cases, people withdraw money from their variable annuities in retirement and may well have retired to a state that imposes no premium tax or income tax. In addition, the annuity may be sold and the proceeds used to purchase a new annuity in a state that does not have a premium tax.

§3004. STATE AND LOCAL TAXATION OF VARIABLE ANNUITIES

Variable annuities are tax-deferred and income taxes, whether federal, state or local, are paid only when withdrawals are made from the variable annuity. Mutual fund proponents claim that ultimately variable annuity owners must pay state and local income taxes just like mutual fund owners. This argument is flawed for two reasons:

- Deferring income taxes on an investment for many years rather than paying income taxes annually will always provide a larger nest egg which will almost always generate a larger *after-tax* stream of income; and

- During one's wealth-building years, one may not be able to choose where they will live. For example, one might be employed in New York or some other high-tax state while working. However, in retirement, one can choose to retire in a low-tax state. Investors with variable annuities often move to a low- or no-income tax state in retirement and effectively exclude their variable annuities from state and local income taxes.

For both of the reasons set out above, one would be better off investing in variable annuities rather than mutual funds for the long-term.

---

[2] $23,750 x 6.06% x 25 year = $103,384.
[3] $23,750 x 5.69% x 25 years = $94,735.

§3005. LOCAL INCOME TAXES

Some large *cities* impose an income tax on their citizens. This tax, together with federal and state income taxes, will greatly increase the tax burden owners will pay on their mutual fund distributions.

§3006. CONCLUSION

The tax burden of owning mutual funds does not stop with the annual payment of federal income taxes. Mutual fund owners must also consider the impact of state and local taxes. Variable annuity owners are able to defer federal, state and local taxes until retirement when they are in a position to select an income tax friendly state for retirement.

PART III - THE COSTS OF OWNING MUTUAL FUNDS

[Summary: Once all of the tax and non-tax costs of owning mutual funds are taken into consideration, investors will realize that long-term investing in variable annuities will produce better financial results than investing in similar mutual funds.]

- CHAPTER 31 -

THE TRUE ANNUAL COST OF MUTUAL FUND AND VARIABLE ANNUITY OWNERSHIP

§3101. INTRODUCTION

When comparing mutual funds and variable annuities most laypeople, as well as many financial professionals, look only to the annual expense of owning these investments. For example, if the average annual expense for owning a mutual fund is 1.5% (including 12b-1 fees) and the average annual expense for owning a variable annuity is in the range of 2.4% to 2.7%, a conclusion that is often drawn is that the mutual fund is the less expensive investment to own on an annual basis. Such a conclusion would be seriously flawed. When contemplating any investment it is important to take into consideration *all* of the costs associated with the investment in order to make a correct investment decision.

§3102. THE TRUE ANNUAL COST OF MUTUAL FUND AND VARIABLE ANNUITY OWNERSHIP

In the chapters that follow, the four major costs of mutual fund ownership are reviewed and discussed. They are

- Annual income taxes
- Annual money management expenses
- Trading costs
- Commissions or contingent deferred sales charges

These chapters also review and discuss the four major costs of variable annuity ownership. They are:

- Annual money management fees
- Mortality and expense (M&E) fees
- Trading costs
- Contingent deferred sales charges

These chapters should demonstrate that mutual funds are subject to many costs of ownership that are often overlooked. When *all* of the costs of owning mutual funds are considered, it usually becomes clear that the mutual fund is more expensive to own on an annual basis than the variable annuity.

§3103. OTHER COSTS OF MUTUAL FUND OWNERSHIP

Chapters 35 through 36B deal with miscellaneous costs of owning mutual funds.

§3104. CONCLUSION

Investors, in order to make correct investment decisions, must understand all of the costs associated with the ownership of mutual funds. Once investors are aware of these costs, the variable annuity will often prove the more cost efficient long-term investment vehicle.

- CHAPTER 32 -

THE ANNUAL TAX COST OF MUTUAL FUND OWNERSHIP - A REVIEW

§3201. INTRODUCTION

One of the major costs of mutual fund ownership is the income tax burden that must be paid annually by fund owners.

§3202. MUTUAL FUND INCOME TAXATION – A REVIEW

The income taxation of mutual funds was discussed in §706 above. This chapter is intended to act as a mere review of the income tax cost of owning mutual funds. As discussed in Chapter 7, several of the country's top researchers have determined that the typical, equity based mutual fund loses 20% of its net gain to *annual* incomes taxes. This is a significant recurring cost of owning mutual funds. Even a conservative 20% annual income tax reduction in a mutual fund's net annual return can have a dramatic impact over time. For example, a $100,000 investment that grows at a 10% net rate of return for 25 years will grow to slightly more than one million dollars.[2] By reducing this return by 20% to an 8% net rate of return, the same $100,000 investment would grow to only $684,848.[3] The 20% annual income tax reduction, compared to the variable annuity, would result in a tax loss to the fund's owner of $398,623 over 25 years![4] The comparisons and examples in this book use a 20% annual tax loss for net mutual fund gains. However, comparisons of actual mutual funds and variable annuities should use the actual annual tax loss which can me more or less than 20%. A front page story in section C of the Wall Street Journal for May 16, 2006 examines this issue.

§3203. OTHER TAX COSTS

In addition to the 20% annual income tax imposed on the net gain of a mutual fund, there are several additional tax costs associated with mutual fund ownership. These additional tax costs were discussed in Part I of this book. They are summarized below:

1. **Late Year Purchases.** Mutual fund purchases late in the year will often result in purchasers having to pay income taxes on distributions that do not increase the value of their mutual fund holdings. (See Chapter 12).

2. **Embedded Gains.** When mutual fund owners hold funds while others are selling

---

[1] A 2010 study conducted by Lipper, Inc., found that equity mutual fund investors give up 20% of their annual net returns to federal income taxes. State and local taxes could increase this tax loss. See Note 2 in Chapter 7.

[2] $100,000 x 25 years x 10% = $1,083,471. Ownership costs are ignored to isolate the tax impact.

[3] $100,000 x 25 years x 8% = $684,848. Ownership costs are ignored to isolate the tax impact.

[4] $1,083,471 - $684,848 = $398,623.

the fund, the fund's annual distribution must be divided among fewer fund owners resulting in larger distributions and therefore larger taxes to remaining fund owners. When this occurs while the fund's value is dropping, remaining fund owners not only pay larger tax bills but often must do so when their fund is losing value. In some cases, this can result in an income tax that can hit triple digits! (See Chapter 13).

3. **Alternate Minimum Tax (AMT).** Mutual fund ownership can result in increased taxes by requiring fund owners to pay taxes under the alternative minimum tax (AMT) structure. (See Chapter 16).

4. **Lost Income Tax Exemptions.** The ownership of mutual funds can cause mutual fund owners to lose tax exemptions, thereby increasing their income tax burden. (See Chapter 19).

5. **Lost Income Tax Deductions.** The ownership of mutual funds can cause mutual fund owners to lose tax deductions, thereby increasing their income tax burden. (See Chapter 20).

6. **Lost Income Tax Credits.** The ownership of mutual funds can cause mutual fund owners to lose tax credits, thereby increasing their income tax burden. (See Chapter 21).

7. **National Sales Tax.** Mutual fund owners will be the losers if a national sales tax is adopted in the future. (See Chapter 22).

8. **A Flat Tax.** Mutual fund owners will be the losers if a flat tax is adopted in the future. (See Chapter 23).

9. **Stepped-up Basis.** In most cases, beneficiaries who inherit from the estates of those who die with mutual funds may receive less than if the decedent died with variable annuities even if a stepped-up basis is available to the beneficiaries receiving the mutual funds. The stepped-up basis provided by variable annuities often produces larger tax savings than the stepped-up basis provided by mutual funds. (See Chapter 25).

10. **Retirement Accounts.** The ability to fund a traditional IRA or Roth IRA or convert from the former to the latter may be lost to mutual fund owners. Variable annuity owners do not lose these tax benefits simply because they own variable annuities. (See Chapter 26).

11. **Social Security Taxation.** Mutual fund ownership, unlike variable annuity ownership, can result in from 50% to 85% of the owner's Social Security retirement

income being subject to income taxes. (See Chapter 27).

12. **Estimated Taxes.** Ownership of mutual funds can result in the owner having to pay state and federal estimated taxes. Ownership of variable annuities does not trigger the requirement for paying estimated taxes by the annuity's owner. (See Chapter 29).

13. **Deductible Losses.** The tax treatment of losses resulting from the sale of a variable annuity is better than the tax treatment of losses resulting from the sale of a mutual fund. (See Chapter 28).

14. **State and Local Taxes.** Annual state and local taxes negatively impact mutual fund owners but not variable annuity owners. (See Chapter 30).

15. **Tax Traps.** Mutual funds are subject to tax traps that variable annuity owners don't face. (See Chapter 14).

16. **Taxation in a Declining Stock Market.** Mutual fund owners frequently are required to pay income taxes on mutual fund distributions even when their funds are losing value. Variable annuity owners never face this situation. (See Chapter 15).

17. **Estate Tax Reduction.** Variable annuities are easy to adjust so that estate taxes and income taxes can be avoided. Mutual funds do not offer their owners the same benefit. (See Chapter 18).

18. **Capital Gains Rates and Holding Periods**. The possibility that capital gains rates or the holding period to obtain these rates will increase is more likely than a reduction in these rates or holding periods. An increase would place a tremendous tax burden on mutual fund owners. (See Chapter 24).

Detailed tax studies are not needed for most mutual funds owners to realize that the annual tax burden they pay on their funds will substantially reduce their long-term investment returns.

§3204. ANNUAL TAX COST OF VARIABLE ANNUITY OWNERSHIP

Variable annuities do not generate an annual income tax liability because they grow tax-deferred.

§3205. CONCLUSION

The annual income tax loss suffered by mutual fund owners is one of the largest costs of owning a mutual fund. Mutual fund owners are also subject to income taxes on the unrealized long-term capital gains that have built up in their funds when they are sold. Investors must understand that when the total tax cost of owning a mutual fund is considered, these tax costs alone can exceed all of the other costs associated with owning a mutual fund. When non-tax costs are combined with income tax costs, the total expense of mutual fund ownership will almost always exceed that of variable annuity ownership. The next several chapters discuss the other major costs associated with mutual fund and variable annuity ownership.

> For more information on the costs of owning mutual funds and variable annuities, please see the report titled "Mutual Funds Vs. Variable Annuities – The True Annual Cost of Ownership."
> This report is available by calling Parker-Thompson Publishing at (919) 832-2687.

- CHAPTER 33 -

MUTUAL FUND AND VARIABLE ANNUITY ANNUAL EXPENSES – A REVIEW

§3301. INTRODUCTION

Mutual funds, like variable annuities, charge an annual expense that pays the money managers who manage the investments held by the mutual fund or variable annuity. Included in this annual expense are 12b-1 fees and administrative fees that pay for marketing and some of the other costs of running the mutual fund or variable annuity company.[1] This annual cost of ownership must be considered when an investor is comparing mutual funds and variable annuities as long-term investments.

§3302. MUTUAL FUND ANNUAL EXPENSES

The average annual expense charged for the typical mutual fund purchased through a financial professional, including 12b-1 fees, is approximately 1.5%. This figure is used in the comparisons examples in this book. If an investor is contemplating the purchase of a mutual fund with an annual expense that is higher or lower than 1.5%, that *actual* annual expense should be used in any comparison with a competing variable annuity. As mentioned above, the annual expense is used to pay the money managers who do the investing for the mutual funds that generate the expense.

§3303. VARIABLE ANNUITY ANNUAL EXPENSES

The annual expense of owning the typical variable annuity obtained from a financial professional can range from less than 2% to nearly 3%. Like mutual funds, the annual expense of owning a variable annuity includes 12b-1 fees and is used to pay the money managers who do the investing for the variable annuity and cover marketing efforts. The average variable annuity sold to the public by financial professionals has a total annual expense of approximately 2.2%. This 2.2% figure is a combination of money management and administrative fees of 0.9% and a mortality and expense fee of 1.3%. Approximately 0.20% of this 1.3% is used to pay for the variable annuity's death benefit. This figure is used in examples that appear in this book. If an investor is contemplating the purchase of a variable annuity with an annual expense of more or less than 2.2%, then any comparison to a competing mutual fund should be adjusted to use the *actual* annual expense charged by the variable annuity issuer being considered by the investor.

---

[1]   The term annual expense is used herein to denote all annual fees charged by a mutual fund or variable annuity for management expenses, providing a death benefit, etc.

§3304. MORTALITY AND EXPENSE CHARGES

Mutual funds do not provide a death benefit to the purchasers of their funds and therefore do not have charges related to this insurance. Variable annuity issuers typically provide a death benefit that will make up the difference between the value of a variable annuity at the death of the owner and the net amount invested in the variable annuity by the deceased owner if this difference is a loss. For example, if Bill buys a variable annuity for $100,000 and dies when it is worth $70,000, the variable annuity issuer will add a $30,000 death benefit to the $70,000 value so as to ensure the deceased variable annuity owner's beneficiaries will get back all net investments made in the annuity by the deceased owner. If Bill's variable annuity was worth $140,000 at his death, his family would get $140,000 and no death benefit would be paid. The typical mortality and expense charge made by most variable annuity companies to provide a death benefit and profit to the variable annuity issuer is 1.3%. (As mentioned earlier, the 0.9% money management and administrative fees result in the 2.2% average annual expense of owning a variable annuity).

§3305. COMMISSIONS PAID BY THE FUND COMPANY

When mutual funds buy investments they have to pay brokerage commissions like any other investment purchaser. These commissions are referred to as trading costs. Mutual fund companies are able to obtain commission discounts that regular investors rarely receive. However, these commissions are paid and passed on to the fund purchasers in a less than straightforward manner. A mutual fund prospectus *does not* have to disclose the commissions the fund company pays in that part of the prospectus that deals with costs. These commission costs are usually found only in a fund's *supplemental* prospectus or statement of additional information (SAI). These commissions are passed on *in full* to fund owners in the form of a reduction in the return a mutual fund owner receives on his fund. These trading costs are estimated to reduce a mutual fund's annual gain by $1/2$% to 1% per year according to various sources.[2] This book uses 0.7% as the trading cost figure for mutual funds.

§3306. VARIABLE ANNUITY TRADING COSTS

Variable annuities have trading costs just like mutual funds. Variable annuity companies do not have to list this cost in their primary prospectus. Just as with mutual fund companies, variable annuity companies report this figure in their supplemental prospecti. Because variable

---

[2] *The Great Mutual Fund Trap*, Baer and Gensler, p. 104, and *Better Investing*, July 2001, p.29. The Wall Street Journal, March 15, 2010, Section C.

annuity companies trade less than variable mutual fund companies by approximately 30%, their trading costs will usually be about 30% less than that of mutual funds. As mentioned above, this book uses 0.7% as the trading cost for a mutual fund.[3] For this reason, this book will use 0.5% as the trading cost figure for a variable annuity (70% of the 0.7% mutual fund trading cost = 0.49%). Actual trading costs should be used whenever actual mutual funds and variable annuities are compared.

§3307. CONCLUSION

Annual expenses and trading costs of both mutual funds and variable annuities must always be considered when a purchase of either of these two investments is contemplated. In addition, the mortality and expense charge made by variable annuity issuers must also be factored into an analysis of the overall cost of owning a variable annuity.

---

[3] Trading costs for mutual funds are slightly higher than the trading costs for a variable annuity because of the year-end selling activity of the mutual fund industry referred to as "window dressing." This activity arises because mutual fund companies need to sell off losers to reduce potentially large year-end capital gains distributions.

- CHAPTER 34 -

COMMISSIONS AND SALES CHARGES

§3401. INTRODUCTION

As a general rule, the money used to compensate a financial professional (i.e., commissions), for helping a client select a variable annuity and monitor it in the future is paid by the *issuer* of their variable annuities. These commissions are paid out of the 2.2% average annual expense the issuer imposes annually on the owners of their variable annuities. Mutual fund companies have several methods they use to compensate the financial professionals who sell their mutual funds. Some of these methods require the mutual fund purchaser to pay a commission out of his pocket at the time of purchase and others do not. The four most common methods of paying commissions to purchase mutual funds are:

- An up-front out-of-pocket commission averaging 2% to 6% (commonly called A-share load) with the average being about 4% before breakpoints.

- A deferred sales charge where no up-front commission is charged but the annual expense of owning the fund (i.e., 1.5%) is increased by approximately 0.8% to approximately 2.3%. This arrangement is referred to as a B-share transaction. B-share purchasers do not pay an up-front out-of-pocket commission but are subject to a declining contingent deferred sales charge.

- An annual expense of approximately 0.8% more than the A-share load of 1.5% is charged and remains in place as long as the funds are owned (commonly called a C-share load).

- An annual money management fee of $1/2$% to $1^1/2$% is paid to a fee-only financial planner to select and manage a purchaser's mutual fund portfolio.

Each of the four major methods of paying loads or commissions is discussed in the sections that follow.

§3402. UP-FRONT COMMISSIONS (A-SHARES)

Many mutual fund owners believe that paying an up-front load or commission for their mutual funds at the time of purchase is the most cost-efficient method of owning mutual funds. Mistakenly, they believe that once an up-front commission is paid they will not be affected by such commissions in the future. This is not accurate. In actuality, up-front commission will affect mutual fund investors more than they realize.

Example

Jack wanted to invest $10,000 in a mutual fund. He chose to pay a 5% up-front commission or load of $500, thus reducing his investment to $9,500. Over a five-year period, Jack's investment increased five-fold to $47,500. Had he not paid an up-front load, his mutual fund account would have grown to $50,000. Jack's single 5% up-front load of $500 has resulted in Jack losing $500 every year for five years for a total loss of $2,500. Jack's belief that he would pay $500 one time and be done with loads and commissions has cost Jack a lot of money. Jack would not have been any better off if he had paid the $500 commission out of other funds so his full $10,000 would be working for him. After five years, Jack's investment would still be worth $50,000 but the $500 commission he paid from another source would have grown to $2,500 had it been invested in the mutual fund Jack bought. Either way, Jack loses an average of $500 a year for buying his A-share mutual fund.

§3403. CONTINGENT DEFERRED SALES CHARGES (B-SHARES)

Many mutual fund purchasers prefer to have 100% of their investment working for them rather than lose a portion to up-front commissions. Such mutual fund purchasers often elect to pay loads or commissions in the form of B-shares. This is accomplished by the mutual fund issuer increasing the fund's normal A-share annual expense by approximately 0.8%. This allows the mutual fund company to pay a commission to the professional who sells the fund and then recoup this advanced commission over a period of time. B-share mutual funds impose a contingent deferred sales charge (CDSC) of approximately 6% on B-share fund purchasers. This charge typically declines 1% a year over six years. If a B-share mutual fund is held only one year, a 5% surrender charge (CDSC) will be imposed on the sale proceeds. If the fund is held for over six years, there would be no CDSC. B-share mutual funds have annual expenses of approximately 2.3% whereas the typical annual expense for an A-share mutual fund is 1.5%. When the CDSC expires (usually after six years), the B-share mutual fund's annual expense drops by 0.8% to the A-share load level of approximately 1.5%.

§3404. CONTINUING ANNUAL COMMISSION (C-SHARES)

When a mutual fund is purchased on a C-share basis, the investor agrees to pay an additional annual fee of approximately 0.8% to own his fund. This fee is added to the basic $1^1/_2$% annual cost of owning the A-share version of the mutual fund. As long as the fund is owned, the fee is paid. In addition, when the C-share form of commission is elected, the mutual fund company frequently imposes a 1% contingent deferred sales charge for at least the first year of the fund's ownership. In some cases a 1% load for the first year of the C-share mutual fund's ownership.

§3405. FEE-ONLY PLANNING

Many mutual fund owners pay their fee-only financial planners a flat fee to select and manage their mutual fund portfolios for them. This management fee is typically 1% a year. If this form of payment is chosen, the mutual fund purchaser must realize that this 1% fee reduces his rate of return on his mutual funds by 1% each year for as long as the funds are owned. Over 10 years this can be 10%. In addition, the fund may charge an annual ownership costs of 1.5% or more.

§3406. VARIABLE ANNUITY DEFERRED SALES CHARGES

Variable annuities, like B-share mutual funds, do not charge up-front, out-of-pocket commissions. Typically, variable annuities impose contingent deferred sales charges (CDSCs) of 6% or 7% that decline 1% a year until they disappear. If a variable annuity is sold before its holding period expires, the appropriate CDSC will be imposed. A CDSC is imposed in any comparison or example used in this book where a hypothetical variable annuity owner does not hold his variable annuity for the full surrender or holding period. Most variable annuities allow surrender charge-free withdrawals of 10% to 15% a year.

§3407. SALES CHARGES USED IN COMPARISONS

For comparisons in this book, it is not as critical to know how a commission or load is paid but that such commissions or loads *are* paid. The important thing for investors to understand is that those who purchase A-share mutual funds or use a fee-only financial planner must pay some form of up-front, out-of-pocket load or commission when they purchase their mutual funds. On the other hand, B-share mutual fund investors and variable annuity investors generally do not pay up-front, out-of-pocket commissions or loads to buy their mutual funds or variable annuities. The financial professional who sells B-share mutual funds or variable annuities receives his commission from the company issuing the mutual fund or variable annuity. This is one reason why the average annual cost of owning a B-share mutual fund is 2.3% and that of the variable annuity is 2.2%. In short, the B-share mutual fund issuer and variable annuity company charge a larger annual cost for owning a mutual fund or variable annuity in order to recoup the cost of advancing commissions to the financial professionals who sell their mutual funds and variable annuities to the public.

The examples in this book will assume a 5% A-share mutual fund is used. Break-point commissions are applied for larger mutual fund purchases. Occasionally, comparisons will assume B-share mutual funds are involved. When this occurs the author will set out any cost assumptions used. Variable annuities will be deemed to have annual expenses of 2.2%. The important thing to remember is that investors must use the *actual* commissions that they might pay when comparing actual mutual funds and variable annuities.

§3408. TOTAL ANNUAL MUTUAL FUND AND VARIABLE ANNUITY EXPENSES

This chapter in conjunction with Chapters 31 through 33 discussed the four major costs of long-term investing with mutual funds and variable annuities. The table below summarizes these costs:

Table of Annual Costs for an Average A-Share Mutual Fund and Variable Annuity

Expense	A-share Mutual Fund	Variable Annuity
Annual Expense Ratio (Incl. 12b-1 fees)	1.50%	2.20%[2]
Annual Income Tax Loss	1.44%[3]	0.00%
Commission	0.80%[4]	0.00%
Trading Costs	0.70%	0.50%
Total	4.44%	2.70%

Although A-share mutual fund owners pay their commissions up-front at the time they purchase their mutual funds, it would not be fair to allocate this full commission to the cost of owning a mutual fund in its first year. A-share mutual funds should be spread over the full period of time a mutual fund is owned. For example, if an A-share mutual fund commission is 5% and the fund will be held for five years, then the commission would be annualized to reflect a 1% commission for each year the fund is owned. In the examples used in this book any A-share commission will be spread over the entire holding period of the fund even if it is twenty years or more. The net ending value charts that are discussed in the next section will demonstrate how the above costs and taxes should be applied to mutual funds and variable annuities.

§3409. NET ENDING VALUE WORKSHEETS

On the following two pages are worksheets that may help financial professionals determine whether a mutual fund or a variable annuity will be the better investment for a client. The first worksheet indicates that on an after-cost and after-tax basis the hypothetical

---

[2] 0.9% money management fee and 1.3% mortality and expense cost.

[3] In this book the gross gain in a mutual fund will be set at 10%. A 20% tax on the smaller net gain will result in a 1.44% tax on the gross mutual fund gain (see §706).

[4] 5% A-share commission for a mutual fund to be held for approximately six years.

variable annuity will provide the investor with a larger gain. The second worksheet, because the investment is shorter term in nature, indicates the investor will be better off financially by purchasing the mutual fund. (Note: If the investor is older or in poor health, he may still want to consider the variable annuity although a few hundred dollars more costly because it provides a death benefit which is included in the cost of buying the variable annuity).

Sample Non-Qualified A-share Mutual Fund/Variable Annuity Net-to-Net Worksheet (53-Year-Old Investor)

NO	DESCRIPTION	MF	VA	MF	VA
1.	Holding Period (Same for MF/VA)	7 years	7 years		
2.	Amount Invested (Lump or Periodic - same for MF/VA)	$25,000 (lump sum)	$25,000 (lump sum)		
3.	Gross Return (Same for MF/VA)	10.0%	10.0%		
4.	Annual Exp. Ratio/12b-1 Fee/M&E	1.5%	2.2%		
5.	Gross Commissions or fee (Zero for VA) A-share	5.0%	-0-		
6.	Trading Costs	0.7%	0.5%		
7.	Annual Taxes (% of Net Gain)	20%	-0-		
8.	Net Return (3 less 4, 5, 6 and 7)	6.064%[1]	7.03%[3]		
9.	Gross Value at End of Holding Period (1x2x8)	$35,862	$40,223		
10	After-tax and Expense Gain (9-2)	$10,862	$15,223		
11.	Surrender Charges	-0-	-0-		
12.	10% IRS Penalty on Gain (Line 10) (If <59½ for VAs but not MF)	-0-	-0-		
13.	Unrealized Cap. Gains 30% of Line 10 (None for VA)	$3,258[2]	-0-		
14.	Taxes on unreal. Cap. Gains (15% of Line 13 for MF)	$489	-0-		
15.	Taxes on VA Gain (25% of Line 10)	-0-	$3,806		
16.	Net Value at End of Holding Period (Line 9 less 11, 12, 14, 15)	$35,373	$36,417		

1. $25,000 - 5% + 10% - 2.2% (1.5% + 0.7%) = $25,550 - $23,750 = $1,800 - 20% tax = $1,440 ÷ $23,750 = 6.064%

2. May be higher or lower than 30%.

3. $25,000 + 10% - 2.7% (2.2% + 0.5%) = $26,758 - $25,000 = $1,758 ÷ $25,000 = 7.03%

4. A client's average tax rate may be higher or lower than 20%.

Sample Non-Qualified B-share Mutual Fund/Variable Annuity Net-to-Net Worksheet (53-Year-Old Investor)

NO	DESCRIPTION	MF	VA	MF	VA
1.	Holding Period (Same for MF/VA)	4 years	4 years		
2.	Amount Invested (Lump or Periodic - same for MF/VA)	$50,000 (lump sum)	$50,000 (lump sum)		
3.	Gross Return (Same for MF/VA)	11.0%	11.0%		
4.	Annual Exp. Ratio/12b-1 Fee/M&E	2.3%	2.2%		
5.	Gross Commissions or fee (Zero for VA) A-share	0% (B-share)	-0-		
6.	Trading Costs	0.7%	0.5%		
7.	Annual Taxes (% of Net Gain)	20%	-0-		
8.	Net Return (3 less 4, 5, 6 and 7)	6.136%[1]	8.00%[3]		
9.	Gross Value at End of Holding Period (1x2x8)	$63,448	$68,032		
10	After-tax and Expense Gain (9-2)	$13,448	$18,032		
11.	Surrender Charges (1% of $50,000)	$500	$578[4]		
12.	10% IRS Penalty on Gain (Line 10) (If <59½ for VAs but not MF)	-0-	$1,803		
13.	Unrealized Cap. Gains 30% of Line 10 - Line 11 (None for VA)	$4,034[2]	-0-		
14.	Taxes on unreal. Cap. Gains (15% of Line 13 for MF)	$605	-0-		
15.	Taxes on VA Gain (25% of Line 10)	-0-	$4,508[5]		
16.	Net Value at End of Holding Period (Line 9 less 11, 12, 14, 15)	$62,343	$61,143		

1. $50,000 + 11% = $55,500 - 3% (2.3% + 0.7%) = $53,835 - $50,000 = $3,835 - 20% tax = $3,068 ÷ $50,000 = 6.136%
2. May be higher or lower than 30%.
3. $50,000 + 11% = $55,500 - 2.7% (2.2% + 0.5%) = $54,002 - $50,000 = $4,002 ÷ $50,000 = 8.00%
4. One year surrender charge of 85% of 1% of $68,032 (15% of withdrawals are surrender-fee free)
5. A client's average tax rate may be higher or lower than 25%.

§3410. CONCLUSION

Commissions for buying financial products must be considered when comparing investments. When commissions are added to annual income taxes and annual ownership costs of mutual funds and variable annuities it should become clear that mutual funds can be significantly more expensive to own on an annual basis than variable annuities.

> For more information on mutual fund and variable annuity commissions, please see the report titled "The Impact of Commissions on Variable Annuity and Mutual Fund Performance." This report is available by calling Parker-Thompson Publishing at (919) 832-2687.

- CHAPTER 35 -
TRANSACTION COSTS

§3501. INTRODUCTION

In addition to sales charges and annual expenses, mutual fund owners may be exposed to additional income taxes and commissions whenever they sell their mutual fund or exchange it for another one. These additional taxes and commissions are referred to as transaction costs. Variable annuity owners do not incur transaction costs because selling or exchanging sub-accounts within a variable annuity neither triggers an income tax nor generates additional commissions or fees.

§3502. MUTUAL FUNDS AND TRANSACTION COSTS

After their initial purchase, mutual fund owners may continue to generate taxes and fees in addition to those incurred to originally buy their fund. On average, mutual fund owners completely sell their portfolios approximately every three years, thus increasing their cost of mutual fund ownership. Such transaction costs are common but rarely do mutual fund owners realize how much these expenses impact overall mutual fund performance. For example, a mutual fund owner who sells a mutual fund to buy another most likely will generate income taxes and possibly new commissions or other costs to purchase a replacement fund.

§3503. VARIABLE ANNUITIES AND TRANSACTION COSTS

When a sub-account held within a variable annuity is sold or exchanged for another sub-account within the same variable annuity, there are no additional commissions or income taxes to pay. Variable annuities, unlike mutual funds, are free of such transaction costs.

Another major benefit of owning variable annuities is that one variable annuity can be exchanged for another variable annuity issued by a different variable annuity company without triggering any income tax liability. Such exchanges are referred to as §1035 exchanges after the tax code provision allowing these tax-free exchanges.[1] As mentioned above, when mutual funds are exchanged for different mutual funds of the same or a different fund company, a taxable event occurs if there is a gain. These potential taxes must be considered when contemplating the purchase of either a mutual fund or variable annuity.

§3504 CONCLUSION

Transaction costs can be significantly higher with mutual funds than variable annuities.

---

[1]   §1035 exchanges should not be made if there will be a large surrender penalty imposed by the transferring variable annuity issuer.

These costs must be considered when considering the purchase of either a mutual fund or variable annuity. Mutual fund transaction costs are ignored in the comparisons made in this book.

- CHAPTER 36 -

RECORD-KEEPING COSTS

§3601. INTRODUCTION

The complexity of mutual fund ownership and the detailed records that must be kept by mutual fund owners generates costs in both time and money that must be considered before buying a mutual fund. Variable annuities do not present these complexities or the attendant record-keeping problems.

§3602. THE COMPLEXITY OF MUTUAL FUND OWNERSHIP

In order to minimize the costs and taxes associated with mutual fund ownership, mutual fund owners must be familiar with concepts such as:

- FIFO (First In, First Out)
- Stepped-up and Stepped-down Basis
- Cost Basis Adjustment
- Realized vs. Unrealized Gains
- Short- vs. Long-term Capital Gains
- Average Cost Method
- Specific Identification Method
- Wash Sales

Most mutual fund owners have no idea what these terms mean. They must often retain the services of a tax expert to help them traverse the complexities of mutual fund ownership or risk making costly mistakes. If tax professionals (i.e. CPAs, attorneys) are hired, their cost must be factored in to the expense of owning mutual funds. If a mutual fund owner decides not to pay for professional guidance, he may expose himself to even larger losses. The following example demonstrates what happens when a mutual fund owner enters into a simple sales transaction without fully understanding the complexities of mutual fund ownership.

Example:
Victoria purchased 10,000 shares of Piedmont Growth mutual fund for $200,000 two years ago when its per share price was $20. This year, Victoria bought another 10,000 shares of Piedmont mutual fund for $300,000 when its price hit $30 a share. In December of this year, Victoria realizes long-term stock market gains of $50,000 and needs some long-term losses to offset these stock market

---

[1] Victoria figured the sale would generate $250,000 but the cost of the fund (i.e. $300,000) would provide the $50,000 investment loss she needed.

gains. Because Piedmont mutual fund was currently selling for $25 a share, Victoria decided to sell the most recent 10,000 shares of the Piedmont fund that she purchased for $30 in an effort to generate the $50,000 investment loss needed to offset her $50,000 stock market gain.[1] After selling the fund and claiming the $50,000 loss, Victoria was audited by the IRS and learned that current tax law requires that, unless a taxpayer clearly specifies to the contrary, the first mutual funds purchased are considered the first funds sold when one sells any of their mutual fund holdings. Victoria did not do this. For this reason, instead of a $50,000 loss to offset her stock market gains of $50,000, Victoria will have a $50,000 mutual fund *gain* ($250,000 - $200,000 = $50,000) that must be *added* to her stock market gains of $50,000 for a total investment gain of $100,000. This error, with penalties and interest, could cost Victoria $25,000 or more.

§3603. VARIABLE ANNUITIES AND RECORD-KEEPING

Record-keeping for variable annuity owners is not necessary. Because income taxes are deferred, there is no reason to keep track of sales and purchases. The only two things a variable annuity owner needs to know is the total amount invested in their variable annuity and its value when withdrawals are taken. The variable annuity issuer always keeps track of these two figures and reports them at least quarterly to variable annuity owners. When withdrawals are made from a variable annuity, it is the responsibility of the issuing company to inform the variable annuity owner of how much of the variable annuity withdrawal is taxable and how much is not.

§3604. THE DOUBLE TAXATION PROBLEM

Because mutual funds are much more complex to own than variable annuities, many mutual fund owners often pay income taxes on mutual funds when such taxes are not owed. This is referred to as the "double taxation" problem of mutual fund ownership. The following example demonstrates this problem.

Example:
Steve's aunt, who is 74, just gave Steve $400,000 worth of Apex Growth Fund. The aunt received the mutual fund from her brother several years ago by gift. He has since died. The aunt had no records regarding the fund. Documents belonging to the deceased brother indicate he purchased Apex Growth for $50,000 in 1953. Apex Growth was taken over by Paramount Funds in 1988. Steve is unable to obtain any information about distributions, reinvestments, redemptions, etc. Steve recently decided to sell the fund for $400,000 and reported its cost basis as $50,000 generating a taxable capital gain of $350,000. Steve used the $50,000 cost basis to avoid an IRS audit that would disclose he had no documentation for using a larger cost basis. If proper documentation were kept by the prior owners of the fund, it might have shown that the cost basis of Paramount Fund was as high as $350,000 saving an unnecessary tax payment of $70,000 or more. If a variable annuity were given to Steve instead of a mutual fund, there would be no

record-keeping problems. Variable annuity companies *must* keep track of cost basis for variable annuity owners. As a matter of fact, Steve would have received stepped-up basis upon the transfer of a variable annuity from his aunt and would have owed *no* taxes on the sale of the variable annuity if it were sold for $400,000 or less. (See Chapter 25).

§3605. CONCLUSION

Incomplete and inaccurate record-keeping can be costly for mutual fund owners. Such problems do not arise where variable annuities are owned. Investors must consider these potential problems, and their potential costs, when comparing the purchase of a mutual fund with that of a variable annuity.

- CHAPTER 36B -
MISCELLANEOUS COSTS OF MUTUAL FUND OWNERSHIP

§36B01. INTRODUCTION

The cost of owning mutual funds is generally limited to a discussion of the following:

- Annual expense ratios
- Annual income taxes
- Commissions
- Trading costs

However, mutual funds have *many* other potential costs that should be considered. This chapter briefly discusses several of these miscellaneous costs.

§36B02. REDEMPTION/EXIT FEES

Many mutual funds have recently decided to impose redemption or exit fees when mutual fund owners sell or exchange their mutual fund shares. Mutual fund companies usually invoke redemption fees to cover two situations:

- When poorly performing markets increase redemptions; and
- When strong markets result in mutual fund owners exchanging one fund for another in an effort to time or trade the market.

Recently, many mutual fund companies have begun, for new customers, to impose redemption fees on their funds when owners sell or exchange these funds within a 90-day period. This fee can be 1% or more and is designed to discourage frequent trading.[1] Even traditionally low-cost mutual funds are imposing redemption fees. These redemption fees are imposed in addition to B-share surrender fees or other commissions. Needless to say, these redemption fees increase the cost of mutual fund ownership.

§36B03. INVOLUNTARY LIQUIDATION

Mutual funds can unilaterally decide, without warning, to close up and liquidate whenever they chose. Since 2000, hundreds of mutual funds elected to merge or fold and distribute remaining assets to their shareholders.[2] When this occurs, fund owners usually suffer losses and incur tax liabilities at the same time. Involuntary liquidation of mutual funds can be very costly for mutual fund owners. Variable annuities do not liquidate involuntarily.

---

[1] See *The Wall Street Journal*, March 7, 2001, p.C21 for a discussion on this issue.
[2] *Ticker* magazine addressed this issue in its March 2001 issue at p.48.

§36B04. REDEMPTION WINDOWS

Some fund companies have started *prohibiting* owners of its funds from selling or exchanging their funds except on specific dates. Often, these dates arise only two to four times a year. For example, *The Wall Street Journal* reported that Tiger Management, LLC will allow redemptions by its fund owners only twice a year on predetermined dates.[3] Other mutual funds may follow suit. The inability to sell one's mutual fund when desired can exact a tremendous cost. If one wants to sell their fund and they must wait to sell it, a large loss can occur if the fund drops in value while the owner is waiting for a redemption window to open. Variable annuities do not pose this problem for their owners.

§36B05. COMMISSIONS ON REINVESTMENT OF DISTRIBUTIONS

Some mutual fund companies actually charge a commission on distributions that mutual fund owners reinvest automatically. This practice of charging multiple commissions can greatly reduce an owner's return on his mutual fund.

§36B06. MARKET TIMING COSTS

A study reported in the *Senior Market Advisor*[4] found that mutual fund owners tend to sell when the market is low and buy when the market is high. The study indicated that the cost of such trading resulted in a reduction of the return a mutual fund owner received over the long-term by 2.22% a year. This is *in addition* to paying extra taxes and commissions that could reach another 3% or so each year. This combined loss does not take into consideration the 1.5% annual cost of ownership of the fund, the original commissions or the 20% annual income tax burden mutual fund owners pay each year on their net gains. When these costs are factored in, the annual cost of some mutual funds can approach *double digits*! A study done by Dalbar, Inc. in 2003 found that mutual fund investors usually obtain about $1/3$ of the stock market's return. This loss is directly attributed to mutual fund owners trying to time the stock market.

§36B07. TRANSACTION COSTS

Chapter 35 should be reviewed for a discussion of mutual fund transaction costs.

§36B08. CONCLUSION

There are several miscellaneous costs associated with mutual fund ownership that should be considered when buying mutual funds.

---

[3] *The Wall Street Journal*, October 7, 1999.
[4] Senior Market Advisor, June 2001, p.36

- CHAPTER 36C -

VARIABLE ANNUITY PERFORMANCE

§36C01. INTRODUCTION

A common myth involving variable annuities is that they do not perform as well over time as do similar investments such as mutual funds. This is rarely the case. This chapter examines this issue.

§36C02. THE COST ERROR

Those who claim mutual funds perform better than variable annuities over the long-term cite as the reason for this out-performance the lower annual cost of mutual fund ownership as compared to a variable annuity. The problem with this is that it is the variable annuity that has the lower annual costs of ownership not the mutual fund. This fact was pointed out in previous chapters. Many studies have been conducted demonstrating that mutual funds are more expensive to own on an annual basis than variable annuities. The typical variable annuity will rarely have total annual costs of ownership that will exceed 3%. However, equivalent mutual funds will nearly always have total annual costs of ownership that exceed 5%. Prior chapters have discussed these studies. For this reason, it is the variable annuity that will nearly always outperform the mutual fund over time.

§36C03. THE PERFORMANCE ADVANTAGE

Often the investing public has the perception that variable annuities do not perform as well as similar investments such as mutual funds. This is rarely the case. As discussed in previous chapters, the total cost of owning a mutual fund on an annual basis can easily reach 4.8% or more. A similar variable annuity will have a total annual cost of ownership of approximately 2.65%. Over time, it would be very difficult for a stock mutual fund to outperform a similar variable annuity if they are both invested for the same period of time and at the same rate of return. For example, a mutual fund purchased for $25,000 and held for ten years will grow to $41,439 at a 10% average rate of return if it charges a 5% commission and has typical annual costs and an average annual tax loss.[1] A variable annuity purchased for $25,000 and held for ten years will grow to $49,317 assuming the same 10% rate of return and average annual ownership costs.[2] Even assuming that the gain in the variable annuity is going to be taxed at 25% (and liquidation taxes on the mutual fund are ignored), the variable annuity

---

[1] $25,000 - 5% = $23,750 x 6.064% x 10 years = $41,439.

[2] $25,000 x 7.03% x 10 years = $49,317.

on an after-expense, after-tax basis will yield $43,238 and will outperform the mutual fund by nearly $1,800 over the ten year investment period. [This difference does not factor in transaction or the concept of time value of money (See Chapter 10B)]. Because the annual cost of owning the typical mutual fund can be as much as two percentage points more than the annual cost of owning a similar variable annuity, it is not surprising that the annual performance of variable annuities is usually better than that of similar investments such as mutual funds.

§36C04. MISLEADING MUTUAL FUND PERFORMANCE DATA

Mutual fund companies report net performance based on the difference between their gross return and their annual expenses, 12b-1 fees and trading costs. For example, if a fund has a gross return of 10% and annual expenses, 12b-1 fees and trading costs totaling 2.2%, the net return is reported as 7.8%. Variable annuity companies report net performance in a similar fashion. For example, a 10% gross rate of return is reduced by annual expenses, 12b-1 fees, trading costs and other administrative fees. Assuming these costs are 2.8%, the net return (i.e., NAV) reported is 7.2%. Investors can often be fooled into thinking that the mutual fund's performance at a 7.2% net return is better than the variable annuity's net return of 6.6%. The mutual fund company's method of reporting net returns can be misleading because the net (i.e., NAV) return for the mutual fund is not a true net return. It does not reflect each mutual fund investor's annual tax liability or initial commission costs. In defense of the mutual fund companies, it is only fair to point out that they do not have access to these two pieces of data and therefore cannot be expected to take them into consideration when reporting their "net" returns. However, investors must take these two additional costs into consideration. It should be remembered that these two costs will differ among mutual fund investors. If the 7.2% "net" return reported by the mutual fund company is reduced by income taxes and annualized commissions that total 3%, the true net rate of return for the hypothetical mutual fund discussed above is 4.2% not 7.2%. Because variable annuity investors do not incur up-front, out-of-pocket commissions or pay annual income taxes, the net return of 6.6% in the hypothetical case would remain unchanged. Thus, the true annual performance of the mutual fund is not 7.2% but 4.2% while the variable annuity's true net rate of return is 6.6%. Investors must be aware of how performance is reported for mutual funds and variable annuities if they hope to make correct investment decisions. It is also important to factor in potential income taxes at liquidation because these taxes are almost always higher for the variable annuity than the mutual fund. However, once these taxes are considered, the true net rate of return will often be greater for a variable annuity than a mutual fund.

§36C05. CONCLUSION

Variable annuities will, as a general rule, outperform equivalent mutual funds over time simply because the annual cost to own mutual funds is greater than it is for variable annuities. Annual costs of owning investments have a major impact on net-ending values of their underlying investments. Long-term investors need to look at the impact cost might have on the potential net-ending value of any investment they are considering.

PART IV – BENEFITS OF VARIABLE ANNUITY OWNERSHIP

[Summary: Variable annuities have many benefits not offered by mutual funds. Part IV of this book discusses 15 of these benefits.]

- CHAPTER 37 -

PROTECTION FROM CREDITORS

§3701. INTRODUCTION

Mutual funds are much more susceptible to the claims of creditors than are variable annuities. Potential forfeiture to creditors is a risk faced by mutual fund owners that must be considered when investing in mutual funds. [See mosessinger.com (search creditor protection) for additional information].

§3702. STATUTORY PROTECTION

No state currently exempts mutual funds from the reach of creditors. One-third of the states provide protection from creditors for owners of variable annuities. This protection can range from moderate to the near absolute protection found in states like New York, Florida and Texas.

§3703. ESTATE CREDITORS

Mutual funds are at the greatest risk of loss to creditors where the mutual fund owner has died. Mutual funds are typically probate assets which are transferred to a deceased owner's estate. Once in the estate, mutual funds become available to creditors of the deceased fund owner. The following example demonstrates how this process can put a deceased owner's mutual fund portfolio at risk.

> **Example**
> Tom was married and had two children. His largest asset was his $700,000 mutual fund portfolio. Tom was a part owner of a large software company that recently went out of business. Tom died shortly thereafter. His estate was sued by his creditors and was required to pay $700,000 to the creditors. Tom's mutual funds were assets of his estate and were available to pay his creditors. This wiped out Tom's mutual fund portfolio and left Tom's wife and two children in financial difficulty.

Variable annuities, being insurance products, are almost always non-probate property. Variable annuities pass at an owner's death directly to a named beneficiary and not to the variable annuity owner's estate. In the last example, had Tom owned a $700,000 variable annuity instead of a mutual fund portfolio, his wife and children would have received the $700,000 instead of his creditors.

§3704. JOINT OWNERSHIP AND MUTUAL FUNDS

Proponents of mutual funds claim that they can get the same protection from creditors that variable annuity owners receive when they die by simply owning their mutual funds jointly with rights of survivorship with their spouse or another person. This is not the case. Many states require that any portion of a mutual fund jointly owned by a decedent be paid into the decedent's estate if unpaid taxes or other debts owed to creditors are involved. In addition, placing mutual funds in joint ownership with survivorship rights can result in significant losses. This problem is demonstrated in the following example.

Example
Dave, who is 65, owned a mutual fund portfolio worth $1,000,000. It was his major asset. Dave owed $500,000 to several creditors before he got married and wanted to prevent his mutual funds from passing through his estate and being depleted by his debt. Several years ago Dave decided to create a joint tenancy with right of survivorship in his mutual fund account. Dave's wife was named as the other joint owner of the mutual fund. Dave recently died. Under state law, Dave's portion of the mutual fund portfolio was required to be brought back into his estate to pay Dave's debts. Had Dave owned a variable annuity, his wife would not have lost half of her inheritance to creditors. In addition, the half of the mutual fund portfolio that did pass to Dave's wife has created problems. Dave's wife is not entitled to a stepped-up basis in her half interest in the mutual fund. This will increase her income taxes.[1]

§3705. CONCLUSION

The potential loss of most or all of one's mutual fund portfolio to creditors is a cost that should be considered when comparing mutual funds with variable annuities.

---

[1] Some states provide Pay-on-Death (POD) or Transfer-on-Death (TOD) procedures that, if elected, could prevent the stepped-up basis loss discussed in this problem but POD and TOD statutes would not protect mutual funds from creditors on the facts of this problem.

- CHAPTER 38 -
PROBATE COSTS

§3801. INTRODUCTION

As the last chapter pointed out, mutual funds are almost always probate assets that must pass through the probate process before becoming available to beneficiaries of a deceased mutual fund owner. Variable annuities, on the other hand, are almost always non-probate assets and avoid the delay and costs associated with the probate process. The cost of probate may impact the rate of return one receives on their mutual fund portfolio. The potential cost associated with the probate of mutual funds must be considered when comparing the cost of mutual funds or variable annuity ownership.

Example

A year ago, John purchased a variable annuity for $100,000. John recently died with the annuity still worth $100,000. John's sister Judy was his beneficiary and received a check for $100,000 from the annuity company a week after John's death. She had no time delays or probate costs to deal with because the annuity was non-probate property.

Example

Mark purchased a mutual fund for $100,000. Mark recently died with the mutual fund still worth $100,000. Mark's wife Lisa had to wait nine months before getting the mutual fund from Mark's estate. Additionally, the cost of probate was 5% of the estate's value. Because of this, Lisa only received $95,000 instead of the full $100,000 value of the mutual fund. The probate cost of 5% was, in effect, a 5% additional cost of mutual fund ownership.

§3802. COSTLY ATTEMPTS AT AVOIDING PROBATE

Some mutual fund owners go to great lengths to avoid probate and the costs associated with probate regarding their mutual fund portfolios. Often these attempts fail and result in large losses. The following example demonstrates this problem.

Example

Jack, who is 65 years old, has a mutual fund portfolio worth $1,000,000. He and his wife purchased the portfolio over several years. Jack's cost basis in the portfolio is $400,000. Jack was concerned that at death his portfolio will have to go through the probate process. To avoid this, several years ago Jack changed the ownership of the funds from himself to a joint ownership with rights of survivorship equally with his wife and daughter. Recently, the daughter (at the behest of her new boyfriend) sold one-third of the fund. By doing so, she lost the benefit of a stepped-up basis and caused her parents to lose a large part of their estate tax unified credit because they had to use it to offset the gift tax imposed when the sale of the mutual fund was made by the daughter. The daughter also generated a huge income tax for herself. The wife, if she is the surviving spouse, will also forfeit her stepped-up basis in a large portion of the mutual fund portfolio. This will increase her income taxes. The total actual and potential tax cost to Jack, his wife and his daughter for attempting to avoid probate of their mutual funds could easily run in excess of a hundred thousand dollars. This tax loss is *in addition* to a loss of one-third of the portfolio's value to the daughter. Had Jack owned a $1,000,000 annuity, he could have named his wife and daughter as beneficiaries of the annuity. By doing so he would have avoided probate and eliminated many of the costs and problems associated with joint mutual fund ownership.[1]

§3803. AVOIDING MUTUAL FUND PROBATE COSTS

Financial and legal professionals can help mutual fund owners avoid probate costs on their mutual funds. When this is done, it will often generate additional fees to establish trusts or perform detailed estate planning. These additional costs must be factored into the total cost of mutual fund ownership.

§3804. CONCLUSION

When investors are considering the purchase of mutual funds or variable annuities, it is important that they factor into their decision-making process the potential expenses of probate or the costs of avoiding probate on a portfolio of mutual funds.

---

[1] State pay-on-death (POD) or transfer-on-death (TOD) statutes can, if available and if elected, prevent the problems discussed in this example.

- CHAPTER 39 -

COLLEGE TUITION ASSISTANCE QUALIFICATION

§3901. INTRODUCTION

Mutual fund ownership may prevent the owner from receiving tuition assistance for himself or a child. Variable annuities do not, as a general rule, disqualify annuity owners from receiving tuition assistance.

§3902. COLLEGE FINANCIAL AID PROBLEMS

The ownership of a mutual fund portfolio may prove problematic for parents with college-bound children. Parents who have applied for college financial aid are learning that large mutual fund holdings may disqualify them, in whole or part, form obtaining such aid. What many parents don't realize is that most financial aid sources do not count assets held in variable annuities when determining eligibility for financial aid if these annuities are in the accumulation phase. Many financial aid applications used by colleges (e.g., FAFSA) do not require life insurance or variable annuities to be listed as assets but do require mutual funds and stock to be listed. The following examples demonstrate how ownership of mutual funds may result in the loss of tuition assistance.

> **Example**
> Jane's parents applied to obtain college financial aid to put Jane through college. Their total income for each of the past three years was $50,000. Of this amount $15,000 was a distribution from a mutual fund. Their mutual funds were worth $250,000. Because of their income level and the value of their mutual fund portfolio, Jane's parents were not eligible for college tuition assistance. Had their investments been in a variable annuity their reportable income would have been $35,000. In addition, variable annuities are not required to be reported as assets while they are in the accumulation phase. In short, with variable annuity ownership, Jane's parents would have been eligible for tuition assistance.

§3903. CONCLUSION

Investors must understand that if they are disqualified from receiving tuition assistance due to their ownership of mutual funds, the cost of this disqualification must be added to the cost of owning their mutual funds.

- CHAPTER 40 -

MEDICAID QUALIFICATION

§4001. INTRODUCTION

Owning mutual funds can disqualify one from receiving Medicaid benefits. Variable annuities that have been annuitized do not cause Medicaid disqualification.[1]

§4002. NURSING HOME (MEDICAID) DISQUALIFICATION

Mutual fund ownership may pose a serious problem if the owner of such funds, or his spouse, needs Medicaid assistance should they go into a nursing home. The reason for this is that all states count the value of mutual funds in determining eligibility for nursing home coverage under Medicaid. On the other hand, most states do not count the value of annuities that are making payments to either or both spouses as an asset for Medicaid eligibility. A portfolio of mutual funds can result in Medicaid disqualification, as the following examples demonstrate.

Example #1

Mary, age 72, went into a nursing home three years ago. Her only asset at that time was a variable annuity worth $144,000 that she bought eight years ago. Mary had a handicapped daughter that she was concerned about. Shortly before going into the nursing home, Mary annuitized her annuity and started to receive $1,222 per month for life with payments being guaranteed for ten years. Mary had to use this income toward her nursing home care expenses of $4,000 a month. Medicaid only counts annuity *income* to determine Medicaid eligibility. Mary recently died. Her daughter will receive the remaining monthly annuity payments of $1,222 for seven years, for a total of $102,648.

Example #2

Mark, age 72, went into a nursing home three years ago. His only asset at that time was a mutual fund and stock portfolio worth $144,000 he purchased eight years ago. Mark had a handicapped son that he was concerned about. The cost of Mark's nursing home care was $4,000 per month. Medicaid requires that both the *income* and *principal* of mutual fund and stock portfolios be exhausted before Medicaid will pay for nursing home care. Mark made each month's nursing home payment from his mutual fund and stock portfolio. Mark recently died. Mark used the $144,000 value of his mutual fund portfolio for his nursing home assistance care over the three years he was in the nursing home. His son will receive nothing. Had Mark liquidated his fund portfolio and bought an annuity he would have had a smaller nest egg and would have incurred transaction costs and income taxes that Mary, in the prior example, avoided because she had invested her money in a variable annuity initially. Additionally, many states require that the variable annuity involved be owned for at least six

---

[1] The author will leave to readers the appropriateness of Medicaid planning. Some states are restricting the use of Medicaid qualifying annuities.

years prior to applying for Medicaid.

§4003. LOOK-BACK

There is no "look-back" penalty period involved with the annuitization of a pre-existing variable annuity as long as it was owned for some period (usually for six years) prior to applying for Medicaid.

§4004. MEDICAID QUALIFYING ANNUITIES

Elder care lawyers are a great source of information regarding how annuities can be used to preserve family assets or qualify a family member for Medicaid assistance. As a result of the Deficit Reduction Act of 2005, major changes occurred in 2006 regarding Medicaid rules. These new rules still allow a spouse or disabled child to be the primary beneficiary on an immediate annuity that was once a variable annuity even if the annuity is owned by a Medicaid recipient who passes away. Annuitizing a variable annuity for Medicaid qualification should never be attempted without the guidance of a lawyer or other professional familiar with elder law.

§4005. CONCLUSION

Investors who own variable annuities are in a much better position to protect these assets from depletion due to nursing home costs. Mutual fund owners rarely, if ever, are able to put themselves in the same position as variable annuity owners when confronted with possible admission to a nursing home.

- CHAPTER 41 -
THE RIGHT OF RESCISSION

§4101. INTRODUCTION

Purchasers of variable annuities have the right to review their variable annuity contract when it is delivered and are given a period of time to make a final decision as to whether they want to accept the variable annuity or not. Mutual funds don't provide this advantage. Once a mutual fund is purchased the buyer is obligated to accept and pay for the fund.

§4102. THE RIGHT TO RESCIND A VARIABLE ANNUITY PURCHASE

Today, by state law, variable annuity issuers must provide a period of time after a variable annuity is issued for the buyer to revoke or cancel his purchase. The period of time allowed for such revocations ranges from ten to 30 days. The time frame involved does not begin until the variable annuity is actually *delivered* to the purchaser. If a timely revocation occurs, the purchaser is, in most cases, entitled to a full refund of his purchase price in the majority of states. The following example demonstrates how the right of revocation might save an investor from a possible loss.

> **Example**
> Dave and Sara both have $100,000 to invest. They both wanted to become involved in technology investments. On January 2, Dave purchased a variable annuity that invested in Internet stocks. On the same day Sara purchased a technology mutual fund that invested exclusively in Internet stocks. Three weeks later Dave's variable annuity was sent to his financial planner. On February 1, the planner delivered the annuity to Dave and told him he had 20 days to decide whether he wanted to keep the annuity. By February 19 the stock market had dropped 20%. Internet stocks were particularly hard hit and Dave's annuity was worth only $75,000. Sara's mutual fund was also worth $75,000. Dave revoked his annuity purchase and received a $100,000 refund check from the annuity issuer. Sara could not do the same thing and was stuck with her mutual fund loss.

§4103. CONCLUSION

The right of revocation is just another example of a benefit or safety feature of buying a variable annuity that is not offered by a mutual fund.

- CHAPTER 42 -
INVESTMENT SAFETY

§4201. INTRODUCTION

Variable annuity assets must be held in separate accounts and not held by the annuity issuer in their general account. This creates a layer of safety for variable annuity investors.

§4202. WHO HOLDS YOUR MONEY?

The safety of money held in variable annuities is usually greater than with other investments. Examples abound regarding investment losses arising from investing. A few of these are discussed below.

§4203. THE HEARTLAND MUNICIPAL BOND MUTUAL FUND DEBACLE

A prime example of the things that can go wrong with a mutual fund is the case of the Heartland Municipal Bond Fund. In a single day owners of this fund saw their supposedly conservative fund drop by 70% due to the improper accounting activities of the fund's managers. In the August 9, 2001 issue of *The Wall Street Journal* it was reported that the SEC had taken action against Heartland's managers but the likelihood that investors would fully recover their losses was remote. The SEC's action merely consisted of issuing a cease and desist order to Heartland. This same article stated that 25 similar cases have occurred since adoption of the federal statutes that regulate mutual funds.

§4204. SCHWAB BOND MUTUAL FUND COLLAPSE

One of Charles Schwab's bond funds that was touted as a safe alternative to cash dropped by 25% by April of 2008. There was no protection for the conservative investors who invested in this mutual fund.

§4205. MONEY MARKET MUTUAL FUND SUFFERS LOSS

The safest mutual fund one can own is a money market mutual fund. However, even they can expose investors to losses. Reserve Primary Fund reported in the fall of 2008 that it had lost money and froze redemptions.

§4206. VARIABLE ANNUITY SEPARATE ACCOUNTS

Money invested in variable annuities is, by law, not allowed to be held in the general account of the issuing variable annuity company. All investor funds *must* be held in separate trust accounts held by trustees not associated with the issuing variable annuity company. Because variable annuity investors have their money held by trustees in separate accounts not associated with the issuing variable annuity company, the insolvency of a variable annuity

193

company would have no impact on investors' account values. Several years ago, Conseco Insurance Company, a major variable annuity issuer filed bankruptcy. Although thousands of investors owned variable annuities issued by Conseco, none of them lost a cent because their variable annuities were held in separate accounts. Guarantees offered by variable annuity issuers may be impacted by insolvency. Investors should remember that it is the general claims-paying ability of a variable annuity company that backs up the various *guarantees* offered by variable annuity issuers. The financial strength of variable annuity companies should be an important consideration when selecting a variable annuity company offering any guarantee. As the next section points out, state guarantee funds may provide additional protection to variable annuity purchasers where guarantees are offered by the annuity issuer.

§4207. STATE GUARANTY FUNDS

Every state provides a financial mechanism that ensures that any guarantees made by a variable annuity issuer are honored. If a variable annuity company *guarantees* that their annuity will provide a stated protection or result (i.e. the investor will not lose principal, the variable annuity will grow at a certain rate, the death benefit will increase periodically, etc.)[2] state guaranty funds may be available to back these protections or other benefits. Typically, state guaranty funds protect each annuity owner for up to $300,000. State guaranty funds are not available and never provide protection to mutual fund owners who own their mutual funds outside of a variable annuity.

> **Example**
> Bill purchased a variable annuity for $200,000. The variable annuity company guaranteed that he would not lose his investment if he held his variable annuity for at least six years. After owning his variable annuity for six years, Bill decided to sell it. Just before he sold his variable annuity, the market went down sharply and his variable annuity was worth only $150,000. The variable annuity company then went out of business. The state guaranty fund would pay Bill the $50,000 loss he suffered. The remaining $150,000 is held in a separate account in Bill's name. In short, Bill will get the $200,000 he was promised from his variable annuity company. Had Bill owned a mutual fund, he would have suffered a loss because state guaranty funds do not protect mutual fund owners.

§4208. REQUIRED RESERVES

Insurance law in all states requires that variable annuity issuers set up reserve accounts with each state in which their variable annuities are sold. These reserve accounts must equal the

---

[2] State guaranty funds do not protect variable annuity owners from general stock market downturns unless the variable annuity guarantees that the variable annuity owner will be protected from such downturns.

194

withdrawal value of all variable annuities sold in a given state. In addition, surplus requirements and required minimum levels of capital imposed on variable annuity issuers add another level of protection for those who own variable annuities.

§4209. SECURITY INVESTORS PROTECTION CORPORATION (SIPC)

Brokerage firms and other institutions that sell mutual funds often carry private insurance through Security Investors Protection Corporation (SIPC) to protect mutual fund owners from losses. Many mutual investors have little understanding of how SIPC insurance works. The following example demonstrates one of the limitations of SIPC coverage.

Example
Linda, who is single, had been investing in mutual funds for several years. Her mutual fund currently was worth $500,000. Linda's brokerage firm carried $1,000,000 worth of SIPC coverage on every customer account. Linda, who was 57, wanted to reduce the risk she had in her current mutual fund portfolio. Her stockbroker told her of a fund that was less risky but historically provided a return very close to what Linda was used to receiving. Because of erratic movements in the stock market, Linda sold her mutual fund for $500,000 and held the cash proceeds in her brokerage account. She intended to buy the more conservative fund recommended by her broker when the stock market settled down. A few weeks later, Linda's stock brokerage firm filed for bankruptcy. Linda was not overly worried because of the million-dollar SIPC coverage she had on her $500,000 account. A short while later, Linda received a letter from SIPC explaining that cash accounts are only covered by SIPC for a maximum of $100,000. Linda lost $400,000 because she was not aware of the limitations of coverage provided by SIPC.

Mutual fund owners relying on SIPC coverage may be in for a surprise even where their losses are covered by SIPC insurance. SIPC has a poor track record of paying valid claims. In a recent issue of *Ticker* magazine, Mark Maddox, in an article he wrote, reports that of the 3,369 claims filed in 1997 when the brokerage firm of Stratton Oakmont collapsed, only nine of the claims had been paid as of October 1999.

Newspapers frequently report stories involving the improper activities of financial advisors who attempt to cheat the public. SIPC insurance does not protect the public against such fraud. For example, in 2002 a stockbroker working for Lehman Brothers in their Cleveland office defrauded clients out of tens of millions of dollars over a decade and a half. Although many clients lost everything they invested with the stockbroker, SIPC did not cover these losses.

To the author's knowledge, no one has ever lost a cent because of fraud involving variable annuities or as the result of a variable annuity company running into financial difficulties.

Because the funds of investors are held in separate accounts monitored by variable annuity companies, the possibility of losses arising from fraudulent activity is reduced to practically zero.

In non-variable annuity settings, many investors have lost money to fraudulent activities. The following are examples:

- Wesley Rhodes, a financial advisor who handled client funds, bilked many of his clients over a 15 year period. Some clients were forced into poverty and some retired clients had to go back to work. (See www.lifeafterrhodes. blogspot.com/). SIPC coverage was not available.

- The brokerage firm Stratton-Oakmont collapsed due to fraudulent stock activities. Many clients lost large amounts of money in the collapse. Although Stratton-Oakmont was successfully sued, clients have never been able to collect on their judgments. In addition, SIPC coverage was not available.

- A stockbroker for LPL Financial stole $5 million from 40 clients. SIPC insurance does not cover theft.

§4210. CONCLUSION

If an investor is concerned about losing his investment due to the insolvency of the issuing company or financial firm the investment is purchased from, such investors need to understand that variable annuities often offer more protection against such losses than do other investments.

- CHAPTER 43 -
THE DEATH BENEFIT

§4301. INTRODUCTION

A standard benefit offered by all variable annuities is the death benefit which guarantees the beneficiaries of a variable annuity that they will receive, at a minimum, the total net amount invested in a variable annuity by a deceased owner. Mutual funds do not offer this benefit.

§4302. THE BASIC DEATH BENEFIT

All annuity issuers provide a guaranteed minimum death benefit to beneficiaries when an annuity owner dies. Generally, this benefit pays beneficiaries the greater of contributions (less withdrawals) paid into the annuity or the annuity value at date of death. For example, if an annuity owner contributes $85,000 to his annuity and it's worth $70,000 at his death, his beneficiaries will receive $85,000. If the annuity were worth $100,000 at death, then the beneficiaries would receive $100,000.

§4303. THE RATCHET EFFECT

Not only do variable annuities provide a death benefit to beneficiaries when the owner of the annuity dies, but in many cases this benefit ratchets up every few years. Assume Mark purchases $200,000 in mutual funds and Martha buys a variable annuity for $200,000. A few years later the mutual funds and annuity are worth $300,000. At that point Martha's guaranteed minimum death benefit ratchets up or is increased to $300,000. Later the market falls, causing the mutual funds and annuity to be worth $200,000 each. If Mark and Martha were to die, Mark's beneficiaries would receive $200,000 but Martha's beneficiaries would receive $300,000.

§4304. EXCHANGING ANNUITIES CAN INCREASE THE DEATH BENEFITS

Each time one variable annuity is exchanged for another, the death benefit is raised to the value of the new annuity. Such exchanges should only take place after considering any surrender penalties that might apply. The following example demonstrates how death benefits can be increased by using IRC §1035 (See Chapter 35) to make tax-free exchanges of variable annuities.

> **Example**
> Judy purchased two variable annuities eight years ago for $250,000 each. One variable annuity was with the ABC Company and one was with the XYZ Company. Today, each annuity is worth $800,000. The annuities do not contain language that increases or ratchets up the basic $250,000 death benefit over time. Judy's death benefit on each annuity offers little protection to her beneficiaries because the market value of each of her annuities would have to drop $550,000 in value before Judy's death to reach her $250,000 death benefit level. Judy

decided to exchange her ABC variable annuity for an XYZ variable annuity and vice versa. After making the tax-free exchange Judy is in the *identical* investment position she was before the exchange except both of her annuities now have minimum death benefits of $800,000. Judy would want to make sure she planned on holding her exchanged annuities long enough to avoid any new surrender penalties.

§4305. INCREASING DEATH BENEFITS

Many variable annuities today allow the purchaser to pay a small annual fee to guarantee that the death benefit provided by the annuity will increase at a set rate. For example, Beth could purchase a variable annuity that would increase her death benefit by 7% a year. If the stock market does better than 7%, the higher market rate of return would be used for the annual increase.[1] If she bought an annuity for $205,000 and died ten years later, Beth would provide her beneficiaries with a minimum death benefit of $403,266 even if her variable annuity had an investment value of less than this. If her investment value exceeded $403,266, her beneficiaries would receive this larger amount.

§4306. INVESTING THE DEATH BENEFIT

The death benefit provided by a variable annuity not only protects beneficiaries, but provides a significant benefit when invested by beneficiaries. The following examples demonstrate this.

Example

Andy purchased a growth mutual fund for $300,000. A few years later it had dropped in value to $150,000. Shortly thereafter, Andy died. His daughter inherited the mutual fund. She sold the fund for $150,000 and purchased an S&P 500 index mutual fund. The fund went up three-fold in ten years to $450,000. Andy's daughter then sold the index fund. The gain of $300,000 was taxed at 15% leaving her with $405,000.

Example

Tara purchased a variable annuity for $300,000. A few years later it had dropped in value to $150,000. Shortly thereafter, Tara died. Her son inherited the variable annuity at its original cost of $300,000 due to the death benefit. Tara's son sold the variable annuity for $300,000. Tara's son reinvested the $300,000 in an S&P 500 index fund offered by another variable annuity company. The index fund went up in value by three-fold over ten years to $900,000. Tara's son decided to sell his variable annuity. He had to pay taxes on the gain of $600,000 at 35% leaving him with $690,000.[2] This is, on an after-tax basis, $285,000 more than

---

[1] Variable annuity companies refer to this benefit as The Guaranteed Minimum Ratcheting Death Benefit, or GMRDB.
[2] $600,000 x 35% tax = $390,000 after tax + $300,000 principal = $690,000.

Andy's daughter received in the last example on identical facts where mutual funds were involved.

§4307. PENDING DEATH AND VARIABLE ANNUITIES

The death benefit provided by variable annuities can be of critical importance where one's life expectancy may be reduced by disease or illness. The following example demonstrates this important benefit:

Example

John is a conservative investor. He has $500,000 in bank CDs. The money is earmarked for retirement. He has a 40-year-old wife and twins in college. John has just learned he has a form of cancer that has reduced his life expectancy to five years. John would be well advised to purchase a variable annuity for four reasons:

- Knowing that he cannot leave his wife and children with less than a $500,000 death benefit, John can be more aggressive with his investment choices.

- If the variable annuity, for example, doubles in value, John's wife will have $1,000,000. If the variable annuity goes down in value, John's wife will still have $500,000 as a death benefit when John dies. Mutual funds don't provide this benefit.

- John can purchase an increasing death benefit that could provide his family with a minimum death benefit well in excess of $500,000.

- Many variable annuities offer a death benefit that increases by a set amount each year. For example, a death benefit that increases at 5% a year would provide John's wife with an account value of $638,141 in five years even if the variable annuity's account value goes down.

Purchasing a variable annuity to obtain its death benefit is possible without taking a physical exam or answering health questions that traditional life insurance companies require. Additionally, such insurance is available to people as old as 80.

§4308. EARNINGS ENHANCEMENT BENEFIT

The earning enhancement benefit, commonly called an EEB, is essentially an increasing death benefit. It was discussed in §2508.

§4309. CONCLUSION

Investors need to understand that one of the major benefits of variable annuities is the death benefit they provide in those cases where the owner dies. Mutual funds do not have a similar benefit.

- CHAPTER 44 -

AUTOMATIC DOLLAR-COST AVERAGING
AND ASSET ALLOCATION/REBALANCING

§4401. INTRODUCTION

Automatic dollar-cost averaging and portfolio rebalancing are useful tools that variable annuity owners can benefit by much more than mutual fund owners.

§4402. DOLLAR-COST AVERAGING

Many variable annuities allow purchasers to use dollar-cost averaging to purchase their variable annuities. This procedure allows investors to purchase variable annuities over time rather than in a lump sum. By doing so, an investor buys fewer shares when the stock market is moving up and more shares when the market is moving down. Money awaiting investment into a variable annuity by way of automatic dollar-cost averaging earns above market rates of return. Although dollar-cost averaging can be accomplished with mutual funds, these funds do not offer above average market rates of interest on money awaiting dollar-cost averaging. [It must be remembered that dollar-cost averaging will not guarantee profits and may result in a loss in a declining stock market.] The following example generally demonstrates how dollar-cost averaging works where a single stock is involved:

> **Example**
> Dave and Donna both invested $8,000 in Federated Electric (FEC) stock. Eight months ago, Dave purchased 80 shares of FEC at $100 a share for a total investment $8,000.[1] Today, his investment is worth $8,000 because FEC is currently selling for $100 per share. Eight months ago, Donna started buying FEC at $100 a share by making $1,000 investments in FEC over this eight months. In short, she was using dollar-cost averaging. As the chart below shows, Donna had a gain of 37.9% by using dollar-cost averaging. Over the same eight-month period, Dave broke even.

---

[1] Commissions and other costs are ignored for this example.

Price	Cost per share	#of shares bought with $1000	Total shares owned	Total amount invested	Current value of shares (2) x (4)	% Net gain or loss (6) - (5)
(1)	(2)	(3)	(4.0)	(5)	(6)	(7)
1	$100	10.0	10.0	$1,000	$1000	0
2	80	12.5	22.5	2,000	1,800	-10.0
3	70	14.3	36.8	3,000	2,576	-14.1
4	60	16.7	53.5	4,000	3,210	-19.7
5	50	20.0	73.5	5,000	3,675	-26.5
6	70	14.3	87.8	6,000	6,146	+2.4
7	80	12.5	100.3	7,000	8,024	+14.6
8	100	10.0	110.3	8,000	11,030	+37.9

The following example demonstrates dollar-cost averaging with mutual funds and variable annuities.

Example:

Bill had $120,000 to invest. He selected a variable annuity that would allow him to move his money into the annuity over a 12-month period by using dollar-cost averaging. Bill chose the XYZ Electronics Fund for his variable annuity investment. Money pending investment would earn 8%. The following table reflects Bill's investment over the 12-month period:

Month	Amount invested[2]	Price	Shares bought
1	$10,000	20	500
2	$10,067	18	559
3	$10,133	17	596
4	$10,200	15	680
5	$10,267	13	790
6	$10,333	15	689
7	$10,400	16	650
8	$10,467	17	616
9	$10,533	18	585
10	$10,600	19	558
11	$10,667	20	533
12	$10,733	20	537
			7293

In the 12th month, Bill has 7,293 shares of XYZ Electronics Fund. At $20 per share, Bill's investment is worth $145,860, which is a 21.55% annual increase in value. Had Bill done the same thing with a mutual fund it is unlikely that he could have received a *guaranteed* 8% return on money awaiting investment.

---

[2] Reflects an 8% increase while funds are awaiting investment. 8% is used for illustrative purposes. In 2008 these rates are usually in the 4% to 5% range. However, mutual funds are currently paying less than 2% on money market funds.

Because mutual funds don't provide automatic dollar-cost-averaging with a guaranteed interest rate on money awaiting investment, many mutual fund purchasers buy their funds in a lump sum rather than by using dollar-cost averaging. Had Bill invested his $120,000 in XYZ Electronics via a lump sum mutual fund investment, he would have purchased 6,000 shares of XYZ at $20 per share. Twelve months later his investment would still be worth $120,000. This election would have caused Bill to underperform an equivalent variable annuity investment by more than 21%!

§4403. AUTOMATIC PORTFOLIO REBALANCING

In addition to providing investors with automatic dollar-cost averaging, variable annuities also provide investors with automatic portfolio rebalancing. Because of increased taxes and other transaction costs, constant portfolio rebalancing of mutual funds may be cost-prohibitive. The following example demonstrates how automatic asset allocation/rebalancing works:

Example #1
Larry purchased a variable annuity three years ago and invested equal amounts in the following three funds:

- Apex Large Cap Fund
- Blue Chip Mid Cap Fund
- Capital Internet Fund

Larry's variable annuity automatically (and without cost) rebalances his investment every three months so they remain equal in value. As Internet's stock rose in value, rebalancing would move money from Larry's Internet holding to his Large and Mid Cap holdings. When stocks dropped dramatically in the 2008 bear market, Larry was not hurt as much as his sister Fran who owned mutual funds. Fran's situation is set out in the next example.

Example #2
Fran purchased, in equal amounts, three mutual funds in the Apex Family of Funds three years ago. The funds she chose were:

- Apex Large Cap Fund
- Blue Chip Mid Cap Fund
- Capital Internet Fund

By 2007, 80% of the value of her mutual funds were in Capital Gogo Fund due to the run up in growth stocks through 2007. When the 2008 bear market occurred, Fran lost half of the value of her mutual fund and lost much more than her brother Larry who, as the last example pointed out, had taken advantage of automatic portfolio rebalancing through his variable annuity.

§4404. THE 2000 PRICEWATERHOUSECOOPERS STUDY

In October of 2000, PricewaterhouseCoopers, LLP, one of the largest accounting firms in the world, conducted a study comparing variable annuities and mutual funds and how dollar-cost averaging and automatic portfolio asset allocation/rebalancing affected the long-term returns on their investments. The accounting firm had previously determined that long-term investing with variable annuities provided better results than similar investing with mutual funds. By factoring in dollar-cost averaging and asset allocation/rebalancing, the gains provided by variable annuities were increased even more.

§4405. CONCLUSION

The advantages of dollar-cost averaging and automatic portfolio rebalancing are helpful investing tools. They can be used with variable annuities without any additional cost. This is not true where mutual funds are concerned.

- CHAPTER 45 -
LIVING BENEFITS

§4501. INTRODUCTION

Variable annuities, in addition to their death benefit that protects beneficiaries, offer benefits to the owners of variable annuities. Such benefits are referred to as living benefits.

§4502. LIVING BENEFITS

Today many variable annuity issuers provide living benefits to purchasers of their variable annuities. A living benefit is different than a death benefit. For decades, variable annuity issuers have provided death benefits to protect beneficiaries. The great majority of variable annuities sold today guarantee that if the owner dies his beneficiaries will receive at least what the decedent invested in his annuity even if the market value is less than this. For example, if Sara invests $100,000 in a variable annuity and dies a few years later when her annuity is worth $80,000, her beneficiaries will receive $100,000 rather than the lower market value. Variable annuity issuers, in an effort to make annuities even more attractive as investments, have begun to provide benefits to the annuity owner if he *lives*. Thus the term living benefits.

§4503. THE MAJOR LIVING BENEFITS

An example of a few of the major living benefits currently provided by many variable annuity issuers today include:

- Guaranteed minimum income benefit (GMIB)
- Guaranteed minimum accumulation benefit (GMAB)
- Guaranteed minimum withdrawal benefit - term certain (GMWB - Term Certain)
- Guaranteed minimum withdrawal benefit - for life (GMWB - For Life)

The list of living benefits will continue to grow in the future. Generally, living benefits are not free. However, the small cost associated with them can make these benefits attractive to variable annuity purchasers. The material that follows briefly discusses the living benefits set out in the above list.

§4504. GUARANTEED MINIMUM INCOME BENEFIT (GMIB)

Many variable annuity companies will guarantee a stated minimum return on a variable annuity if it is held for a certain period that is usually around ten years. This rider or benefit carries an annual cost of 40 to 75 basis points.

Example

Betty, a 55-year-old widow, wants to retire in ten years. She has a bank account containing $300,000. Because Betty is a conservative investor, her money is invested in CDs. In order for Betty to have the retirement income she needs when she retires, she estimates she will need for her $300,000 to grow to a minimum of $600,000 in the next ten years to generate the $30,000 annual income she will need. Betty has talked with two financial experts about how she should invest her money to reach her retirement goal. The results of her two consultations were:

Consultation #1:

The first financial expert was a fee-only planner who suggested that Betty invest her $300,000 in mutual funds and become a more aggressive investor. When Betty questioned the planner, she determined the following:

- The total annual cost of owning the fund would be 5.2% (20% annual income tax loss on net gains; 2.2% annual fee and trading costs; 1% commission);

- Betty could lose money if the mutual funds went down in value; and

- Betty had no assurances that this mutual fund account would ever go up in value much less double in value in the next ten years.

Consultation #2:

The second financial professional Betty saw was a financial planner who suggested Betty place her $300,000 in a variable annuity. The annuity provided the following benefits:

- The annuity company would add a $15,000 bonus to Betty's $300,000 premium (see §4508 and §4509).

- If the variable annuity were held for ten years, Betty was guaranteed at a minimum her account would double to $630,000 (2 x $315,000). This $630,000 benefit base would be available in the form of an immediate retirement annuity that would provide Betty with retirement withdrawals of more than $30,000 a year for life.

- If the investments Betty made in the annuity exceeded the guaranteed minimum doubling (i.e., $630,000) over the next ten years, she would be free to annuitize the larger amount or take the total account value in cash and do with it as she pleased.

- If Betty held the variable annuity for ten years, she would be guaranteed that her benefit base could not go down in value (at a minimum, it would double).

- The cost of owning such an annuity was only slightly more than the cost of owning the mutual funds that were recommended to her by her fee-only planner.

Based on the above facts, Betty chose the variable annuity that offered living benefits because it provided her with what she needed to guarantee a secure retirement.

§4505. GUARANTEED MINIMUM ACCUMULATION BENEFIT (GMAB)

Many variable annuity companies now offer products that protect the purchaser against the risk of a falling stock market by providing a money back guarantee for investors. Generally, a small fee is charged for this living benefit. Additionally, the purchaser must agree to hold the variable annuity for a period of time ranging from five to ten years.

Example

Dave is 65 years old and has $250,000 to invest for five years. He initially considered a portfolio of stocks and mutual funds but realized that the last time he made a similar decision in 2008 he lost 30% of his investment. Dave has elected to purchase a variable annuity with a rider that guarantees a full refund of his $250,000 in five years if the market should go down again. If the stock market were to double in the next five years, Dave's investment would be worth $500,000 less his normal cost of investing.

§4506. GUARANTEED MINIMUM WITHDRAWAL BENEFIT FOR A PERIOD CERTAIN (GMWB - PERIOD CERTAIN)

Several annuity issuers will guarantee a 100% return of principal to annuity investors. The most common way this guarantee is offered is by allowing investors to withdraw a percentage of their investment (usually 5% to 7%) over a period of time. No matter what the stock market does, the investor is guaranteed to receive 100% of his investment back over time. If the stock market goes up, the investor is entitled to that gain less normal investment costs. The investor is not subject to market loss.

Example:

Mary, who is 60 years old and retired, has $500,000. At age 70, Mary will receive a very large payment from a trust fund. Mary needs to supplement her current retirement income by $50,000 a year for the next ten years. She contacted a brokerage firm to see if they had any stocks or mutual funds that would *guarantee* that she could receive a $50,000 annual stream of principal and income from her $500,000 for ten years. The stockbroker Mary talked to correctly informed her that no such guarantee existed with stocks or mutual funds. Mary later talked with a financial professional who specialized in variable annuity investing. He informed Mary that there were several variable annuity companies that would accept her $500,000 investment and *guarantee* $50,000 annual payments to her for ten years regardless of what the stock market did in the future. If the market were to go down, Mary would be guaranteed to receive her $50,000 annual payments for ten years. (These payments would be income tax free because they are a return of principal). If, on the other hand, the stock market went up in the future, Mary would not only recover her full $500,000 investment in ten annual installments of $50,000, but would be entitled to any gain above her $500,000 investment less the normal cost of investing.

§4507. GUARANTEED MINIMUM WITHDRAWAL BENEFIT FOR LIFE (GMWB FOR LIFE)

The GMWB - For Life is similar to the GMWB - Period Certain, except that the withdrawal amount is guaranteed for *life* plus a period certain (usually 20 years). The withdrawal amount is usually set at 5% to 7% of the initial investment and, as mentioned, is usually guaranteed for life plus a set number of years. The 5% to 7% payout ratchets up (but not down) as the stock market fluctuates.

Example:

Jan is a 63 year old widow with a $700,000 nest egg. Social Security and her husband's pension provide $40,000 in income but Jan needs $75,000 in additional annual income. She elected to buy a variable annuity with a lifetime Guaranteed Minimum Withdrawal Benefit rider (GMWB - For Life). The annuity provides the following for Jan:

- A guaranteed annual withdrawal of $35,000 for her lifetime guaranteed for a set number of years

- The annual withdrawal can increase (but never decrease) with the upward movement of the stock market

- Jan is free at anytime to take her account value

- The variable annuity provides a death benefit to protect Jan's beneficiaries

- If withdrawals are postponed by Jan, the withdrawal amount increases for every year of delay.

- Jan never has to annuitize her variable annuity

- Jan will receive a $35,000 bonus that will be added to her account (see §4508 and §4509).

§4508. PREMIUM BONUS

Many variable annuity issuers pay those who purchase their living benefit annuities a bonus from 3% to 5% on premiums paid for the annuity. The tax deferral of a guaranteed 5% bonus makes annuities with this feature very attractive to people who traditionally have their money in CDs, money market accounts, etc. Mutual funds do not offer similar bonuses. Most variable annuity companies impose a small charge to provide such bonuses. Some variable annuity companies make no charges for such bonuses but require, for example, that the annuity owner will be subject to a nine-year surrender charge rather than a seven-year surrender charge.

208

The following examples discuss this feature: (see §5405 *infra* also).

Example #1
Tim purchased a mutual fund for $30,000 15 years ago. Like all mutual funds, Tim's fund did not offer any bonus at the time of purchase. His fund grew at 10% a year. His costs were typical for a mutual fund (see §709). Tim's mutual fund is currently worth $68,884 after annual taxes and expenses.[3]

Example #2
Phil invested $30,000 in a variable annuity 15 years ago. It paid no premium bonus. The variable annuity returned 10% and had normal ownership costs (see §709). Phil's variable annuity is now worth $83,120.[4] Assuming the growth of $53,120 is taxed at an average rate of 25%, Phil's variable annuity, on an after-tax, after-cost basis would be worth $69,840.[5]

Example #3
Paula invested $30,000 for 15 years in a variable annuity that paid a 5% premium bonus. The variable annuity returned 10% and had normal ownership costs (see §709). To receive the 5% Paula had to agree to a surrender penalty period of nine years rather than seven. Today, Paula's annuity is worth $87,276.[6] If the annuity's growth of $57,276 is taxed at an average 25%, Paula's annuity, after taxes and costs, would be worth $74,457. This is $4,617 more than Phil got in Example #2 and $5,573 more than Tim got in Example #1.

§4509. THE COST OF THE PREMIUM BONUS

Premium bonuses offered by variable annuity issuers can, in many cases, provide variable annuity owners with the opportunity to greatly increase the value of their variable annuity over time. Premium bonuses should only be added to a variable annuity if the cost associated with such an election is reasonable. Where the only cost involved in obtaining a premium bonus is the requirement that the annuity be held for a longer surrender period (e.g. nine years versus seven years), then electing the premium bonus almost always makes sense for long-term investors. A monetary charge to obtain a premium bonus should be reviewed more carefully. Such bonuses should be viewed as loans and evaluated as such. A fee of 1% over a five-year period or more might not justify adding a premium bonus to a variable annuity.

§4510. CONCLUSION

The list of living benefits provided by variable annuity companies grows each year. In many cases investors can customize a variable annuity so that it provides the exact benefits an

---

[3] $28,500 x 6.06% x 15 years = $68,884. Taxes on unrealized gains are ignored.

[4] $30,000 x 7.03% x 15 years = $83,120.

[5] $53,120 x .75 = $39,840 + $30,000 = $69,840.

[6] $31,500 x 7.03% x 15 years = $87,276.

[7] $57,276 x .75 = $42,957 + $30,000 + $1,500 = $74,457.

investor would like to have. Mutual funds do not offer living benefits.

- CHAPTER 46 -

PREVENTING POTENTIAL LIFE INSURANCE LOSSES

§4601. INTRODUCTION

Variable annuities can be used to prevent losses where one needs to surrender a life insurance policy. Mutual funds cannot provide this same benefit.

§4602. LIFE INSURANCE LOSSES

When a life insurance policy is surrendered for its cash value and this cash value is less than the total premiums paid, the policy owner will have a loss. Losses on life insurance policies are deemed personal losses by the IRS and are not deductible on a policy owner's income tax return.

> **Example**
>
> As part of a business venture Bob entered into four years ago, he had to purchase a $1,000,000 whole life insurance policy on his life. Over this four-year period, his net premiums were $12,500 a year, for a total premium outlay of $50,000. Recently, Bob left this business venture and had no need for his insurance policy. He did not want to continue paying annual premiums of $12,500. He elected to surrender the policy for its cash value of $25,000. The difference between Bob's $50,000 total premium outlay and the $25,000 cash value he received upon surrender represents a non-deductible $25,000 loss.

§4603. LOSS PREVENTION BY USING VARIABLE ANNUITIES

Variable annuities can be used to prevent life insurance losses such as the one mentioned in the previous example. Section 1035 of the Internal Revenue Code allows a life insurance policy owner to exchange a life insurance policy for a variable annuity. Such §1035 exchanges are allowed on a *tax-free* basis. Additionally, the cost basis of the insurance policy becomes the cost basis of the newly acquired variable annuity as does the account value. An IRC §1035 transfer can help prevent a life insurance owner from suffering a loss.

> **Example**
>
> In the previous example, had Bob used IRC §1035 to transfer his insurance policy to a variable annuity, he would have owned his newly acquired variable annuity with a cost basis of $50,000 although its current account value would only be $25,000. Assuming Bob held his variable annuity for a while and it doubled in value to $50,000, Bob could liquidate the variable annuity and take the $25,000 gain he made income tax-free because his $50,000 liquidation value would equal his cost basis. If under age $59^1/_2$, there would be no 10% IRS penalty because there is no *gain* on which to base the 10% penalty.[1] If the annuity did not move

---

[1] If the variable annuity were sold for less than $50,000, it could generate a tax-deductible loss. See Chapter 28.

up from its $25,000 value and Bob elected, at a later time, to sell the annuity, and it reflected a loss, he would have a tax loss that would be immediately deductible against his ordinary income (see Chapter 28 above).

§4604. CONCLUSION

Financial professionals need to be aware of all of the many attributes of variable annuities in order to assist clients with potential financial problems.

- CHAPTER 47 -
DETAILED STUDIES

§4701. INTRODUCTION

Many detailed studies have been conducted by major accounting firms, researchers and universities on the issue of whether variable annuities or mutual funds are a better long-term investment. These studies show that the variable annuity is the better choice for long-term investors.

§4702. ACADEMIC STUDIES

Over the years many detailed studies have been conducted comparing variable annuities and mutual funds as long-term investments. These studies uniformly hold that long-term investors are better off putting their money in variable annuities rather than mutual funds.

A sample of these studies include the following:

- The Carty-Skinner study reported in *Financial Planning Magazine* in November 1996 demonstrated that investing in variable annuities rather than mutual funds would increase net returns to long-term investors.

- A Conning Study done in 1998 concluded in part that "...in nearly every case the variable annuity ultimately outperforms the mutual fund, and the annuity's advantage over mutual funds has much greater upside potential than downside risk."

- A 1997 study by PricewaterhouseCoopers, LLP concluded that where mutual funds and variable annuities were compared as long-term investments, variable annuities were the more attractive investment choice.

- In 1999, a PricewaterhouseCoopers, LLP report concluded that: "[Long-term investors] ...generally receive higher after-tax payouts [from] variable annuity investments, [when compared] to similar investments in mutual funds..."

- In 2000, PricewaterhouseCoopers, LLP found that the long-term advantage variable annuity investors had over long-term mutual fund investors widened when dollar-cost averaging and asset allocation/ rebalancing were applied to these long-term investment vehicles.

- PricewaterhouseCoopers, LLP conducted a study in 2002 that showed that an investment in variable annuities would produce an after-tax stream of income that would be significantly larger than could be received from a similar investment in mutual funds.

§4703. CONCLUSION

Long-term investors need to review some of the studies that have been conducted where mutual funds and variable annuities were compared. These studies clearly show that long-term investors are better off investing in variable annuities than mutual funds.

- CHAPTER 48 -

MAKING TAX-FREE WITHDRAWALS FROM A VARIABLE ANNUITY TO FUND A RETIREMENT DREAM

§4801. INTRODUCTION

Hopefully, earlier chapters demonstrated that variable annuities are better long-term wealth accumulation vehicles than mutual funds. Wealth creation, although highly desirable, should never be an end in itself. Wealth creation should be used to fund a specific dream such as early retirement, traveling, a new home after retirement, etc. To accumulate wealth and not enjoy it is a sad, but commonplace occurrence. Variable annuities are the premier wealth accumulation vehicle for those who want to make their retirement as fulfilling as possible.

§4802. HOW TO MAKE YOUR RETIREMENT GOALS COME TRUE – COMPLIMENTS OF THE IRS

As investors approach retirement, they begin to think more seriously about how and where they want to live in retirement as well as what they want to do during this exciting period in their lives. Investors who have planned and saved for their retirement by funding variable annuities have an unequaled opportunity to exchange their variable annuities tax-free for their retirement dream. The amazing thing about exchanging a variable annuity for a retirement dream is that such exchanges can frequently be structured so that *no income taxes are paid* on the variable annuity withdrawals used to purchase the retirement dream!

§4803. A NEW HOME AFTER RETIRING

This chapter will limit its discussion and examples to a retired couple who want to exchange withdrawals from their variable annuity for a new home after they retire. It is important to understand that exchanging variable annuity withdrawals for a new home without having to pay income taxes on the variable annuity withdrawals can be used just as effectively to meet retirement dreams other than buying a new home. For example, the process discussed in this chapter may be used to make a tax-free exchange of money held in a variable annuity to purchase a vacation home, a yacht, recreational vehicle, etc. IRC §72 can be used where a variable annuity owner is under $59^1/_2$ to avoid any early withdrawal penalty.

§4804. THE PROCESS OF EXCHANGING A VARIABLE ANNUITY TAX-FREE FOR A DREAM HOME IN RETIREMENT

The process of exchanging a variable annuity tax-free for a dream home in retirement is quite simple. An investor need only coordinate withdrawals from his variable annuity so they exactly match any interest charged to purchase their new home. The interest deduction will exactly offset the variable annuity withdrawal resulting in an income-tax neutral transaction.

Example

Dave has funded a variable annuity for several years. It is held in an SEP retirement account. He and his wife are both 60 and want to purchase a new $800,000 home on a golf course in an upscale retirement community in Florida. They recently sold their current home for $500,000. Under current income tax law, these proceeds were untaxed. The $500,000 was invested in long-term municipal bonds yielding 4.812%. Dave's annuity contains $350,000.[1] Dave talked with his variable annuity company and learned that he could expect, without having to annuitize, to make withdrawals of $48,000 a year for ten years if his variable annuity earned a 6.2% annual return. These withdrawals would be considered income. Dave had a bank that would loan him and his wife $800,000 for the new home they wanted to buy in Florida. The loan was set up so it would require interest only payments in the amount of $48,000 a year at a 6% interest rate.[2] If Dave and his wife buy the house and pay interest payments with annuity withdrawals of $48,000, the withdrawals will be exactly offset by the $48,000 in tax-deductible interest charged by the bank.[3] This will result in the annuity withdrawals escaping taxation. Ten years from now, assuming that the new home increases in value to $1.3 million, Dave and Ellen will:

- Have a new home in Florida worth $1.3 million.

- This new home could be sold tax-free for $1.3 million if Dave and his wife elected to do so.[4]

- The home can be passed to beneficiaries with a stepped-up basis thus avoiding any income taxes on the gain in value.

- The $500,000 in proceeds from the sale of their prior home (which were invested in municipal bonds at 4.812%) would now be worth $800,000[5] and could be used at any time to pay the $800,000 loan balance owed on their Florida home.[6]

- Dave and his wife would have lived in their dream home for ten years (with many years of enjoyment left).

- Dave will have withdrawn $480,000 in income from his variable annuity over ten years without ever paying income taxes on these withdrawals. It is important to remember that Dave accumulated this $480,000 on a tax-deferred basis.

---

[1] The $350,000 variable annuity was the result of Dave investing $9,500 a year in his SEP for nearly seventeen years and obtaining an average 9% net rate of return.

[2] Any type of mortgage will work.

[3] An informal assignment of these withdrawals can be made directly to the bank to simplify payments.

[4] $800,000 is cost and $500,000 is a tax-free capital gain.

[5] $500,000 x ten years x 4.81224% = $800,000

[6] The loan should not be repaid until the variable annuity reaches a value of zero.

§4805. MUTUAL FUNDS AND THE EXCHANGE PROCEDURE

The exchange procedure discussed above cannot be used with mutual funds effectively because mutual funds are taxed annually and, by the time of an owner's retirement, most of the taxes on a mutual fund portfolio have already been paid and the mutual fund value will be significantly less than the variable annuity value. Because the exchange procedure does not work well with mutual funds, many investors fund the purchase of retirement homes and other retirement goals in more traditional ways that rarely provide the advantages of the tax-free exchange procedure discussed above.

§4806. FINE TUNING

The tax-free exchange procedure discussed in this chapter has many variations. Financial professionals should discuss these variations with a tax professional. For example, with non-qualified variable annuities, annuitization might be used to obtain fixed payments of which a portion could be recovered as tax-free income by application of the exclusion ratio. The remaining taxable portion could be used to buy a vacation home, etc. to eliminate income taxes. The assistance of a tax advisor would be helpful in determining which variation of the tax-free exchange process discussed in this chapter would be most advantageous to the client.

§4807. CONCLUSION

A major advantage of variable annuity ownership is that such annuities grow on an income tax-deferred basis. In the future, withdrawals can be made from variable annuities to purchase retirement homes, yachts, etc. in such a way that the variable annuity withdrawals are not ever subject to income taxes. Mutual funds cannot provide this advantage.

- CHAPTER 49 -

FIXED COSTS VS. INCREASING COSTS

§4901. INTRODUCTION

When a variable annuity is purchased, the variable annuity company is contractually obligated to set contract expenses for the variable annuity and then *guarantee* that these expenses will never increase as long as the variable annuity is held even if it is later annuitized. Mutual funds are under no such obligation. Historically, mutual funds have constantly increased the annual cost of mutual fund ownership.

§4902. THE FIXED COSTS OF VARIABLE ANNUITY OWNERSHIP

When one purchases a variable annuity, the contract expenses for owning the variable annuity are set out in the prospectus. Once the variable annuity is purchased, these expenses cannot be changed. For example, a variable annuity purchased a few years ago with a mortality and expense charge of 1.7% will have the same 1.7% M&E cost of ownership today. These rates may be based on old payout figures where the life expectancy of a variable annuity owner was much shorter than it is today. Variable annuity companies are contractually bound not to increase these contract costs.

§4903. THE INCREASING ANNUAL COST OF MUTUAL FUND OWNERSHIP

Mutual funds, unlike variable annuities, are not obligated to hold expenses to a set amount. Mutual funds are free to increase their annual cost of ownership whenever they deem it necessary. Over the years, mutual funds have increased their annual costs of ownership constantly. Since 1980, the average annual mutual fund expense ratio has more than doubled.[1]

§4904. CONCLUSION

Investors need to understand that a mutual fund with a 1.5% annual expense ratio may not be a bargain if these costs increase to 2% in the future. Investors who buy variable annuities today know that their contract cost will remain fixed during the period of ownership and later if they elect to annuitize.

---

[1] *Better Investing*, p.28, June 2001.

- CHAPTER 50 -

THE VARIABLE ANNUITY'S FIXED INCOME BENEFIT

§5001. INTRODUCTION

Variable annuities allow conservative investors to obtain a guaranteed fixed rate of income on their investments. Mutual funds do not provide this benefit.

§5002. GUARANTEED FIXED RATE OF INCOME

Nearly all variable annuities sold today have one or more fixed income investments to choose from. When these investments are selected, the variable annuity owner is guaranteed the stated rate of interest for a set number of years. Mutual funds do not provide this same guarantee. Mutual funds offer money market and similar cash options which pay interest, but the interest rate is not guaranteed. The interest rates offered by mutual funds fluctuate frequently depending on what the market does. The following example demonstrates the advantage of obtaining fixed rates of interest with a variable annuity.

> **Example**
> Dora is 53 and wants to retire at age 60. She has $380,000 in savings, but realizes that she will need $500,000 by the time she retires. Dora did some reading and called a few financial professionals and found out that if she put her $380,000 in an investment that would provide a 4% return for seven years, she would be able to meet her $500,000 retirement goal. Dora decided to purchase a variable annuity with her money. The variable annuity Dora selected offered a 4% rate of return compounded for seven years on its fixed account. This would *guarantee* the $500,000 nest egg Dora would need for retirement. One stockbroker suggested Dora buy a mutual fund or consider a money market or bond fund. Dora declined because she knew the income paid on such funds was not *guaranteed*.

§5003. CONCLUSION

For investors needing a *guaranteed* rate of return for a long period, the variable annuity is a better investment vehicle than a mutual fund.

- CHAPTER 50B -

TEN GOOD REASONS TO CONSIDER VARIABLE ANNUITIES

§50B01. INTRODUCTION

For over thirty years I have taught law and finance courses at a major university in addition to being a partner in a law firm. As a finance professor and tax attorney, I am often asked by other professionals, as well as members of the general public, how I have invested for my retirement. My response, that most of my retirement funds are invested in variable annuities, often generates both curiosity and several questions.[1] The most common questions I receive deal with the reasons why I have invested in variable annuities over the years. Although there are many reasons why variable annuities make excellent long-term investments, there are basically ten reasons why I have chosen variable annuities as the financial foundation for my retirement. Each of these reasons is discussed in the sections that follow:

§50B02. COMMISSION-FREE INVESTING

The investing public has been led to believe that if they purchase a variable annuity, the commission that they will pay to buy the annuity will be significantly larger than if they chose to buy mutual funds or stocks. Over the years I have found just the opposite is true. When common stocks and standard mutual funds are purchased, the *investor* is required to pay an up-front, out-of-pocket commission to buy these products.[2] Whether these investments are held for one day or several years, the commissions paid are a foregone expense. Investing in the typical variable annuity does not require that an up-front, out-of-pocket commission be paid by the investor who purchases the annuity.[3] Variable annuity commissions earned by financial professionals who help their clients purchase these annuities are actually paid by the company that issues the annuity. The variable annuity issuer recoups these advanced commissions over time from the fees it charges the variable annuity owner each year.

The major advantage of not having to pay an up-front, out-of-pocket commission when buying a variable annuity is that all of an investor's money goes to work for him right away. An investment in mutual funds or stocks, because of their up-front, out-of-pocket commissions creates an immediate economic reduction in value which reduces the return earned on the mutual

---

[1] The majority of my liquid assets are invested in variable annuities.

[2] B-share mutual funds do not require the payment of up-front, out-of-pocket commissions. However, the annual cost of owning these funds is nearly 1% more than for A-share mutual funds.

[3] A-share variable annuities, which are exceptionally rare, do impose up-front, out-of-pocket commissions like A-share mutual funds.

funds or stocks purchased.[4] For example, a $25,000 investment that earns an average 8% rate of return for ten years will grow to $53,973.[5] However, that same investment, if reduced by a 5% up-front, out-of-pocket commission, will grow to only $51,274.[6] This $2,699 commission loss amounts to nearly 11% of the original $25,000 mutual fund investment.[7] The only time the typical variable annuity investor would pay any out-of-pocket commission would be if he failed to hold his variable annuity for the annuity's stated holding period which averages six to seven years.[8] These potential annuity commissions are technically called contingent deferred sales charges (CDSC) and are commonly referred to as surrender fees. For each year that a variable annuity investor holds his annuity, his potential liability for having to pay a surrender fee to the annuity company decreases and eventually disappears completely at the end of the agreed surrender or holding period. In short, what this means is that investors who purchase variable annuities and keep them for the agreed holding period can *completely avoid* having to pay commissions when they buy their variable annuities. This is not true for the purchaser of the typical mutual fund or stocks.

One of the analogies I use with my students to help them understand the difference between paying an up-front, out-of-pocket commission and having someone else pay this commission and ultimately have it disappear after a specified holding period is set out in the following example:

Example

Jack is getting ready to move three states away to go to work for one of two potential new employers. Employer A has told Jack that he will not pay any of Jack's moving expenses should he decide to work for Employer A. Employer B has agreed to pay the $24,000 commission that Jack will incur to sell his $400,000 house if Jack comes to work for Employer B. However, Employer B will require Jack to work for him for at least six years. Should Jack decide not to work for the full six years, the $24,000 real estate commission advanced by Employer B must be repaid to Employer B on a pro-rata basis. In this example, the real estate broker is going to receive the exact same commission whether Jack decides to go to work for Employer A or B. However, it should be obvious that Jack can save $24,000 by going to work for Employer B and remaining an employee for six years. Even if Jack decides to stay for less than six years, he will still be better off working for Employer B than Employer A.

---

[4] An investment of $10,000 growing at 10% a year will always grow to a larger amount than a $10,000 investment returning 10% if the second investment is subject to an up-front, out-of-pocket commission.

[5] $25,000 x 8% x 10 years = $53,973.

[6] $25,000 - 5% = $23,750 x 8% x 10 years = $51,274.

[7] $53,973 - $51,274 = $2,699. $2,699) $25,000 = 10.8%.

[8] A-share variable annuities, which are exceptionally rare, do impose up-front, out-of-pocket commissions like A-share mutual funds.

Today, investors can purchase variable annuities that have very short or no surrender periods at all.[9] Investors, who take the time to understand how the commission structure for variable annuities works, can enjoy commission-free investing for decades. Of all the variable annuities I have, I've never paid a commission to own any of them. The reason for this is that when I buy a variable annuity, I hold it for the surrender period I have selected which results in the elimination of all up-front, out-of-pocket commissions.

Many investors believe that because variable annuity companies advance commissions to the financial professionals who help investors buy their annuities, that these companies must increase the annual cost of owning their variable annuities to a level that is higher than the annual cost of owning mutual funds and stocks. I have found that this is rarely the case, as is pointed out in the next section.

§50B03. LOW ANNUAL COST OF OWNERSHIP

The investing public has been led to believe that variable annuities are more expensive to own on an annual basis than similar investments like mutual funds and stocks. The truth of the matter is usually just the opposite. The average variable annuity purchased today will have an annual ownership cost of approximately 2.35%.[10] This 2.35% figure includes the cost of the death benefit provided by the variable annuity, allows the variable annuity company to recoup the commissions they advance to the financial advisors who sell their variable annuities and enables the variable annuity issuer to compensate the professionals who manage the investments held in the variable annuity. As mentioned above, variable annuities do not impose up-front, out-of-pocket commissions on investors. In addition, because variable annuities grow tax-deferred, they do not generate an annual income tax liability to the owner as long as the variable annuity is held.

One reason for the confusion surrounding the annual cost of owning a mutual fund and a variable annuity is that the investing public has been conditioned to believe that the *only* annual cost of owning a mutual fund is the annual expense ratio (including 12b-1 fees) charged by mutual fund companies to compensate those who manage the investments held by the mutual fund. These costs, which average 1.4% to 1.6% a year, are only *one* of the three major annual costs of owning a mutual fund (The lower 1.4% figure is used in this article).[11] Few

---

[9] As a basic rule, the shorter a variable annuity's surrender period the higher the annual cost of owning the variable annuity.

[10] NAVA Outlook, Nov/Dec 2005, p. 6.

[11] Morningstar recently reported this figure to be 1.67%. See Investment News article "Fund Fee Baffle MBA Students" by David Hoffman, April 24, 2006. There are other costs incurred annually by mutual fund owners. One such cost is the fund's trading costs which can approach 1.0%. According to a study done by Lipper, the annual expense ratio of a mutual fund can be 70% more expensive than the same fund held inside a variable annuity.

members of the investing public take into consideration the other two major costs of owning the average stock mutual fund – annual income taxes and commissions. Mutual funds, unlike variable annuities, must distribute virtually all of their gains each year to their mutual fund owners.[12] These distributions force income on the owners of the mutual fund which results in an involuntary income tax that fund owners must pay each year to the IRS (state income taxes are an additional liability). It has been estimated that the annual gross return earned by the average stock mutual fund loses 20% of its gain to income taxes.[13] This is a loss of two full percentage points for a fund returning 10%. In addition to paying annual income taxes to the IRS, mutual fund owners must factor in to the total annual cost of owning their mutual funds the commissions they pay when they buy their funds. Researchers have determined that the average mutual fund commission is 4.1% and that the average holding period for the typical mutual fund is approximately three years.[14] This indicates that the average, annualized commission for owning a mutual fund is approximately 1.37%.[15] Although there are other costs of owning a mutual fund,[16] if only the three major costs discussed above are considered, the average stock mutual fund returning 10% can easily lose 4.8% of this gain each year just to commissions, income taxes, costs and money management fees including 12b-1 fees.[17] This is more than *twice* the 2.35% annual cost of owning a variable annuity. As a tax attorney I have helped many clients over the years complete their tax returns. Many times I find that mutual fund owners believe that they are only giving up 1.4% to 1.6% of their fund's gain each year as the cost of owning their funds, when in actuality, they are often giving up 5% or more. Several researchers have determined that the average equity mutual fund owner pays an annual cost of ownership of between 5% and 6% each year to own their funds when *all* the annual costs of owning a mutual fund are considered.[18]

---

[12] These distributions are reported to fund owners and the IRS on IRS Form 1099-DIV.

[13] A 2010 Lipper study demonstrated the reduction of a fund's net gain due to income taxes was approximately 20%. For example, on a 10% fund gain, 2% will go to the IRS. See also, "Magellan Investors Are Biting The Tax Bullet," by Jennifer Lovitz. *The Wall Street Journal*, May 10, 2006, p.1, section C.

[14] *The Great Mutual Fund Trap*, Gary Gensler (Former Undersecretary of the U.S. Treasury 1999-2001) and Gregory Baer (Former Assistant Secretary for Financial Institutions for the U.S. Treasury) Broadway Books, New York, 2002.

[15] 4.1% ÷ 3 = 1.37%.

[16] See Chapter 35 and §3305 above regarding trading costs.

[17] 1.4% annual expense ratio and 12b-1 fees + 1.37% annual commission and 2% tax loss = 4.8%.

[18] *Your Money, Your Choice...Mutual Funds - Take Control Now and Build Wealth Wisely*, Professor Charles Jones (North Carolina State University), Prentice Hall, 2003. *The Great Mutual Fund Trap*, Gary Gensler (Former Undersecretary of the U.S. Treasury 1999-2001) and Gregory Baer (Former Assistant Secretary for Financial Institutions for the U.S. Treasury) Broadway Books, New York, 2002. Vanguard's John Bogle determined that even a no-load mutual fund could cost 5.2% a year to own. "The Pros and Cons of Mutual Funds." www.windsorwealth.com/mfprosandcons. Another study by Kyle Alkins, CLU, ChFC in the January 2004 issue of the *Journal of Financial Service Professionals*, page 33, mirrored Bogle's results.

In many cases, the commission's incurred to own stocks and the income taxes paid on their gains is not much less than owning mutual funds. On average, individuals who own stocks buy and sell them over holding periods that are significantly less than the typical three-year holding period for a mutual fund. If one pays a 1.5% commission to buy $20,000 worth of stock and pays another 1.5% commission to sell the stock at $22,000 a year later, his total commissions and capital gains taxes will come to $930.[19] These costs will reduce a 10% annual stock gain by 4.65%.[20] I frequently review brokerage statements for tax clients and find that they are paying total commissions and income taxes that approach 5% a year. The total annual cost of many managed money accounts can also be in the range of 3% to 5%.

The difference between owning an investment that imposes a 2.35% total annual ownership cost and one that imposes a cost of nearly twice this figure can be dramatic. For example, a $25,000 mutual fund investment held for ten years will grow to $45,002 if it can earn a 10% rate of return but is subject to a typical 5% purchase commission, income taxes of 2% and annual ownership expenses of 1.4%.[21] On the other hand, a $25,000 investment made in a variable annuity will grow to $52,249 in ten years if it can earn a 10% rate of return less an annual ownership expense of 2.35%.[22] This is a difference of more than $7,200 over ten years.[23] Even after reducing the variable annuity's ending value for income taxes at a 20% rate upon liquidation (and ignoring liquidation taxes for the mutual fund), the variable annuity still nets nearly $1,800 more to the annuity investor over ten years.[24] The basic annual cost of the variable annuities I own averages 2.3%. This 2.3% annual cost provides me with:

- A death benefit to protect my family;
- Tax-deferred trading for as long as I hold my variable annuities;
- The ability to trade among the investments held in my variable annuities without having to pay new commissions;

---

[19] 12% of $20,000 = $300 + 12% of $22,000 = $330 + 15% of $2000 or $300 = $930.

[20] $930 ÷ $2,000 = 46.5%. 46.5% of 10% = 4.65%.

[21] Because the holding period is assumed to be ten years, the commission cost is reduced in this example from the 1.37% annualized rate to a rate closer to 0.50%. Mutual fund commissions for trading in the mutual fund after it is purchased are also ignored. $25,000 - 5% = $23,750 x 6.6% (10% - 3.4%) x 10 years = $45,002. This calculation reduces the commission from 1.37% to about 2% a year.

[22] $25,000 x 7.65% x 10 years = $52,249.

[23] $52,249 - $45,002 = $7,247.

[24] $52,249 - $25,000 = $27,249 - 20% = $21,799 + $25,000 = $46,799 - $45,002 = $1,797.

- Free professional advice and research relating to my variable annuities;[25] and

- The ability to exchange any variable annuity I own for another one without incurring income taxes or commissions.[26]

Neither stocks nor mutual funds provide all of these benefits.

§50B04. TAX-DEFERRED GROWTH

One of the major advantages provided to variable annuity investors is the fact that income taxes on all gains generated by a variable annuity are deferred until these gains are withdrawn.[27] Tax deferral allows all gains made in a variable annuity to compound and increase in value without having to share these gains with the IRS. For the typical mutual fund, this is not the case. Mutual fund companies are required to distribute their gains each year resulting in forced income for the fund's owners which in turn creates an income tax liability for them. Mutual funds are the only investment that can distribute taxable gains while losing value. In the 2000-2002 bear market and 2008 credit crisis, mutual fund owners saw the value of their mutual funds drop almost daily yet they still received distribution notices each year that required them to pay income taxes on their funds. If investors buy and hold stocks, they will not pay income taxes on their gains, except for dividend distributions. However, unlike variable annuities, when one stock is sold and replaced with another, income taxes must be paid on all gain generated by the transaction. The advantage of tax deferral should not be overlooked by investors. Considering *only* annual income taxes, a $25,000 investment made in a mutual fund that grows at 9% annually but loses two percentage points of this gain to income taxes each year, will grow to $68,976 in fifteen years.[28] The same investment made in a variable annuity, because it is tax-deferred, will grow to $91,062 over the same period of time.[29] Even after taxing the variable annuity's entire gain at one time at 20% (and *ignoring* any taxes due on the fund's sale), the variable annuity investment will have an after-tax value of $77,850 which is nearly $9,000 more than the mutual fund investment.[30] This calculation also ignores the exclusion ratio, which

---

[25] For as long as one owns a variable annuity, they are entitled to free research and data on the variable annuity and the assistance and advice of financial professionals who work for the variable annuity issuer.

[26] IRC §1035 allows a variable annuity owner to exchange one variable annuity for another without having to pay taxes on any realized gain. This same Internal Revenue Code provision also allows the variable annuity owner to avoid IRS penalties if the owner is not $59\frac{1}{2}$. §1035 is most effective when the annuity being exchanged is beyond its holding or surrender period. In such a case, any exchange would also avoid having to pay a surrender fee.

[27] Such withdrawals are usually made in retirement when the variable annuity owner is most likely in a lower income tax bracket.

[28] $25,000 x 7% (9% - 2%) x 15 years = $68,976.

[29] $25,000 x 9.0% x 15 years = $91,062.

[30] $91,062 - $25,000 = $66,062 - 20% = $52,850 + $25,000 = $77,850 - $68,976 = $8,874.

when used can greatly reduce the annual income tax liability on a stream of income generated by a variable annuity. The exclusion ratio is not available to mutual fund or stock investors.[31] Many of the variable annuities I own have grown on a tax-deferred basis for decades. The tax deferral provided by variable annuities offers other benefits. For example, bookkeeping is greatly simplified with tax-deferred investments. When the annuity is ultimately sold or used to generate income in the future, the withdrawals representing gain in the annuity will be subject to taxation. This tax liability is calculated by the variable annuity company issuing the annuity. With investments such as mutual funds, it is often necessary for the owner to keep detailed annual records relating to cost basis adjustments, etc. Because many people do not keep good records regarding their mutual funds, they will often pay more in income taxes on their funds than they would normally be required to. In addition, each year, due to mutual funds distributions, many individuals are required to complete and submit a Schedule D with their income tax returns. This schedule is complex and often results in individuals having to hire tax professionals to help them with this schedule. Many income tax clients retain me each year to help them with their income taxes solely because they cannot figure out how to complete Schedule D.

§50B05. COMMISSION FREE TRADING

Another major advantage of owning variable annuities is that once one is purchased, and for as long as it is owned, all trading among the variable annuity's investment selections may be accomplished, not only on a tax-deferred basis, but without having to pay any commissions.[32] This is true even if such trading involves moving from one fund family to a different one. This benefit is not available with either mutual funds or stocks. For example, a variable annuity investor who owns an annuity purchased for $50,000 that has doubled in value can move his entire $100,000 investment from one investment management company's sub-account to an entirely different one within his annuity without incurring any income tax liability on his $50,000 gain or incurring any commissions for making this transaction. An investor who purchases and sells a mutual fund or stocks on the same facts, would incur income taxes and possibly new commissions. Most of the annuities that I own I have had for many years. I actively trade in these annuities and yet do not incur either income taxes or commissions. However, many of my friends who own mutual funds and stocks find themselves constantly having to pay new commissions and income taxes every time they want to change their

---

[31] The exclusion ratio excludes a portion of annuitized income generated by a variable annuity.

[32] Some variable annuity issuers impose small (i.e., $10-$15) administrative fees for excessive trading.

investments. Over a long period of time, the ability to invest and re-invest without having to pay commissions or incur income taxes will greatly increase one's net investment results.

§50B06. COST-FREE REBALANCING AND REALLOCATION

Most investors understand that rebalancing and reallocation of their investments on a regular basis is important. Nearly all variable annuity companies allow automatic rebalancing and reallocation of their investments on a tax-deferred, no-commission basis. Investors who own mutual funds and stocks will often find themselves paying additional income taxes or new commissions or both in order to accomplish the very important function of rebalancing and reallocating and their portfolios. Mutual fund companies do not provide free asset rebalancing and reallocation nor are they able to avoid creating an income tax liability for their owners should the owners decide to rebalance or reallocate their investments themselves. In many cases, mutual fund investors do not understand how much commissions and income taxes generated by trading can erode their gains. A $25,000 mutual fund purchase that is held for ten years that grows to $75,000 will generate income taxes and commissions of $10,250 if the mutual fund is sold to buy another.[33] In making an identical trade, a variable annuity owner would incur no commissions or income taxes thus saving over $10,000.[34] Attempts at rebalancing and reallocation by investors who own stocks will almost always result in additional income taxes and commissions. During the course of a given year, the trading that I do within the many variable annuities I own can often involve large amounts. However, in all the years that I have owned my variable annuities, I have never had to pay a commission or incur an income tax liability when implementing these trades. If the same investments where held in mutual funds or stocks, the income tax burden and additional commissions of trading would result in a significant reduction in the rate of return received on my investments.

§50B07. TAXATION IN RETIREMENT

Because variable annuities grow on a tax-deferred basis, income taxes are not due until the owner withdraws money from his variable annuity, which usually occurs near or in retirement. The investing public has been led to believe that owning mutual funds and stocks and paying long-term capital gains taxes on these investments in retirement is more

---

[33] Because the holding period is assumed to be ten years, the commission cost is reduced in this example from the 1.37% annualized rate to a rate closer to 0.50%. Mutual fund commissions for trading in the mutual fund after it is purchased are also ignored. $25,000 - 5% commission = $1,250. $50,000 gain taxed at 15% (paid from non-mutual fund sources) = $7,500. $50,000 reinvested with a 3% commission = $1,500. $1,250 + $7,500 + $1,500 = $10,250.

[34] In buying a new variable annuity, the annuity owner will incur a new surrender period unless he selects a variable annuity without a surrender period or a short surrender period.

advantageous than owning a variable annuity because withdrawals from these annuities are subject to ordinary income taxes. I have found this to be a costly error made by many investors. The current *temporary*[35] 15% long-term capital gains tax treatment that is available to mutual fund and stock owners is not that big a benefit to retired investors because the great majority of retired individuals already pay their income taxes at the 15% level.[36] The following example demonstrates this:

Example
John and Mary Smith are both 61 and retired. Their retirement income in 2010 consisted of pensions and miscellaneous income totaling $90,000. They withdraw $10,000 from variable annuities they had invested in over the years. Their combined gross retirement income for the year was $100,000. With normal exemptions and deductions of $26,650, they had a taxable retirement income of $76,350. This taxable income, although it was all ordinary income and placed the Smiths in a 25% marginal tax bracket, but only generated a tax to the IRS in the amount of $11,450.[37] This figure amounts to 15% of the Smiths' taxable income.[38]

What the above example demonstrates is that retired couples who have gross incomes of as much as $100,000 a year and have normal exemptions and deductions will pay ordinary income taxes at the same rate as the current 15% long-term capital gains rate. Mutual fund and stock investors must also keep in mind that under current tax law the 15% long-term capital gains rate is scheduled to increase to 20% after December 31, 2012 and may increase sooner if there is a change in administration in Washington.

All of the variable annuities that I have purchased over the years have grown on a tax-deferred basis. As I approach retirement, I plan on supplementing my pensions with withdrawals from my variable annuities so my total retirement income does not exceed $100,000 a year. This will provide my wife and me with a tax liability in retirement of 15%. My friends who purchased mutual funds and stocks over the years have paid both long-term capital gains taxes at rates as high as 28% or more and short-term capital gains rates of up to twice that in an effort to obtain the same 15% income tax liability in retirement I will receive with my variable annuities.[39] By paying these burdensome income taxes over the years, my friends who have

---

[35] Under the current law, these rates are scheduled to increase to 20% after December 31, 2010.

[36] 2010 report by the Congressional Budget Office estimates the 2010 effective individual income tax rate for the *highest* quartile of taxpayers to be 15.7%.

[37] See the IRS tax tables for 2010.

[38] $10,729) $71,525 = 15%.

[39] Not too many years ago top marginal tax rates were 60% and capital gains rates were set at half of a taxpayer's marginal tax rate.

invested in mutual funds and stocks have accomplished nothing more than guaranteeing their nest egg will be significantly smaller than if they had purchased variable annuities. They did this in an effort to obtain 15% long-term capital gains rates, not realizing that their *ordinary* income tax rate in retirement would most likely be 15%.

§50B08. GUARANTEED LIVING BENEFITS

Without a doubt, the greatest single advantage to variable annuity ownership today is the ability to obtain guaranteed living benefits.[40] In years past, the only benefit that was guaranteed by variable annuity issuers was the death benefit. This benefit helped the survivors of a variable annuity owner but not the variable annuity owner himself. Beginning about eight years ago, most of the large variable annuity companies began offering riders to their variable annuities that provided guaranteed benefits to the owners of their annuities while they were alive. These guaranteed benefit riders are commonly referred to as living benefits. There are several living benefits available to variable annuity investors for a slight additional cost. Space does not allow for a detailed description of each of these benefits.[41] There are living benefits designed to protect an investor's principal if the stock market declines. Other living benefits are designed to provide a lifetime stream of income even if the stock market goes down. If the stock market goes up, the lifetime income paid out will increase but never decrease. Most living benefits are designed to ensure an investor receives his full investment back in a lump sum or payments over time. For example, one of the living benefits available to variable annuity investors is referred to as the Guaranteed Minimum Accumulation Benefit (GMAB) and is essentially a money-back guarantee that protects an investor's principal. Assume that an individual invests $500,000 in a variable annuity that has a GMAB rider. Such a rider provides that, at the end of a stated period of time (usually ten years), if the variable annuity is worth more than $500,000, the investor is entitled to keep all of the gain less his normal costs of investing.[42] However, if the $500,000 investment has dropped in value to $350,000 by the end of the agreed holding period, the GMAB rider would protect the variable annuity investor by fully refunding the investor's entire $500,000 investment. In this latter case, the issuer would impose *no charge* of any kind to the investor. By providing a money-back guarantee, individuals are able to invest in a more aggressive manner

---

[40] All guarantees are backed solely by the credit worthiness and financial solvency of the variable annuity issuer.

[41] For a summary of living benefits see, "It May be Time To Take Another Look At Annuities," by Mark Phelan and John Huggard. *Investment News*, March 6, 2006.

[42] As discussed above, the annual cost of owning the variable annuity will not be significantly more than the cost of a typical mutual fund offering none of the benefits provided by the variable annuity.

with living benefits, allowing them the opportunity of seeing their investment grow significantly over time, while knowing that if the stock market does go against them, they will at least receive back their principal.[43] As mentioned above, several variable annuities provide guaranteed living benefit riders that are designed to provide a lifetime stream of income that can increase but not decrease. For example, the last variable annuity that I purchased provided a Guaranteed Minimum Income Benefit (GMIB) rider. The GMIB rider operates differently than the GMAB rider that was discussed above. My GMIB annuity has a ten year holding period. At the end of this ten year holding period, if my annuity has gone up in value, say four-fold, I am entitled to keep all of the gain less my normal costs of investing in the annuity. Prior to buying my variable annuity with the GMIB rider, I determined that its cost was nearly identical to a mutual fund I was considering that offered none of the guarantees provided by the annuity with the GMIB rider.[44] If the stock market goes against me, I will receive a substantial annual income payment for the rest of my life with these payments guaranteed for twenty years.[45] In short, if the market goes up, I get the gain. If the market goes down, I will recover my initial investment over a short period of time by receiving guaranteed minimum annual income payments. After recovering my initial investment, I will still be entitled to annual income payments for the rest of my life.[46] If I die prematurely, the annuity issuer will continue my annual income payments to my spouse until they have made such payments for a combined twenty-year period. Whether I live beyond my normal life expectancy or die prematurely, my annuity company will pay out much more than I invested in the annuity. All of these benefits presuppose that the stock market declines in the future. If it goes up, as mentioned earlier, I will be entitled to all of the market increase less my costs of investing. No mutual fund or stock investment offers this type of guaranteed financial security. When mutual funds or stocks are purchased, investors are entitled to all of the gain they generate less investing costs, but at the same time must bear any losses should the market go against them. My wife and I have several retirement accounts that we are in the process of consolidating. Our goal is to position these accounts so that they will provide us with a financially secure base for our retirement. We would like to generate at *least* 5% a year from these accounts for as long as either of us live. At the same time we want to maintain

---

[43] Some variable annuity issuers require that their investment models be used with and living benefits selected. Other variable annuity issuers provide optional models and do not restrict investments when their living benefits are selected by investors.

[44] See note 42 above.

[45] Receiving these payments requires formal annuitization of the variable annuity contract.

[46] The annual income stream would be increased if the stock market were to spike-up during the ten year holding period.

control of our investments and provide a substantial death benefit to each other. We also want to know that if the stock market does well in the future, that our investments will grow and that our potential income stream can increase (but never decrease). If the stock market does not do well in the future, we want to know that our income stream will never be reduced. We also want the freedom to take our remaining account balance in a lump sum at any time that we desire. The only investment I have found that will provide what we want is a variable annuity with a lifetime Guaranteed Minimum Withdrawal Benefit (GMWB) rider.

§50B09. WEALTH TRANSFER ADVANTAGE

The investing public has been led to believe that dying and passing mutual funds or stocks to one's survivors is more tax-efficient than dying and passing variable annuities to survivors because mutual funds and stocks receive a step-up in basis at death, whereas variable annuities do not.[47] The truth of the matter is that with some minor tax planning, an estate made up in large part of variable annuities is actually more tax-efficient to transfer to survivors than a similar estate consisting in large part of mutual funds and stocks. In short, the step-up in basis that the public has been conditioned to believe is of some tremendous benefit, is really illusory at best. The following example demonstrates the "advantage" of passing an estate to survivors that is made up in part of mutual funds:

Example:
Jill, who is 67, has a net estate worth six million dollars. One million dollars is in a mutual fund she wants to pass to her three sons. If she dies in 2011 her estate taxes will be $350,000.[48] Because of the step-up in basis, the remaining $5,650,000 will pass to her three children without further taxation.

If Jill's mutual fund were a variable annuity, her estate taxes together with her son's income taxes on the gain in the variable annuity would certainly exceed $350,000. However, investors who own variable annuities can pass more to their children than owners of mutual funds if they are willing to do a few *minutes* of tax planning as the next example demonstrates.

Example:
Jack, aged 67, a widower, has an estate worth $6,000,000. One million dollars of his estate is a variable annuity of which half is his contributions and half is growth. The remainder of his estate consists of his house, car, etc. which is worth $5,000,000. If Jack dies in 2011, his estate taxes would be $350,000.[49] Income taxes owed by his children (after any §691 deduction) could bring total

---

[47] As a technical matter, variable annuities provide a step-up in basis for *lifetime* transfers. See IRC §72(e)(4)(c)(i).

[48] $1,000,000 x .35 = $350,000.

[49] See note 48 above.

taxes to $500,000 or more. Jack wants to retire but needs at least $50,000 (after taxes) each year from his annuity to supplement his other retirement income. Jack wants his entire $6,000,000 estate to pass to his three children without death or income taxes if possible. The solution for all of Jack's concerns can be resolved easily. Jack should have his children purchase (and own) a $1,000,000 life insurance policy on Jack's life.[50] The premiums on this policy will be approximately $27,000 a year. After the policy is in place, Jack should convert his variable annuity to an immediate lifetime annuity (i.e., no guarantees other than lifetime payments). The immediate annuity will pay Jack approximately $90,000 a year for life. Jack's exclusion ratio based on a life expectancy of 15 years will be 37%.[51] This will protect a large portion of this income from taxation for several years. The after-tax annuity payment will be $78,660.[52] Jack can give his children $27,000 each year to pay the premiums on the life insurance they purchased. (No gift taxes would be due because of the annual gift tax exclusion). This leaves Jack with more than the $50,000 in income he needs each year. If Jack dies tomorrow, his estate will be worth $5,000,000 and will pass to his children estate tax free due to the current $5,000,000 exemption. The immediate annuity is valued at zero because it is a lifetime annuity that ceases to have any value at death. In addition, the children will receive $1,000,000 estate and income tax free from the insurance company. (Estate taxes are avoided because the insurance is not in Jack's estate. Insurance proceeds are not subject to income taxation.) In short, a combination of annuitization and asset adjustment eliminates all estate and income taxes for Jack's children. They will receive Jack's entire $6,000,000 estate. (Any unrecovered portion of the annuity premium (if non-qualified) can be treated as an income tax deduction on *Jack's* final income tax return). People who own mutual funds and stocks cannot replicate Jack's tax savings technique.[53] If Jack were to live, he would get $90,000 a year from the immediate annuity company with an exclusion ratio.

As can be seen in the last example, some basic tax planning will not only benefit the owner of the variable annuity before he dies by providing a substantial tax-advantaged and guaranteed stream of income for his lifetime, but will also provide a larger inheritance for his beneficiaries. In Jack's case, his complete six million dollar estate passed to his beneficiaries without any reduction for estate taxes, gift taxes, income taxes, probate costs, etc. In the earlier example involving Jill, application of the mutual fund's step-up in basis rule resulted in Jill's beneficiaries receiving $350,000 less than Jack's beneficiaries.

---

[50] Such a policy should be permanent insurance and not term.

[51] $500,000 ÷ ($90,000 x 15) = 37%

[52] $90,000 - 37% = $56,700 - 20% = $45,360 + $33,300 = $78,660.

[53] The primary reason for this is that mutual fund and stock portfolios would be much smaller than the variable annuity portfolio. In addition, costs and taxes would be incurred to liquidate the mutual funds stocks in order to purchase the required immediate annuity and insurance policy. This later transaction would also cause the mutual fund and stock investors to lose their step-up in basis.

Another point that is frequently lost on the investing public regarding the inheritance of mutual funds and variable annuities, is the fact that most mutual funds are subject to taxation on an annual basis for every year they are held prior to the owner's death. A variable annuity is tax-deferred and therefore is not taxed during the accumulation phase of ownership. By understanding these two important facts, many mutual fund owners have learned that the *net after-tax* value of an inherited variable annuity can actually be larger than the value their beneficiaries could receive from a similar mutual fund inheritance, even though the mutual fund inheritance avoids income taxes at the death of the owner by application of the step-up in basis rule. For example, if a $100,000 mutual fund investment, which is taxed every year, grows to $200,000 at the time of the owner's death, his survivors will inherit the $200,000 without owing income taxes due to the step-up in basis rule. However, a $100,000 investment in a variable annuity that grows tax-deferred, might grow to $250,000. If income taxes are paid on the $150,000 gain in the variable annuity, the *net, after-tax* annuity inheritance might only be $220,000 but would net the beneficiaries of the deceased variable annuity owner $20,000 more than that provided by the mutual fund and its step-up in basis.

Another fact that the public is unaware of is that beneficiaries who inherit non-qualified variable annuities from a taxable estate are entitled to a large income tax deduction under IRC §691. Beneficiaries who inherit non-qualified mutual funds and stocks are not entitled to this deduction. As a tax attorney, I often find that a §691 income tax deduction will offset any benefit provided by the step-up in basis that is available to those who inherit mutual funds and stocks. (See §2514 above).

§50B10. THE PERFORMANCE ADVANTAGE

Often the investing public has the perception that variable annuities do not perform as well as similar investments such as mutual funds. I have found that this is rarely true. As mentioned above, the total cost of owning a mutual fund on an annual basis can easily reach 4.8% or more. A similar variable annuity will have a cost of 2.35%. Over time, it would be very difficult for a stock mutual fund to outperform a similar variable annuity if they are both invested in similar investments. For example, a mutual fund purchased for $25,000 and held for ten years will grow to $41,033 at a 9% average rate of return if it charges a 5% commission

---

[54] $25,000 - 5% = $23,750 + 9% = $25,888 - 1.4% = $25,525 - $23,750 = $1,775 - .22 (2% of 9%) = $1,381 ÷ $23,750 = 5.81%.
   5.81% x 10 years x $23,750 = $41,788. $41,788 - $25,000 = $16,788 x .30 x .15 = $755. $41,788 - $755 = $41,033.
[55] $25,000 + 9% = $27,250 - 2.35% = $26,609 - $25,000 = $1,609) $25,000 = 6.44%. 6.44% x 10 years x $25,000 = $46,658.

and has annual costs of 1.4% and a 2.0% annual tax loss.[54] A variable annuity purchased for $25,000 and held for ten years will grow to $46,658 assuming the same 9% rate of return and an annual ownership cost of 2.35%.[55] Even assuming that the gain in the variable annuity is going to be taxed at 25%, the variable annuity on after-expense, after-tax basis will yield $41,238 and will outperform the mutual fund by more than $200 over the ten year investment period.[56] In an effort to counter this result, many individuals claim that low-cost index mutual funds will out-perform the typical variable annuity because of the index fund's lower annual cost of ownership. If low-cost index funds are going to be compared to the variable annuities, then the variable annuities chosen should also be low-cost variable annuities offering index sub-accounts. Contrary to popular belief, the S&P 500 does not weather bear markets any better than other investments. In the 2000-2002 bear market and the 2008-2009 bear market, the S&P 500, from its high to its low, dropped nearly 50%.

§50B11. THE DEATH BENEFIT

Variable annuities, as mentioned above, provide a death benefit to the survivors of a deceased variable annuity owner. Mutual funds and stocks do not provide a similar death benefit. The basic death benefit provided by variable annuity companies guarantees that the survivors of a deceased variable annuity owner will never receive less from the decedent's annuity than the net investments made by the owner of the annuity before his death. For example, assume that Frank purchased a variable annuity for $100,000 and that at his death the annuity was only worth $75,000. On these facts, Frank's beneficiaries would receive an income tax-free check for $100,000.[57] On the same facts, had Frank invested in stocks or mutual funds, his family would have received only $75,000. In addition to the basic death benefit offered by variable annuity companies, many annuity issuers provide enhanced death benefits for a slight additional cost. Typically, these enhanced death benefits will either increase the variable annuity's value at death by a fixed annual, compounded rate (i.e., 6% to 7% a year from purchase to death) or they will pay a lump sum based on the value of the annuity at the owner's death.

People who know little about variable annuities claim that the basic death benefit is not significant because over time most variable annuities usually go up in value and therefore the death benefit is of no value when an annuity owner dies. The problem with this is that the

---

[56] $46,658 - $25,000 = $21,650 - 25% = $16,238 + $25,000 = $41,238. $41,238 - $41,033 = $205.

[57] Because the variable annuity was worth exactly its original cost, no income taxes would be due.

[58] "Death Benefits Payout Exceed Value, Says NAVA." *National Underwriter Life and Health*, October 4, 2004, p. 7.

stock market does not always go up. Annuity companies paid out $2.8 billion in death benefits between 2001 and 2003 to beneficiaries who inherited variable annuities that suffered losses in the bear market of 2000-2002.[58] If the value of one's variable annuities go up in value over time, the ability to increase the annuity's death benefit without cost can be easily accomplished. Several years ago I had a client who had invested $300,000 in two variable annuities issued by two different companies. I will call them Company A and Company B. Over a seven year period, each of these annuities grew in value from $300,000 to approximately $700,000. Based on these facts, there would be no death benefit in either variable annuity because the annuities were worth more than their initial $300,000 investment. However, this investor, who was 58 and in poor health, used IRC §1035 to exchange the annuity originally issued by Company A for a new one issued by Company B and exchange the annuity originally issued by Company B for a new annuity issued by Company A. The investor incurred no costs, penalties or income tax liability for making these two exchanges.[59] However, as a result of these exchanges, the investor was able to obtain a new death benefit that provides $800,000 more in insurance protection than his original $600,000 variable annuity investment.[60] Even if his variable annuities are worth much less at his death, the investor's family will never receive less than $1.4 million from his annuities. If the variable annuities are worth more than $1.4 million dollars, the investor's family would be entitled to the larger amount. The ability to obtain an extra $800,000 in insurance coverage for one's family without incurring any costs, penalties or income tax liability would certainly constitute a significant benefit especially if one is uninsurable. It is important to remember that the increased insurance coverage obtained by Frank required no medical exam or other underwriting. I have increased the death benefit on some of my variable annuities in the same manner. Mutual funds and stocks do not provide a similar death benefit.

§50B12. CONCLUSION

Many people believe that the way to attain financial security is to chase the hottest mutual fund or the next "sure thing" stock they read about in newspapers or financial magazines. Doing so rarely leads to financial security. In fact, such activities will do little more than increase commission costs, income taxes and other expenses which in turn dooms these investors to financial mediocrity.

---

[59] §1035 transfers to obtain an increased death benefit should only be done after considering current potential surrender charges and possible new surrender periods.

[60] Even if the variable annuity owner died a week later, his family would receive $800,000. Any surrender period ends with the annuity owner's death.

What I have learned over the years is that variable annuities offer a way to create a well-diversified investment portfolio at a reasonable cost. If done correctly, variable annuities can be owned for decades without incurring any commissions for purchasing these annuities or trading in them. Variable annuities grow tax-deferred which allows the owner to decide when and under what circumstances he will pay income taxes on his annuities. Variable annuities provide a death benefit, no-cost asset rebalancing and reallocation and other benefits unique to variable annuities. These annuities, among other things, offer guarantees, eliminate fears and provide financial certainty. Such benefits are not available with any other type of investment. Today's variable annuities offer the opportunity to obtain stock market gains while providing a way to reduce or eliminate stock market losses. For those needing income, modern variable annuities can generate a guaranteed, lifetime stream of income which can increase over time, but never decrease. This income benefit still allows the variable annuity owner to control his investment and reap any market gains resulting from his investment selections. In short, variable annuities respond to nearly every need or concern investors might have today. The proof of this lies in the fact that the sales of variable annuities have reached record highs over the past two decades.[61] The investing public holds over a *trillion* dollars in their variable annuities.[62] Long-term investing in variable annuities has laid the foundation for secure and comfortable retirements for millions of Americans – I'm one of them.

---

[61] Variable Annuity Research and Data Service (VARDS); National Association for Variable Annuities (NAVA); *National Underwriter* (Life and Health), March 7, 2005, p. 6, March 13, 2007, p. 12, September 7, 2007, p. 8-9, June 18, 2007, p. 8 and January 7, 2008, p. 7.

[62] National Association for Variable Annuities and *National Underwriters* (Life and Health), June 26, 2006, p. 8 and LIMRA International statistics for 2008-2009.

PART V – DO VARIABLE ANNUITIES BELONG IN QUALIFIED PLANS?

[Summary: Many investors have qualified retirement accounts funded with mutual funds. The chapters that follow examine why investors should consider owning variable annuities inside of their retirement accounts.]

- CHAPTER 51 -

DO VARIABLE ANNUITIES BELONG IN QUALIFIED PLANS?

§5101. INTRODUCTION

Today, many individuals have tax-deferred retirement plans and accounts. Some of these individuals believe, or have been persuaded, that because these retirement plans and accounts are already tax-deferred, owning variable annuities inside of these plans and accounts provides no real additional benefit. This belief can result in long- term investors making a major mistake that could prove costly over the years. There are many excellent reasons why variable annuities should be considered as long-term investments for qualified retirement plans and accounts.

§5102. VARIABLE ANNUITIES AS INVESTMENTS FOR QUALIFIED RETIREMENT PLANS AND ACCOUNTS

Over the past few decades, 401(k)s, 403(b)s, IRAs and similar qualified plans and retirement accounts have proliferated. Today, many individuals prepare for retirement by funding one or more of these income tax-deferred retirement vehicles.[1] Over the past few years, articles have appeared in the financial press questioning the practice of selling variable annuities as investments for qualified plans.[2] Those who have challenged the appropriateness of this common transaction attempt to support their position by arguing that:

1. Both variable annuities and qualified plans are income tax-deferred investments. Because tax deferral is duplicated when variable annuities are sold as investments for qualified plans, such transactions are inappropriate;

2. The cost of variable annuities is higher than that of other qualified plan investments. In the long run, these higher costs will reduce overall performance when variable annuities are held in qualified plans; and

3. Government regulations and ethical guidelines indicate that the selling of variable annuities as investments for qualified plans is improper.

None of these arguments, when examined closely, have any merit.

§5103. CONCLUSION

Investors must make their own decisions as to what investments should be held in their qualified plans. A good financial professional should have little trouble demonstrating that variable annuities are frequently one of the best investments that can be held inside a qualified

---

[1] Under recently passed legislation, IRAs, SEPs, 401(k)s, and 403(b)s are all easily transferable and interchangeable.

[2] In this chapter, the term qualified plan will be used generically to refer to all income tax-deferred qualified plans and retirement accounts including 401(k)s, 403(b)s, IRAs, SEPs, etc. Because qualified plans are generally funded for retirement purposes, it will be assumed that all investments are long-term and will remain in place until the owner is at least 59½ years old.

plan. The arguments against holding variable annuities inside qualified plans do not hold up under careful scrutiny. Each of the three arguments set out above are discussed in the following chapters.

- CHAPTER 52 -

THE DUPLICATION ARGUMENT

§5201. INTRODUCTION

Because qualified plans and retirement accounts provide tax deferral as do variable annuities, many investors believe that this is a valid reason not to own variable annuities inside of a qualified plan. This logic can result in long-term financial losses.

§5202. THE DUPLICATION ARGUMENT

Proponents of the duplication argument claim that placing a variable annuity inside a qualified plan duplicates the benefit of income tax deferral provided by the qualified plan and therefore such a transaction is improper because the purchaser receives no benefit from it. The duplication argument would have validity only where a variable annuity offered income tax deferral as its sole benefit. The problem with this is that anyone with any understanding of basic investing knows that variable annuities offer buyers many benefits other than tax deferral.

The duplication argument is usually made by journalists and commentators who misstate or offer no support for this argument. For example, the author of an article appearing in The Wall Street Journal, after making the duplication argument, stated that variable annuity companies charged a premium for the tax deferral offered with their variable annuities.[1] This statement is incorrect. The tax-deferred status afforded to variable annuity owners is not a benefit created by the insurance companies that issue variable annuities, but is the result of congressional mandate. By law, Congress declared decades ago that variable annuities may grow on an income tax-deferred basis. No insurance company issuing variable annuities has ever imposed a specific charge for the income tax deferral provided by their variable annuities.

If purchasing a variable annuity for a qualified plan results in duplicating the benefit of income tax deferral and such duplication costs nothing, it defies logic to claim that the buyer of a variable annuity has somehow been harmed if the annuity provides some benefit to the buyer other than income tax deferral. The defective nature of the duplicity argument can easily be demonstrated by applying it to other everyday transactions. The following two examples are illustrative:

Example 1
Fred has two automobiles and decides to trade one in for a newer model. As an automobile owner, Fred is entitled to use his autos on the public highways

---

[1] *The Wall Street Journal*, annuities watch column by David Frenecki, July 20, 1998, p. C-20

without cost. Likewise, anyone who buys a new car may operate it on the public highways without cost. Proponents of the duplicity argument would claim that any auto dealer selling a new car to Fred would be acting improperly because in doing so, the auto dealer is providing, without cost, a duplicate benefit to Fred (i.e. the right to use the highways without cost).

Example 2

Sally has a radio in her bedroom and has decided to purchase a newer model. Anyone who owns a radio may use the radio airwaves without cost. Every time one purchases a radio, they receive the benefit of free access to these airwaves. The proponents of the duplicity argument would claim that any department store selling a radio to Sally would be acting improperly because such a sale would duplicate, without cost, an existing benefit already enjoyed by Sally.

In both of the above examples the auto dealer and department store provide new products to customers that, if purchased, would duplicate benefits their customers already enjoyed. If the auto dealer and department store do not charge for use of the public highways or use of the radio airwaves, any argument that their selling practices could somehow be construed as improper is baseless. The two examples discussed above, although laughable, are no different than the position taken by the proponents of the duplicity argument regarding the sale of variable annuities as investments for qualified plans. In short, where a variable annuity provides some benefit sought by a qualified plan owner other than income tax deferral, the duplication argument becomes irrelevant. The following examples demonstrate this:

Example

Dave has $100,000 in a Roth IRA that currently provides him with income tax deferral.[2] Dave lives in a state where Roth IRAs are not protected from creditors although variable annuities are. As a young physician, Dave is concerned about lawsuits and the possibility that his Roth IRA could be taken by potential judgment creditors. Dave's financial professional suggested that Dave transfer his Roth IRA to a variable annuity to obtain creditor protection. Dave followed this advice even though the variable annuity, without cost, duplicated the income tax deferral provided by his Roth IRA. Could anyone seriously argue that the recommendation made by the financial professional was somehow improper or unethical? Certainly not.

Example

Jane is 60 and has a $200,000 IRA. She needs a stream of income from this $200,000 of at least $10,000 a year for her lifetime. Jane's financial advisor recommended against investing in a variable annuity because Jane's IRA is already tax-deferred, as is the variable annuity. Instead, the advisor invested Jane's IRA in a portfolio of stocks and mutual funds paying an average dividend

---

[2] The principle and income in a Roth IRA grow income tax deferred. Qualified distributions may be taken free of income taxation.

rate of 2.3%. This would allow Jane to receive $10,000 annual payments of principal and interest for 27 years or until Jane is 87. This assumes the stock market remains constant. Jane's stockbroker told her that if the market goes up, Jane's stream of income would be paid for more years or she could increase her annual payments. However, shortly after Jane invested her $200,000 in the portfolio the stock market dropped 25%. If the stock market does not rebound, Jane's remaining $150,000 IRA balance will pay principal and interest payments of $10,000 for only 18.6 years or until Jane is 78.6 years old.

§5203. CONCLUSION

In summary, the decision to include a variable annuity in a qualified plan should not be discounted simply because the benefit of income tax deferral is duplicated without cost by the variable annuity. The important issue is whether the variable annuity provides a qualified plan owner with some other benefit desired by the plan owner.

- CHAPTER 53 -

THE HIGHER COST ARGUMENT

§5301. INTRODUCTION

Many investors believe that variable annuities are more expensive to own inside their qualified plans than are mutual funds. This is rarely the case.

§5302. THE HIGHER COST ARGUMENT

Those who question the propriety of placing variable annuities in qualified plans frequently attempt to support this position by claiming that variable annuities are more expensive to own than other investments typically held in qualified plans. Making such an argument demonstrates a lack of knowledge regarding basic financial principles. Merely because two products sell for different prices does not necessarily mean the less expensive product is a better buy. In comparing products with different prices one must always take into consideration any additional benefits or value provided by the more expensive product or lacking with the less expensive product. If this were not true, it would be inappropriate for a stockbroker to recommend IBM stock to a client if the broker knew Fly-By-Night Computer stock was available for a lower price. It would be also be improper for a real estate broker to sell a young couple a three bedroom house knowing that a large tent would be a cheaper alternative. Following this flawed logic, the local Cadillac dealer would have his morals questioned if he sold a Cadillac to a customer knowing full well that used Ford pick-up trucks could be purchased for much less. As silly as these examples seem, they mirror the position taken by the proponents of the higher cost argument.

The major flaw with the higher cost argument is that it ignores the fact that variable annuities often provide valuable additional benefits to qualified plan participants that are not available with other investments. The decision to buy a Mercedes or a Honda, a Rolex or Timex, a first class airline ticket or coach ticket is made everyday by consumers. In many cases the more expensive item or service is purchased. This is done because the buyer believes he is receiving some additional value or benefit not provided by the less costly alternative. If a variable annuity provides guarantees, reduces investment risks, provides certainty or offers other benefits not available with less expensive investments, investors should have the economic freedom to decide for themselves whether they want to purchase these benefits.

Example

Gina has $300,000 in an inherited IRA. She, as a recent widow, cannot afford to expose the IRA to risk. She needs to know that her IRA will grow to at least $600,000 in the next ten years. The only investment that can provide such a guarantee is a variable annuity with a guaranteed minimum income benefit (GMIB) rider. If Gina uses her $300,000 IRA to purchase such a variable annuity she will be guaranteed a lifetime stream of income from $600,000 under a worst case scenario. If the stock market increases her account value to more than $600,000, she can walk away with the larger account value less her cost of investing. No other investment will provide such a guaranteed benefit.

Another flaw with the higher cost argument is the inaccurate assumption that variable annuities are more expensive to own than other investments commonly held in qualified plans. The average annual cost of owning an actively managed qualified variable annuity is 2.7%[1] This figure includes commissions, trading costs, insurance costs, money manager fees, 12b-1 fees and administrative fees. When these same costs are added up (excluding insurance costs) for an average actively managed qualified mutual fund, the annual cost for the fund will usually be 3.2%. In short, all the available research shows that it is the mutual fund that is *more* expensive to own than the variable annuity whether these investment vehicles are held in qualified accounts or not.[2]

§5303. CONCLUSION

In short, the true cost of owning a variable annuity in a qualified plan in many cases may be less than owning similar investments in these plans. Even in those cases where the cost of owning a variable annuity in a qualified plan is slightly higher than the cost of owning other investments, the many benefits offered by the variable annuity may, for many plan participants, be well worth the additional cost. The following chapters discuss several of the advantages of owning variable annuities in qualified plans.

---

[1] The joint SEC/NASD report on variable insurance products issued on June 9, 2004 on page 6 states that the average annual expense of owning a variable annuity ranges from 1.3% to 2.2%. The higher figure is used by the author. Trading costs and miscellaneous expenses are included in these figures.

[2] The following are sources that demonstrate that the annual cost of mutual fund ownership (if annual income taxes are ignored) is in the 3.2% range: (1) *Common Sense on Mutual Funds: New Imperatives for the Intelligent Investor*, John Bogle, Wiley & Sons, 1999. (2) *Your Money, Your Choice... Mutual Funds - Take Control Now and Build Wealth Wisely*, Professor Charles Jones, Prentice Hall, 2003. (3) *The Great Mutual Fund Trap*, Gary Gensler (Former Undersecretary of the U.S. Treasury 1999-2001) and Gregory Baer (Former Assistant Secretary for Financial Institutions for the U.S. Treasury), Broadway Books, New York, 2002. (4) *The Trouble With Mutual Funds*, Richard Rutner, Elton-Wolf Pub., 2002.

- CHAPTER 54 -

BENEFITS PROVIDED BY VARIABLE ANNUITIES

§5401. INTRODUCTION

Even in those rare cases where the cost of owning a variable annuity inside of a qualified plan might be slightly higher than owning mutual funds in the plan, variable annuities provide several benefits that mutual funds do not. Once these benefits are considered they more than offset any additional cost of owning a variable annuity inside a qualified plan. The remainder of this chapter discusses several benefits variable annuities offer qualified plan owners that mutual funds do not.

§5402. THE DEATH BENEFIT

Variable annuities provide a death benefit that guarantees the owner that regardless of what happens to the value of the underlying investments held in his annuity, should he die, his beneficiaries will receive the greater of the market value of the annuity at his death or the net value of the contributions paid into the annuity.[1]

> **Example**
> Several years ago, Dave went to work for an employer who offered a 401(k). Dave chose to purchase mutual funds offered through his 401(k). The funds have been in Dave's 401(k) for 20 years and have increased in value to $500,000. Dave is now 66 and his health is not good. He retired last year and initially left his 401(k) with his employer. Dave wants his wife be financially secure should he die. Based on the advice of his financial planner, Dave liquidated the mutual funds in his 401(k) and transferred the balance to an insurance company to purchase a variable annuity. The annuity had more investments to choose from and many of the investments had better performance records than Dave's prior 401(k) plan. More importantly, if a stock market correction were to occur and the value of Dave's variable annuity were to drop, for example, to $300,000, Dave's wife would, if Dave were to die, receive a minimum of $500,000 due to the death benefit provided by the variable annuity. On the same facts, had Dave elected to keep his 401(k), at his death his wife would only receive the $300,000 reduced value of the 401(k). The reason for this is that investments, other than variable annuities, held in qualified plans do not provide a death benefit. By owning a variable annuity as his retirement vehicle, Dave is able to provide an extra measure of financial security for his wife.

In recent years, the death benefit offered by variable annuity companies has been greatly improved. Several annuity issuers pay a death benefit equal to the highest value that the

---

[1] At the death of the owner of a variable annuity, the issuing company will pay to the beneficiaries the larger of the account value or total contributions made to the annuity. Contributions are reduced by withdrawals that may have occurred.

annuity reaches before the owner's death. Other annuity issuers provide death benefits that will automatically adjust or ratchet upward every few years. For example, a variable annuity might increase the owner's death benefit every three years. This could be a significant benefit, especially in light of the fact that the death benefit is provided by variable annuity issuers to purchasers without the requirement of a physical examination or having to prove insurability. Other annuity issuers allow a variable annuity owner to purchase a death benefit that is guaranteed to increase in value each year at a set rate. For example, a variable annuity issuer might increase an annuity owner's death benefit by five to seven percentage points a year. This benefit ensures that the owner's beneficiaries will always receive proceeds that will exceed contributions made by the annuity owner.

Example

Jane, who is 70 years old and in poor health, has an IRA containing $510,000. The IRA is in a bank CD paying $2^{1}/_{2}\%$. She has other assets to live on and plans on leaving her IRA to her grandchildren. She elected to purchase a variable annuity that provides a death benefit that compounds at 7% a year. For the small additional cost of owning such an annuity, Jane can ensure that she can pass an increasing benefit to her grandchildren. For example, if Jane dies at age 80 her grandchildren will receive, at a minimum, more than one million dollars as a death benefit from the variable annuity she purchased for $510,000. In addition, Jane has the opportunity to invest more aggressively because her death benefit protects her beneficiaries against loss. If Jane's investments do well, it is possible that her grandchildren could receive an amount that could easily exceed the million dollar death benefit mentioned above. Under no circumstances would the grandchildren receive less than $510,000 increased by 7% each year until Jane's death.

The death benefit offered by variable annuities is not offered by any other type of investment that can be held in a qualified plan. This benefit, as the next example demonstrates, is so significant that a case for professional malpractice could be made if a financial professional failed to suggest this benefit in certain cases.

Example

Ed has had a 401(k) for several years. He has been a conservative investor over the years and his 401(k) now contains $500,000. Ed is 67 and retired. He just learned that he has cancer and has a life expectancy of about two years. Although the stock market has been extremely volatile lately, Ed feels he must be more aggressive with his 401(k) in order to leave more than $500,000 to his family. Ed sought the advice of a financial advisor who suggested to Ed that he consider using his 401(k) proceeds to purchase more aggressive mutual funds within a new IRA. Ed asked about the death benefit provided by variable annuities but his advisor warned him not to buy a variable annuity with his 401(k) money because the benefit of tax deferral would be duplicated. Ed followed his advisor's advice. Shortly thereafter, the stock market corrected sharply and Ed's new mutual fund IRA dropped in value to $350,000. Ed died shortly thereafter. Ed's family received the $350,000 held in the IRA. Had the advisor transferred Ed's 401(k) to a variable annuity offering aggressive sub-accounts, Ed would have been placed in a win-win situation. Had the variable annuity gone up in value, his family would have received all of the gain. Had the market gone down, as it did in this case, his family would have received, at a minimum, the $500,000 placed in the variable annuity together with all additional contributions less withdrawals. Without a physical exam, Ed would have been eligible to purchase a rider that would have increased the value of his variable annuity by 5% to 7% a year until his death. The advisor's failure to assist Ed in purchasing a variable annuity with his 401(k) proceeds, on these facts, could constitute professional negligence. The National Association of Securities Dealers has held that the death benefit offered by variable annuities may be an appropriate reason for placing a variable annuity inside of a qualified plan.[2]

§5403. INCOME TAX REDUCTION FOR BENEFICIARIES

As a general rule, qualified plans are subject to ordinary income taxes in the hands of beneficiaries following the death of the plan owner. One of the major benefits of having a qualified plan held in a variable annuity is the opportunity to reduce or eliminate the income tax burden facing beneficiaries who inherit qualified plans. Of all the investment vehicles available to qualified plan owners only the variable annuity provides a rider for reducing or eliminating income taxes on inherited qualified plans. This rider is most commonly referred to as an earnings enhancement benefit or EEB. Variable annuities offering the EEB charge a small fee to provide additional cash at the owner's death to help beneficiaries of an annuity to reduce or fully pay all income taxes associated with the inherited annuity.

Example
Judy, age 55, had a SEP containing $100,000. She recently retired early due to poor health. The SEP was not performing well and Judy transferred it to a brokerage firm. Judy earmarked the SEP for her children because she had other assets to cover her retirement needs. Judy's total estate was worth less than $5,000,000. Judy invested her money in growth mutual funds. At age 65 Judy died. Her SEP was worth $350,000 at her death. Her four children inherited the SEP and each paid 20% in income taxes (i.e. $17,500) on their $87,500 share of the SEP's value, netting each child $70,000.

Example
John, age 55, had an IRA containing $100,000. He recently retired early due to poor health. The IRA was not performing well and John transferred it to an

---

[2] NASD Notice to Members 99-35. (Available at www.nasdr.org)

annuity company. John earmarked the IRA for his children because he had other assets to cover his retirement needs. John's total estate was worth less than $5,000,000. John purchased a variable annuity that invested in growth oriented investments. The variable annuity contained an EEB rider that provided, at John's death, that 40% of any growth in his variable annuity would be added to the annuity's value to help beneficiaries defray income taxes. This benefit was capped at $100,000. At age 65 John died. His IRA was worth $350,000 at his death. The EEB rider added $100,000 (40% of $250,000 in growth) to the value of the annuity. John's four children each received $112,500 and paid 25% income tax on this amount, netting each child $84,375 or $14,375 more than Judy's children received on identical facts in the previous example.

§5404. PLAN TRANSFER COSTS

Transferring a qualified plan to another plan is a common transaction today. One of the drawbacks of such transfers is cost. In many cases, when a qualified plan is transferred it frequently must be liquidated after which the cash proceeds are then transferred to the new plan. The reinvestment of the cash account often involves the payment of new commissions and related expenses. This does not occur when qualified plans are transferred to variable annuities. All of the transferring participant's plan balance is fully invested and working for the participant from the date of the transfer.

Example

Andy had an IRA containing $300,000 that was not performing well. He transferred it to a local brokerage firm and set up a new IRA. Andy invested the $300,000 by placing half in stocks and half in mutual funds. The commission for funding the IRA with new investments was $9,000. Only $291,000 of Andy's money went into investments. Had Andy transferred his IRA to a variable annuity, his entire $300,000 would have been invested and working for him.

It could be argued that proceeds from the liquidation of a qualified plan could have been reinvested in an IRA offering B-share mutual funds, thus providing the same advantage as investing in a variable annuity. This argument is defective for two reasons:

1. B-Shares may not be appropriate for an investor with a $300,000 portfolio. Any financial professional working with Andy would most likely point out that an A-share commission (i.e. front end load) would be more cost efficient.

2. Many investors who own IRAs, SEPs, etc., outside of variable annuities buy other investments for their qualified plan (i.e. stocks and bonds) that generate commissions when these investments are bought and sold.

§5405. PREMIUM BONUS BENEFIT

Many annuity companies pay premium bonuses of as much as 5% when their annuities are purchased. Some annuity companies increase their annual fees to provide such a bonus and others charge nothing. In some cases the cost of such bonuses are often recouped by reducing the commission paid to the financial professional selling the variable annuity.[3] Those companies that charge nothing usually require that the annuity be held for between seven and ten years to obtain the full benefit of the bonus. For people funding qualified plans, such holding periods are usually not a concern. (See §4508 *supra* also).

Example
Larry had a poorly performing 403(b) that contained $500,000. He decided to transfer his 403(b) to an annuity company. Larry's $500,000 was increased by $25,000 due to the 5% bonus paid by the annuity company. Larry's $525,000 was invested in good quality sub-accounts within the variable annuity. Ten years later, Larry's annuity tripled in value to $1,575,000.

Example
Linda had a poorly performing 403(b) that contained $500,000. She transferred the $500,000 balance to a brokerage firm, her $500,000 was reinvested in several good quality mutual funds. The brokerage firm charged a 2% A-share commission, or $10,000, to buy the funds for Linda. Ten years later Linda's $490,000 plan balance tripled in value to $1,470,000. This is $105,000 less than Larry received in the previous example. Larry's out-performance was due primarily to receiving a bonus when he purchased his annuity.

It should be remembered that the annual cost of owning the mutual fund would most likely be greater than owning the variable annuity. These costs were ignored in the above examples.

§5406. AVAILABILITY OF FIXED RATE INVESTMENTS

401(k)s, 403(b)s and similar qualified plans rarely, if ever, provide investments that guarantee a fixed rate of interest over a long period of time. Frequently, they do offer money market accounts. However, these accounts do not offer a fixed interest rate, but rates that vary according to market conditions. On the other hand, most variable annuities offer investors account options that provide long-term guaranteed rates of return. In some situations, a long-term guaranteed rate of return can be of importance to a qualified plan participant.

Example
Judy, who is 58 years old and single, plans to retire in seven years. She has $456,000 in her 403(b). Judy has determined that to have the type of retirement she has planned, her 403(b) must grow to at least $600,000 by the time she retires. None of the investments available to Judy in her 403(b) will guarantee the return Judy needs to reach her retirement goal. Judy, following the advice of her financial advisor, transferred her 403(b) balance to a variable annuity. One of the

---

[3] In some cases the cost of a bonus may be paid for entirely by the variable annuity purchaser through higher fees or longer holding patterns. The cost of any bonus should be examined before opting to elect the bonus.

investment choices available to Judy in the variable annuity was a fixed account offering a 4% rate of return guaranteed for a seven year period. In seven years, the 4% compound return provided by the variable annuity will increase Judy's $456,000 qualified plan balance to just over $600,000.[4] In short, by transferring her 403(b) account to a variable annuity, Judy will be assured of meeting her retirement goal.

§5407. TAX SAVINGS AT DEATH

Owning variable annuities purchased with qualified money can provide dramatic estate and income tax savings not often available where other investments are held in a qualified plan.

Example

Bob, who is a 66-year-old widower, recently left his job and transferred his $1,000,000 401(k) into an IRA that was held inside of a variable annuity. The remainder of Bob's estate consists of his house, car, etc., which are worth $5,000,000. Bob wants his entire $6,000,000 estate to pass to his three daughters without having to pay estate taxes. In addition, Bob wants his daughters to inherit his $1,000,000 qualified retirement annuity without having to pay income taxes on it. In addition to other sources of income, Bob has determined that he will need to draw at least $64,000 a year from his annuity. The solution for all of Bob's concerns is quite simple. Bob should have his daughters purchase (and own) a $1,000,000 life insurance policy on Bob's life. Such a policy would carry an annual premium of approximately $26,000. After the policy is in place, Bob should make a tax-free transfer of his variable annuity to a life insurance company in exchange for an immediate lifetime annuity (i.e. no guarantee other than lifetime payments). The immediate annuity should pay Bob approximately $90,000 a year for life. Bob can give $26,000 each year to his daughters free of gift taxes to enable them to pay the premiums on the life insurance policy they purchased. This leaves Bob with the $64,000 he needs each year in addition to his other income. If Bob dies in 2011, his estate will be worth $5,000,000 because the immediate annuity is valued at zero for estate tax purposes. This will allow Bob's $5,000,000 estate to pass to his daughters free of estate taxes due to the current $5,000,000 estate tax exemption for 2011. Most importantly, the daughters will receive an additional $1,000,000 from the life insurance policy they own, bringing their total inheritance to $6,000,000. This $1,000,000 will not be subject to income taxes when received by the daughters because it constitutes life insurance proceeds. Because Bob did not own the insurance policy at his death, it will also pass free of estate taxes. For every year Bob lives, he will receive $90,000 a year. After 12 years, he will have more than recouped his $1,000,000 immediate annuity premium.

In the above example, a combination of annuitization of an existing variable annuity coupled with the purchase of life insurance eliminated all estate and beneficiary income taxes on

---

[4] $456,000 x 4% x 7 years = $600,665. It is important to realize that the 4% return guaranteed to Judy is a net return. Whether or not the additional costs are imposed for owning her variable annuity is immaterial because Judy is guaranteed the 4% return she needs.

Bob's six million dollar estate. Additionally, the benefit of a lifetime stream of income for Bob was preserved. Had Bob initially invested in mutual funds, stocks or other investments in his IRA, he could have obtained a similar result by selling these investments and using the proceeds to purchase the required life insurance and immediate annuity. However, such investments may have a cost associated with their sale. For example, a brokerage commission of just 2% to sell $500,000 in stock could cost $10,000 to obtain a tax benefit variable annuity ownership provided for nothing. Being able to pass a large estate to beneficiaries without a death or income tax burden together with additional savings in commissions may be a benefit that would make owning a variable annuity inside of a qualified plan an excellent financial decision.

§5408. PRINCIPAL PROTECTION

Today, many variable annuities offer a guarantee against loss of invested principal. This benefit should not be confused with the death benefit variable annuities provide. The principal protection benefit is referred to as a living benefit because the annuity owner receives the benefit during his lifetime. In order to obtain this living benefit, annuity owners are required to hold their annuities for a specified period. This period usually ranges from five to ten years. Such holding periods rarely present a problem for people funding qualified plans because such plans are usually long-term investments by their nature. Like all living benefits provided by variable annuities, the annual cost of such benefits can range from 20 to 70 basis points.

Example

Dick is 53 years old and wants to retire at 60. He has $400,000 in his IRA and cannot afford to lose any of this money if he and his wife are to have the retirement they desire. Additionally, Dick also wants the chance to invest in equities in hopes of increasing his $400,000 nest egg. Dick transferred his $400,000 IRA to an annuity company that provided a principal guarantee if the annuity owner held his annuity for seven years. There was a small charge made for this benefit. Assume that just before Dick turns 60 that the stock market suffers a reversal and Dick's annuity is only worth $250,000. By opting for the principal protection benefit, Dick and his wife will have a $400,000 annuity that will provide them with a stream of income during their retirement. They also have the option of taking their $400,000 in a lump sum. If the market doubled over the same seven-year period, Dick and his wife would have $800,000 less normal investment costs. Had Dick placed his IRA in an unprotected equity investment, he would not have been able to obtain the guarantee he would have $400,000 available for his retirement.[5]

---

[5] Investors need to discuss any living benefit they might be interested in owning with their financial professional. The cost must be compared to the benefit that will be received.

§5409. ELIMINATION OF ONGOING COMMISSIONS

When qualified plan owners want to change investments, they may be required to pay commissions or other similar costs. Variable annuities do not charge commissions when the annuity owner changes investments within the annuity. Once commissions are taken into consideration, the cost of owning a variable annuity within a qualified plan can frequently be less than owning other types of qualified plan investments.

Example

Jill has an IRA containing $300,000 with North Star Brokerage. The IRA was invested in several different stocks and mutual funds. Jill's twin brother Jeff, has his IRA, worth $300,000, with Polar Star Insurance Company. Jeff's IRA is invested in a variable annuity. Jeff's IRA is equally divided among several sub-accounts made available to him through his annuity. Jill and Jeff actively trade investments within their IRAs. Jill incurs commissions of $3,000 a year due to the trading she conducts in her IRA. Jeff's trading activity is similar to Jill's, but he pays no commissions on his trades because his IRA is held in a variable annuity. Based on the facts set out above, it can be determined that Jill could lose up to 1% of her IRA's value to commissions each year. This loss will cause Jill's IRA to underperform her brother's IRA over time. Some would argue that Jill could reduce her commission costs by purchasing B-share mutual funds. This argument is unpersuasive for the same three reasons mentioned above under the heading PLAN TRANSFER COSTS.

Individuals who have IRAs, SEPs and similar qualified plans may find that the commissions they are paying may be more costly than they thought. Having a variable annuity hold IRAs, SEPs and similar qualified plans may prove to be a better economic choice.

§5410. ANNUITIZATION BENEFIT

Qualified money held in a variable annuity may be annuitized without cost. Annuitization provides a stream of income that cannot be outlived. Some argue that any investment held in any qualified plan can be transferred to an annuity company for an immediate annuity at any time. Although this is true, such transfers may not be cost-free.

Example

Ben is 60 and has held his SEP in a variable annuity for the past 10 years. The SEP is now worth $800,000. Ben has elected to annuitized the $800,000. This can be done without any cost. Had Ben, for example, held his SEP in a full-service brokerage firm he could face commissions that could reach five figures in order to liquidate his brokerage account to obtain a guaranteed lifetime stream of income provided by the annuitization of a variable annuity.

In addition, when one buys a variable annuity, all contract expenses are fixed at the time of purchase. Additionally, mortality tables in effect at the time of purchase are used to forecast the lifetime payments that will be made upon future annuitization. For example, a variable annuity purchased just a few years ago might show the life expectancy of a 60 year-old to be less than current mortality tables. Someone buying such a variable annuity could receive a larger annuity payment from such an annuity than someone the same age who liquidates mutual funds to buy a variable annuity today. The annuitization benefit and fixed contract expenses offered by variable annuities have been cited by industry regulators as appropriate reasons for placing a variable annuity in a qualified plan.[6]

§5411. GUARANTEED RATES OF GROWTH

Several annuity companies currently guarantee the amount invested in their annuity will grow by a specified rate. This rate is usually between 6% and 7% or more. Like the principal protection benefit discussed earlier, the guaranteed rate of growth benefit, when elected, is paid out as a lifetime annuity and is only available if the variable annuity purchased is held for a specified amount of time, usually ten years. For persons saving for retirement, such holding periods are usually of little concern. In many cases annuitization may be required if this benefit is elected. Most annuity companies charge an annual fee of from 20 to 70 basis points of an annuity's account value for this benefit.

Example
Ken, who is 55, has $400,000 in an inactive 401(k) he had with his prior
employer. He is currently self-employed. Ten years from now he plans to retire.
Ken must have a nest egg that will provide at least $43,000 a year in income for
his lifetime. Ken transferred his dormant 401(k) to a variable annuity that would
guarantee that his $400,000 investment would, at a minimum grow to $800,000
in ten years and provide a minimum lifetime stream of income for Ken in the
amount of $45,000. Over this ten year holding period, Ken may invest in any or
all of the sub-accounts offered by the variable annuity. If, ten years from now,
the value of Ken's account is only worth $250,000 due to a poorly performing
stock market, he could elect to receive an $800,000 annuity that will pay him
$45,000 for life. Because of this living benefit, Ken can afford to invest more
aggressively. If the stock market does well and Ken's account exceeds $800,000
in value ten years from now, Ken can elect to annuitize this larger amount or take
the total account value and invest it elsewhere. If Ken places his 401(k) in stocks
or mutual funds he will not be able to obtain a similar guaranteed benefit.

§5412. MISCELLANEOUS BENEFITS

There are many other benefits offered to qualified plan owners by variable annuity issuers that may not be available in other types of qualified plans. Space limitations do not allow for a

---

[6] See note 3 *supra.*

complete discussion of all of them. Three such benefits are set out below in summary form as examples:

1. Many variable annuities offer automatic dollar-cost averaging at no cost while paying above market rates of return on money awaiting investment. For those investors who prefer to dollar-cost average rather than make lump-sum investments, this benefit may be attractive.

2. Many variable annuities offer automatic asset rebalancing or reallocation at no cost. For investors who believe in asset allocation, this may prove to be a valuable benefit. Automatic asset rebalancing or reallocation on a no cost basis is rarely available with investments other than variable annuities.

3. Some states provide creditor protection for variable annuities. This same protection may not be available for certain qualified plans (IRAs, Roth IRAs, SEPs, SIMPLES, etc.). In such cases, creditor protection may be obtained by transferring qualified plan proceeds to a variable annuity.

§5413. CONCLUSION

Even if it is assumed that owning a variable annuity in a qualified plan is more expensive than owning other investments in such plans, the many exclusive benefits provided by the variable annuity may, for many investors, be well worth the additional cost of receiving these benefits.

There are several situations where variable annuities offer benefits that may also be available with other investments. Just because a benefit is provided by both a variable annuity and another investment does not necessarily mean selecting the variable annuity for inclusion in a qualified plan would be an incorrect decision.

Example
Sara had a 403(b) that was performing poorly. She talked to two financial professionals who made similar suggestions. The first professional suggested Sara purchase a portfolio of mutual funds in order to obtain stock market rates of return. The second professional suggested Sara purchase a variable annuity offering sub-accounts that had a history of providing stock market rates of return. Just because good rates of return are common to both the mutual fund and variable annuity does not mean that Sara should ignore the variable annuity. She should look at costs, commissions, other benefits, etc. before making her decision.

- CHAPTER 55 -

THE IMPROPRIETY ARGUMENT

§5501. INTRODUCTION

Rumors abound that some government regulation or law prohibits variable annuities from being held in qualified plans. Investors need to know that there is no such regulation or law.

§5502. THE IMPROPRIETY ARGUMENT

Just like the duplication argument and the higher cost argument, the argument that there is some government regulation or ethical rule indicating that the sale of variable annuities for inclusion in qualified plans is improper is completely baseless. There is not a single state law, federal statute, government regulation or ethical mandate existing that comes close to supporting the impropriety argument. To the contrary, nearly all guidance dealing with this issue indicates that variable annuities may be considered as possible investments for those who have qualified plans.

It is interesting to note that variable annuities were developed in 1952 *exclusively* for use in qualified plans for college professors.[1] Later, the use of variable annuities, with congressional approval, was expanded to allow their inclusion in other qualified plans. Variable annuities make up a large part of all the 403(b) plans in existence today. In addition, many 401(k) plans are funded with variable annuities.[2]

The most important document existing today dealing specifically with the topic of selling variable annuities as investments for qualified plans is NASD Notice to Members 99-35 (available at www.nasdr.org). Nowhere in this notice is there language that blanketly prohibits the sale of variable annuities as investments for qualified plans. Notice to Members 99-35 is a guide designed to help registered representatives comply with four important responsibilities that have existed for many years. They are:

1. A registered representative should never sell a variable annuity to a client based *solely* on the variable annuity's tax-deferred status if the variable annuity will be held in a qualified plan such as a 401(k), IRA, etc.

2. If a registered representative recommends a variable annuity as an investment to be held in a qualified plan (i.e. 401(k), IRA, etc.) the recommendation *must* rest on one or more of the benefits provided by the variable annuity other than tax deferral.

---

[1] "Why Use a Variable Annuity to Fund a Qualified Plan?" 1997 report issued by the National Association of Variable Annuities.

[2] Today, approximately 65% of all variable annuities are invested in qualified accounts. "Using Variable Annuities in IRAs", Brandon Buckingham, *Trust and Estates*, March 2008, pp. 37-41. "Why Variable Annuities May Make Sense in a Qualified Account", by Kurt Ohlson, *Financial Advisor Pro*, newsletter, p.5.

When such a recommendation is made the registered representative should inform his client that the variable annuity duplicates the tax deferral already enjoyed by the client through his qualified plan and that no additional tax benefit is gained by purchasing the variable annuity.

3. Registered representatives should, in addition to discussing the benefits of variable annuities, fully discuss any potential limitations (e.g. surrender fees, liquidity, etc.) or other material information before recommending a variable annuity (e.g. costs, IRS penalties, treatment of required minimum distributions, etc.). A review of the variable annuity prospectus is a good way to accomplish this.

4. Registered representatives should know, understand and record their clients' financial background so they can better determine the suitability of recommending a variable annuity for inclusion in a client's qualified plan. At a minimum, the basic information obtained from a client for the purchase of any investment (e.g. age, investment experience, investment holding period, etc.) must be reviewed with the client.

Registered representatives need to understand there may be some situations where placing a variable annuity in a qualified plan may be inappropriate. The following list identifies some of these situations.

1. Short-term investing is contemplated

2. Hardship withdrawals are contemplated

3. Large loans from a qualified plan are contemplated (403(b) loans)

4. Surrender penalties could be triggered (B-share commissions)

5. Liquidity problems may arise

6. Death benefit is not realistic

7. Early retirement is contemplated (See the following example).

Example
Mike recently took an early retirement at age 55. His 401(k) contains $800,000. He needs to withdraw $40,000 a year during retirement. Transferring his 401(k) to a variable annuity may not be appropriate because the IRS imposes a 10% penalty on withdrawals taken from a variable annuity if the owner is under $59^1/2$. The IRS does not impose this penalty on 401(k) withdrawals taken by owners if they are retired and over 55 years of age.[3]

Good financial professionals realize how important it is to have written records that reflect why an investment was recommended to a client and the reasoning behind its purchase.

---

[3] Mike could leave $200,000 in his 401(k) and transfer $600,000 to a variable annuity in order to avoid IRS penalties. Additionally, if the variable annuity can be set up as a 401(k), no penalty would be imposed on withdrawals from the variable annuity. §IRC 72(t) (Series of equal periodic payments) would most likely not work in this situation.

The best way for an investor and their financial professional to ensure they have discussed the four responsibilities outlined above is to have a written disclosure form that addresses all of these responsibilities. A suggested disclosure form appears below. Financial professionals and investors must understand that the form provided is merely an example that may need to be modified to reflect the specific variable annuity being considered for purchase. Use of a modified version of this sample form will provide a written record that will reflect the basis for a client's decision to buy a variable annuity for his or her qualified plan. Such a record protects both the client and the financial advisor.

Reluctance to consider placing variable annuities into a qualified account or selling a variable annuity that will be funded with qualified money may raise the specter of malpractice. For example, if a 67-year-old widow has a $500,000 nest egg and needs $30,000 a year in guaranteed lifetime income and her financial planner places her money in mutual funds or stocks, the advisor may get sued if the stock market has a protracted downturn. The reason for this is that a variable annuity could have *guaranteed* a 6% *lifetime* income stream to the widow while mutual funds and stocks can't.

Sample Tax Duplication Disclosure Document

The form below is a sample disclosure document that should be filled out whenever a variable annuity will be placed in a qualified plan or purchased within qualified funds.

MORGAN AND MELLON
FINANCIAL PLANNERS

I.   Product Description:
The undersigned client is contemplating the purchase of a variable annuity issued by the_____ Insurance Company. The specific name of this annuity is _____. This variable annuity will be purchased with qualified money and will be held as a qualified plan.

II.   Type of Qualified Plan or Retirement Account Involved:
The undersigned client is contemplating the purchase of the above-described variable annuity to be held as a qualified plan or retirement account. The specific plan or account involved is a:
☐ 401(k)   ☐ 403(b)   ☐ Traditional IRA   ☐ 457 Plan   ☐ Other_____.

III.   Tax Deferral:
The decision to purchase a variable annuity, which is a tax-deferred investment, should not be based solely on the variable annuity's tax-deferred benefit if the variable annuity is to be held as a qualified plan or retirement account. Qualified plans, retirement accounts and variable annuities all provide tax deferral. The purchase of a variable annuity for a qualified plan or retirement account should be based on one or more of the other benefits available through variable annuities. These benefits are discussed in item IX below.

IV   Client Background:
Because variable annuities are retirement vehicles, they should be purchased with that in mind. No variable annuity should be purchased until the client and his financial professional have discussed all of the following information and data regarding the client and the client's retirement goals.
- Name...
- Address..
- Phone Number ....
- Occupation..
- How long employed: ....
- Employer:..
- Marital status: ....
- Social Security #:..
- Age:...
- Number of dependents:...
- Retirement goals: ....
- Investment time horizon: ....
- Investment objectives: ☐ Growth   ☐ Other ....
- Approximate retirement date: ....
- Life expectancy at retirement: ....
- Risk tolerance: ....
- Marginal tax bracket now:...................................% At retirement:....................................%
- Prior investment experience:..
- Retirement sources other than Social Security: ....
- Total net worth: ....
- Liquid net worth:...
- Client's annual income:...
- Spouse's income:...
- Special situations (i.e. special needs child, etc.)? ....
- Bank used:...
- Are you related to anyone in the securities business?   ☐ Yes   ☐ No
- Other investments: ....
- Liquidity needs: ....
- Life insurance coverage: ....

V   Surrender Fees:
The annuity contemplated for purchase by the undersigned client imposes a surrender fee that will be in effect until _____. The annuity allows withdrawals of up to_____% a year without a surrender fee. Variable annuities are long-term investments that provide less liquidity than other investments. If withdrawals of more than _____% a year are contemplated or large withdrawals will be required prior to the date set out above, the purchase of the variable annuity should not be considered. If large withdrawals are not required before the date set out above, the surrender fees will have little impact on untaxed withdrawals. All variable annuities and qualified plans, regardless of the investments held in such plans, may be subject to a 10% penalty imposed by the IRS if such investments are withdrawn prior to a specified age (usually 59$^1/_2$). The prospectus more fully discusses the surrender fees involved with the purchase of the above-described annuity and has been discussed with the client.

VI. Prospectus:

A prospectus is a detailed explanation of every aspect of a variable annuity. Variable annuities are subject to market risk. This is set out in detail in the prospectus. Any investor contemplating a variable annuity purchase must be given a copy of the prospectus for any variable annuity to be purchased. It should be reviewed by the prospective variable annuity purchaser and his financial advisor. Special attention should be paid to IRS required minimum distributions (RMDs) and surrender charges. The client has received a prospectus and reviewed it with the undersigned financial advisor.

VII. Pricing Structure:

No investment should be considered for purchase unless the prospective purchaser understands the various costs that may be charged for owning the investment. The variable annuity prospectus for the annuity being contemplated for purchase by the undersigned client fully discusses mortality and expense charges, administrative charges, investment advisor fees, etc. The client and financial advisor have completely reviewed the prospectus mentioned above, giving special attention to the expenses and pricing structure. Sub-account choices have been reviewed by the client and financial advisor also.

VIII. Tax Treatment:

All investments held in tax-deferred qualified plans including stocks, mutual funds, variable annuities, etc. receive the same tax treatment under current IRS rules. Withdrawals from all qualified plans and variable annuities funded with before-tax dollars are subject to ordinary income taxes.

IX. Variable Annuity Features:

For the reason mentioned in item III above, a variable annuity should not be purchased for a qualified plan (401(k), IRA, etc.) *solely* based on the fact that the variable annuity provides tax-deferred growth. The purchase of a variable annuity for a qualified plan should be based on one or more of the other benefits offered by the variable annuity contemplated for purchase. The annuity under consideration by the undersigned client offers the following benefits other than tax-deferred growth. The undersigned client has checked those benefits that are the basis of his/her decision to purchase the variable annuity described above. The undersigned financial professional has discussed each of these benefits fully.

☐ Death benefit (basic or enhanced)	☐ Guaranteed increasing death benefit
☐ Guaranteed fixed contract expenses	☐ Guarantee against loss of principal
☐ Potential estate and income tax savings	☐ Premium bonuses
☐ Guaranteed minimum growth rates on benefit base	☐ Creditor protection
☐ No cost automatic reallocation and rebalancing	☐ Guaranteed income without annuitization
☐ No cost dollar-cost averaging of contributions	☐ Long-term fixed rates of return
☐ Eliminate transaction costs	☐ Medicaid planning
☐ Lifetime income benefits through annuitization	☐ College tuition planning
☐ Spousal continuation	☐ Other..

Variable Annuities may not be appropriate for holding qualified money where:

Each of the following issues have been discussed between the client and financial advisor:

- Large loans from a qualified plan are contemplated
- Surrender penalties could be triggered by RMDs
- Early retirement is a consideration
- Hardship withdrawal may be needed
- Short-term investments are planned
- There may be liquidity concerns
- Benefits limited by age

X. Summary:

Each of the following topics was fully discussed between the undersigned client and financial advisor:

- The specific variable annuity being recommended (see item I)
- The qualified plan that will hold the annuity (see item II)
- The duplication of tax deferral (see item III)
- Client background (see item IV)
- Surrender fees (see item V)
- Prospectus for the variable annuity was delivered to and discussed with the client (see item VI)
- Pricing structure of the variable annuity (see item VII)
- Tax treatment of the variable annuity (see item VIII)
- Variable annuity features (see item IX)
- Loss of creditor protection status

_____   _____
Client   Date

_____   _____
Financial Advisor   Date

§5503. CONCLUSION

Variable annuities are no different than any other type of investment that a financial professional might recommend to a client for inclusion in the client's qualified plan. The fact that both variable annuities and qualified plans provide tax deferral is of no significance. Clients who elect to have some or all of their qualified money invested in a variable annuity are not charged anything for the duplication of this tax benefit. The recommendation of a variable annuity for inclusion in a qualified plan should always be based on some benefit provided by the variable annuity other than tax deferral. Today, variable annuities exist that respond to nearly every need or concern qualified plan owners might have. These annuities, among other benefits, offer guarantees, eliminate fears and provide certainty. Such benefits are not available with any other type of qualified plan investment. If a financial professional knows of a variable annuity that provides a needed benefit to a client not offered by the client's qualified plan, he or she would be obligated to fully discuss this option with the client. Whether any financial product, including a variable annuity, is an appropriate investment for inclusion in a qualified plan must be determined by what is best for the client.

Variable annuities, for over a half a century, have been one of the most common investments held in qualified plans. Long-term investment in these annuities have laid the foundation for secure and comfortable retirements for millions of Americans. This trend will continue as qualified plan participants begin to learn of the many unique benefits provided by variable annuities.

INDEX